FROM THE TABLES of BRITAIN

FROM THE TABLES of BRITAIN

Exploring the Exciting New English Cuisine: 250 Contemporary Recipes

Elisabeth Lambert Ortiz

M. EVANS AND COMPANY, INC.

NEW YORK

Some of the recipes in this book first appeared in Gourmet magazine copyright © by Condé Nast Publications Inc., April, September 1983, July 1984, May, June 1985.

Library of Congress Cataloging-in-Publication Data

From the tables of Britain.

Includes index.
1. Cookery, British.   I. Ortiz, Elisabeth Lambert.
TX717.F877   1986   641.5941   86-24280

ISBN 0-87131-486-X

M. Evans and Company, Inc.
216 East 49 Street
New York, New York 10017

Design by Dana Sloan

Manufactured in the United States of America

9 8 7 6 5 4 3 2 1

For Elizabeth David, C.B.E., whose books have given much pleasure to a multitude of readers, and inspired a multitude of cooks.

CONTENTS

❖   ❖   ❖

FOREWORD

❖   ❖   ❖

I FIRST MET Elisabeth when she interviewed me for an article she was writing for *Gourmet* magazine in New York. She told me then of her interest in the new young chefs of Britain, with whom she knew I was deeply involved, as many of these young cooks of promise were working in my kitchens at The Dorchester Hotel. We talked of my interest and belief in British cooking and of the revolution that was taking place in the cuisine and in the attitudes of the British public to food. She met *sous-chefs* in my kitchen, many of whom have gone on to become head chefs in their own right.

I think Elisabeth has done a splendid job in collecting recipes created by the many gifted young chefs she talked to and whose cooking she enjoyed. She has interpreted the philosophy behind their cooking. Above all she conveys her enthusiasm for cooks who are seeking to provide good healthy dishes, and whose real satisfaction comes from the enjoyment they give. She also shows their enthusiasm for what is very hard work.

The recipes are written in a clear and easy-to-follow style suitable for home cooks. They sound delicious. I am pleased that Elisabeth, whose work I admire, regards me as a valuable influence on the British kitchen, and as her friend and mentor.

Elisabeth makes it clear that chefs have not abandoned the disciplines of classical technique. They have adapted the greatness of the past to contemporary needs, using modern foodstuffs and modern kitchen technology. In this collection she has not hesitated to keep favorites of traditional cuisine, or to value the work of older chefs who were the pioneers of today's new cuisine.

It is not always easy to translate a recipe from a chef's kitchen to a domestic one, but this she has done admirably without falsifying the chef's intention. She also suggests ways for the health- and diet-conscious to cut down on such temptations as heavy cream by using other dairy products—for example, junket cheese. I think she understands the profound revolution that has taken place in the British kitchen, with young, creative chefs meeting the challenge of today's needs with wonderfully innovative dishes that are nevertheless linked with the traditions of the past, in the continuous process of renewal and change that is the heart and essence of good cooking.

Anton Mosimann,
Maître Chef des Cuisines,
The Dorchester Hotel,
London

INTRODUCTION

❖　　　❖　　　❖

NOT SO VERY long ago travelers came to Britain to see historic houses, castles, museums, cathedrals and theater. Now they come for food as well, especially to the restaurants of the country house hotels, small elegant places converted from country mansions set in wide tree-filled parks and gardens, too big for modern families and often impossible for a private family to keep up. The hotels are luxurious and in exquisite taste; the dining rooms are not large but they are beautifully furnished and filled with flowers, often from the hotel's own gardens. And their kitchens are presided over by gifted young chefs whose cooking has caused a revolution in the food of this island.

I first found out what was happening when I met Anton Mosimann, the brilliant young Maître Chef des Cuisines at The Dorchester Hotel in London, author of two important cookbooks and a fervent believer in British cuisine. He encouraged young cooks in his kitchen to turn into important young chefs. He is so devoted to his profession that he founded Club 8, a group of eight young London chefs who met once a month to eat, exchange ideas, discuss recipes and help each other to raise standards. His club inspired young Nicholas Gill, the gifted chef at Hambleton Hall in Leicestershire, to found Country Chefs Seven with the same aim of raising culinary standards.

Nick is still at Hambleton Hall where I met him and enjoyed, more than once, his inspired cooking. The others of the Seven have all moved to other country house hotels, or to restaurants, and are still cooking sublime dishes: Murdo MacSween, Ian McAndrew, John Webber, John Hornsby (now in the United States), Shaun Hill and Michael Quinn, who left Gravetye Manor in Sussex to become the first British chef ever to head the kitchens of the Ritz in London, and has now returned to the country at Ettington Park Hotel, near Stratford-upon-Avon. They and a host of talented young men and women cooked for me, and were generous enough to give me their recipes for this book. There are also recipes from great cooks like George Perry-Smith, Francis Coulson and Kenneth Bell, now older men, who pioneered the change and helped train and inspire many of today's young chefs. When George Perry-Smith opened his restaurant, the Hole in the Wall in Bath, it was an oasis in a desert of indifferent food. Now there are very few desert areas in Britain from Cornwall, where George now has a restaurant with rooms in Helford, all the way north to Scotland. I made a gastronomic pilgrimage round Britain, meeting chefs and eating well. I also enjoyed good wine. It took some time as chefs are no longer thin on the ground. This book is the result of those happy journeys.

I have tested all the recipes in my own kitchen and, without changing essentials, have written them so they will work coherently in a domestic kitchen rather than in a kitchen with a brigade of cooks. The home cook may lack many of the advantages of a restaurant kitchen, especially trained helpers, but we do have the advantage of a captive audience.

I have also taken the opportunity to suggest ways to avoid too much cream and so on, for today's health-conscious diners. Chefs want to produce food that is not just good to eat but is good for one as well, so they are downright stingy with any sauce that is very rich; palate and health are both satisfied. John Webber, whom I met when he was head chef at Gidleigh Park Hotel at Chagford in Devon, and who is now at Cliveden,

Taplon, Buckinghamshire, summed up the new attitude nicely for me when he said that people in Britain used to eat out when they had to, now they eat out for entertainment. They also feel privileged to meet the chefs in their tall starched white hats, stars of the kitchen, when they make their rounds of the restaurant. My thanks go to Michael Harris, proprietor of The Bell Inn, Aston Clinton, Buckinghamshire, a noted wine authority, who has kindly given me suggestions for the wines to serve with some of the dishes.

Writing this book has been great fun, and I hope readers will cook and enjoy the recipes as I have done.

Elisabeth Lambert Ortiz

BASIC
RECIPES

STOCKS

❖   ❖   ❖

EXCELLENT canned chicken and beef stock are available in super-markets nowadays and there are also acceptable stock cubes for beef, chicken, lamb and fish stocks, useful in a crisis, or to enrich a thin-tasting mixture. Many home cooks still prefer to make their own stock, and British cooks, fond of game, like to make a simple game stock. These recipes are not as formal as those of a restaurant chef who has at his or her disposal not only the ingredients and special equipment but storage space, which most of us lack in small kitchens.

I have used Lyn Hall's (principal of La Petite Cuisine School of Cooking in London) excellent recipes for fish stock, and clarified fish stock, which should be used when a strong fish stock is called for. They add wonderfully to the flavor of fish soups.

CHICKEN STOCK

❖   ❖   ❖

4 pounds chicken carcasses, raw or cooked, necks, gizzards, hearts, backs and wings
12 cups water
2 carrots, scraped and chopped
2 celery ribs, chopped
2 medium-size onions, unpeeled, halved, each stuck with 2 cloves
1 leek, trimmed, split, thoroughly washed and chopped
Bouquet garni: 1 thyme sprig, 6 parsley sprigs, 1 bay leaf
6 peppercorns
Salt

Combine all the ingredients, with salt to taste, in a large saucepan or kettle. Bring to a boil over low heat and skim for 5 minutes, to remove any scum that rises to the surface. Cover and simmer over low heat for 2 hours. Strain the liquid into a bowl or jug; discard the solids. Chill the cooled stock in the refrigerator and remove all the fat. The stock can be frozen.

M A K E S 8 cups.

BEEF STOCK

❖   ❖   ❖

4 pounds oxtail, shank or chuck,
   chopped into 2-inch pieces
2 pounds beef bones
12 cups water
2 medium-size carrots, scraped
   and chopped
2 medium-size onions, chopped
2 garlic cloves, chopped

2 celery ribs, chopped
2 medium-size tomatoes, chopped
3 parsley sprigs
1 bay leaf
6 peppercorns
1 thyme sprig
Salt

Combine all the ingredients, with salt to taste, in a large saucepan or kettle. Bring to a boil over low heat and skim for about 5 minutes. Cover and simmer over low heat for 4 hours, skimming from time to time. Strain the liquid into a bowl or jug; discard the solids. Chill the cooled stock in the refrigerator and remove the solidified fat. The stock can be frozen.

M A K E S 8 cups.

Veal Stock

Use 4 pounds veal trimmings (neck or shank) and 1 large veal knuckle bone, cut into 2- to 3-inch pieces, in place of oxtail and beef bones. Cook as for Beef Stock.

LAMB STOCK

❖   ❖   ❖

Lamb stock is not as much used as other stocks, and when it is needed it is usually for a sauce.

1 tablespoon butter
1 tablespoon vegetable oil
1 medium-size onion, chopped
   fine
1 small carrot, scraped and
   chopped
1 celery rib, chopped

1 garlic clove, minced
1 thyme sprig
Lamb bones (from rack of lamb,
   or loin)
4 cups water
Salt, freshly ground pepper
2 teaspoons arrowroot (optional)

Heat the butter and oil in a saucepan and sauté the onion, carrot, celery and garlic over moderate heat, stirring from time to time, until the vegetables are lightly browned, about 10 minutes. Add the thyme and bones, stir and cook for a few minutes longer. Add the water, bring to a simmer, and cook, uncovered, over low heat for 30 minutes. Season with salt and pepper. Strain stock through a fine sieve and return it to the saucepan. If liked, the stock may be thickened. Mix the arrowroot with cold water, stir into the stock, and simmer until the stock is lightly thickened.

M A K E S about 2 cups.

GAME STOCK

❖   ❖   ❖

The carcasses of roast game make wonderfully rich stock which can be frozen and used to enrich sauces or gravies for the next batch of game.

Carcasses of any game such as
  pheasant, grouse, partridge,
  etc., using 2 or 3 birds
  according to size and type,
  chopped
2 tablespoons butter
1 medium-size onion, chopped
1 medium-size carrot, scraped
  and chopped

1 celery rib, preferably with
  leaves, chopped
1 bay leaf
½ teaspoon dried thyme or 1
  sprig of fresh thyme
Salt, freshly ground pepper
4 cups water

Sauté the game bones in the butter in a large saucepan or heavy casserole. Add the onion, carrot and celery and sauté for a few minutes longer. Add the bay leaf and thyme, season with salt and pepper, and pour in the water. Simmer, covered, for 2 hours. Taste for seasoning and strain through a fine sieve.

M A K E S about 2 cups.

N O T E : Any necks or giblets may be added with the bones, as well as any leftover bits of meat.

TO CLARIFY MEAT STOCK

❖ ❖ ❖

3 egg whites for every 8 cups
  stock
3 eggshells, crushed

4 ounces chopped lean beef
  (optional)
Stock (beef, veal, chicken, game)

In a large saucepan beat the egg whites until they are foamy. Stir in the crushed eggshells, and the beef if using it. Mix thoroughly. Pour in the stock and bring to a simmer over low heat, whisking constantly. Simmer, partially covered, over very low heat for 20 minutes. Let the stock rest, uncovered, for 10 minutes. Strain it through a sieve lined with a double thickness of dampened cheesecloth into a bowl or jug, taking care to disturb the crust as little as possible. The crust may be lifted off carefully with a skimmer before straining the stock.

FISH STOCK

❖ ❖ ❖

This very good recipe for fish stock is from Lyn Hall, principal of La Petite Cuisine School of Cooking in London.

2 pounds fish heads and bones of
  any nonoily white fish, cleaned
  and chopped
¼ cup olive oil
½ cup chopped tomatoes
½ cup thin-sliced carrots

1 cup thin-sliced onions
Bouquet garni: 1 thyme sprig, 6
  parsley sprigs, 1 bay leaf
6 cups water
Salt, freshly ground pepper
½ cup dry white wine

In a large saucepan sauté the fish heads and bones in the oil for 2 or 3 minutes. Add the tomatoes, carrots, onions, bouquet garni and water. Season to taste with salt and pepper and simmer, covered, for 30 minutes. Strain the stock into a jug. Rinse out and dry the saucepan and return the stock to the pan with the wine. Bring to a simmer, skimming the froth from the top. Simmer for 4 minutes, then strain through a sieve lined with a double layer of dampened cheesecloth. Cool. Skim all the fat from the top. Measure and reduce over brisk heat to 4 cups to concentrate the flavor.

M A K E S 4 cups.

TO CLARIFY FISH STOCK

❖ ❖ ❖

Use whenever strong fish stock is called for in a recipe.

2 ounces (¼ cup) any nonoily   4 cups fish stock
   white fish, skinned and boned   Salt, white pepper, cayenne
2 egg whites

In a blender or food processor reduce the fish to a purée. Scrape into a bowl. Beat the egg whites until foamy and gradually beat them into the fish purée. Pour the stock into a saucepan, add the egg white and fish mixture, and whisk briskly. Bring to a boil over low heat, whisking. As soon as the stock comes to a boil, remove from the heat. Taste for seasoning and add salt and white pepper and a pinch of cayenne. The stock should be strongly seasoned at this point as the clarifying process thins the flavor. Return the saucepan to the heat and simmer gently for 20 minutes. Remove from the heat and carefully lift off the crust formed by the egg whites and fish with a perforated spoon or skimmer. Strain stock through a sieve lined with a double layer of dampened cheesecloth set over a deep bowl.

M A K E S 3 cups strong fish stock.

SHELLFISH STOCK

❖ ❖ ❖

This is a useful, easy-to-make stock for enriching the flavor of shrimp, lobster or crab sauces.

Shells and heads from 1 pound   1 garlic clove, chopped
   shrimps or 1 lobster or   6 parsley sprigs
   equivalent crab shells, chopped   1 bay leaf
2 tablespoons olive oil   1 thyme sprig
1 small onion, chopped fine   3 or 4 chervil sprigs (optional)
1 small carrot, scraped and   Salt, freshly ground pepper
   chopped   5 cups water
1 celery rib with leaves, chopped   ½ cup dry white wine

(recipe continues)

Sauté the shells in the oil in a large saucepan, stirring with a wooden spoon until they turn pink, 2 to 3 minutes. Add all the remaining ingredients, using very little salt as the stock will be reduced. Cover and simmer over moderate heat for 30 minutes. Strain and measure. Return the liquid to the saucepan and reduce over fairly brisk heat to 4 cups, if necessary. Cool, refrigerate and remove any fat. The stock can be frozen.

M A K E S 4 cups.

ASPIC

❖ ❖ ❖

Most stock will set into a light jelly when cold, but this may not be firm enough for an aspic. Use a little unflavored powdered gelatin to reinforce the stock. One envelope (7 grams), about 1 tablespoon, will set 2 cups of liquid into a firm aspic. One envelope will set 3 cups of liquid into jellied soup.

To use gelatin, sprinkle 1 envelope of the powder onto ¼ cup cold water and let it stand until softened. Stir into the liquid to be jellied and simmer over moderate heat until the gelatin has completely dissolved, stirring once or twice; this needs a minute or two. Pour the liquid into a bowl and refrigerate to set.

There are commercial aspic jelly powders available in specialty shops. These are flavored and have salt. If using these, do not salt the stock.

BÉCHAMEL SAUCE
(White Sauce)

❖ ❖ ❖

This is a sauce far less used by today's young chefs than it was in the past, but it is a classic sauce, and still has its place in the kitchen.

3 tablespoons butter
3 tablespoons all-purpose flour

2 cups milk
Salt, white pepper

In a heavy saucepan over low heat melt the butter and stir in the flour with a wooden spoon. Cook, stirring, without letting the mixture color, for 2 minutes. Remove from the heat and gradually stir in the milk until the mixture is smooth. If there are any lumps, beat with a wire whisk. Season with salt and pepper and return the saucepan to the heat. Bring to a simmer and cook, stirring constantly, for 5 minutes.

M A K E S 2 cups.

Velouté Sauce

Make as above, using white stock made from poultry, veal or fish in place of milk.

SAUCE DEMI-GLACE

❖ ❖ ❖

This has become part of the international repertoire although it originated in France. Cooks everywhere find it useful. It is not difficult to make, or very time-consuming, once you have beef stock on hand.

1 tablespoon butter
1 medium-size onion, chopped
  fine
1 medium-size carrot, scraped
  and chopped
½ cup fine-chopped mushrooms
2 parsley sprigs
1 garlic clove, chopped
1 celery rib, chopped

1 thyme sprig
1 small bay leaf
1 cup chopped tomatoes, fresh or
  canned
5 cups Beef Stock (see Index)
¼ cup dry Madeira wine
  (optional)
Salt, freshly ground pepper

In a saucepan heat the butter and sauté the onion and carrot until they are soft and lightly browned. Add the mushrooms, parsley, garlic, celery, thyme, bay leaf, tomatoes and beef stock. Simmer, uncovered, over very low heat, skimming from time to time if necessary, for 1½ hours. Strain through a fine sieve. Stir in the Madeira if liked. Taste for seasoning and add salt and pepper if needed.

M A K E S about 2 cups.

HOLLANDAISE SAUCE

❖ ❖ ❖

3 egg yolks
1 tablespoon cold water
½ pound (2 sticks) butter, cut
  into pieces

Salt
Pinch of cayenne pepper
1 tablespoon lemon juice

Combine the egg yolks and water in the top pan of a double boiler over hot water and whisk until they are light. Set the double boiler over very, very low heat and whisk in the pieces of butter, one by one, adding a new piece when the previous one has been incorporated into the sauce. Be very careful not to overheat the sauce as it will not thicken into a smooth creamy mixture if it is too hot. The water in the double boiler should not boil but be at just under a simmer. Remove from the heat if necessary.

When all the butter has been beaten into the egg yolks and the sauce is thick and creamy, season to taste with salt, cayenne and lemon juice. Serve as soon as possible. The sauce is always served warm, not hot; it can be kept warm for a time over tepid water. If the water is too hot, the sauce will thin or curdle.

Hollandaise can also be made, with care, in a small, very heavy saucepan set directly over low heat.

M A K E S about 1 cup.

BÉARNAISE SAUCE

❖ ❖ ❖

This is a first cousin of hollandaise sauce. It is more strongly flavored and uses vinegar instead of lemon juice.

¼ cup tarragon vinegar
¼ cup dry white wine
1 tablespoon mixed minced fresh
  tarragon and chervil or ½
  tablespoon dried
2 tablespoons minced shallots

3 egg yolks, lightly beaten
Salt, freshly ground pepper
½ pound (2 sticks) butter, cut
  into bits
2 tablespoons minced fresh
  tarragon, chervil or parsley

In a small saucepan combine the vinegar, wine, herbs and shallots and simmer over low heat until the liquid is reduced to 2 tablespoons. Strain into the top pan of a double boiler set over low heat. Beat in the egg yolks and add 1 tablespoon cold water; continue to beat over low heat until egg yolks are thick. Season to taste with salt and pepper. Beat in the butter, bit by bit, until the sauce is thick and creamy. If it seems to be getting too hot, lift it off the heat for a minute or two. Stir in the minced herbs and pour into a sauceboat.

M A K E S about 1 cup.

BEURRE BLANC
(White Butter Sauce)

❖   ❖   ❖

This is another of the sauces that has become an indispensable part of every cook's repertoire. It can transform an everyday dish into a special one.

¼ cup shallots, chopped fine
¼ cup dry white wine
¼ cup white-wine vinegar

½ pound (2 sticks) chilled butter,
    cut into bits
Salt, white pepper

Combine the shallots, wine and vinegar in a small heavy saucepan and simmer, uncovered, over low heat until the liquid has reduced to about 1 tablespoon. Still over low heat whisk in the butter, one piece at a time, adding a new piece as soon as the previous one has melted into the sauce. Continue until all the butter is used up, beating constantly. Do not let the sauce get too hot or the butter will turn oily. Simply remove the saucepan from the heat briefly if it seems too hot. When all the butter is used and the sauce is thick and creamy, remove it from the heat and season with salt and pepper. Serve as soon as possible.

M A K E S about 1 cup.

V A R I A T I O N : Some cooks use strained lemon juice instead of white-wine vinegar.

TOMATO SAUCE

❖　　　❖　　　❖

If ripe, red tomatoes are not available, use the best canned tomatoes possible.

1 medium-size onion, chopped
　fine
2 tablespoons olive or vegetable
　oil, or butter
1 garlic clove, minced
2 pounds tomatoes, peeled,
　seeded and chopped
2 tablespoons tomato purée

Salt, freshly ground pepper
⅛ teaspoon sugar
1 bay leaf
1 tablespoon chopped basil or
　chervil, or 1 sprig of thyme,
　marjoram or orégano
½ cup water

In a heavy saucepan or casserole sauté the onion in the oil or butter until it is soft. Add the garlic and sauté for 1 minute longer. Add the tomatoes, tomato purée, salt and pepper to taste, sugar, bay leaf and herbs. Stir in the water. Cover and simmer for 15 minutes, stirring with a wooden spoon from time to time. The sauce should be thick and well blended. If it is too thick, add a little water; if too thin, cook uncovered for a few minutes longer. Before serving, remove and discard the bay leaf.

M A K E S　about 3 cups.

MAYONNAISE

❖　　　❖　　　❖

2 large egg yolks
1 teaspoon Dijon mustard
Salt, freshly ground white pepper
1½ cups oil (olive or vegetable or
　a mixture of both)

4 teaspoons vinegar (any type),
　or lemon juice

In a shallow bowl whisk together the egg yolks, mustard, and salt and pepper to taste until they are well blended. Whisk in the oil, drop by drop, until the mixture is thick and creamy. When about half of the oil has been absorbed by the egg yolks, whisk in the vinegar or lemon juice. Add remaining oil, pouring it into the mayonnaise in a thin, steady stream and beating constantly with a whisk. When all the oil has been absorbed, taste for seasoning and add more salt and pepper,

vinegar or lemon juice to taste. If the mayonnaise is too thick it may
be thinned by adding a tablespoon of water or light cream.

M A K E S about 2 cups.

OIL AND VINEGAR DRESSING

❖   ❖   ❖

This is the basic salad dressing that is usually called by its French
name, *vinaigrette*. It can be made with a great variety of oils—vegetable, olive, hazelnut, walnut and so on, used in varying proportions.
The vinegars available are legion—from malt, cider, wine, both red
and white, tarragon, and other herb vinegars, to raspberry vinegar and
Japanese rice vinegar. Lemon juice can also be used. Almost endless
variations can be played on this theme though the basic proportions
for the sauce remain the same. Dijon mustard and garlic may also be
added.

¼ cup vinegar   *¾ to 1 cup oil*
Salt, freshly ground pepper

Combine the vinegar with salt and pepper to taste in a bowl and whisk
in the oil in a steady stream until the mixture is well blended.

M A K E S about 1 cup.

GARLIC CROUTONS

❖   ❖   ❖

2 garlic cloves, peeled   *½ cup olive oil*
¼ teaspoon salt   *French or other firm white bread*

Crush the garlic with the salt and beat into the olive oil. Cut the
crusts off slices of bread and cut the slices into enough ¼-inch cubes
to make 2 cups.

In a skillet heat the oil and garlic mixture and sauté the bread cubes
over low heat until they are browned all over, tossing them frequently.
Alternately they may be sprinkled with the oil and garlic mixture and
baked in a preheated moderate oven (375°F.) until browned, about
10 minutes.

DUXELLES

❖ ❖ ❖

½ pound mushrooms
4 tablespoons (½ stick) butter
¼ cup fine-chopped shallots or
scallions

Salt, freshly ground pepper

Wipe the mushrooms and chop fine, using both caps and stems. In a small heavy saucepan heat the butter and sauté the mushrooms and shallots or scallions over moderate heat, stirring from time to time, until the mushrooms have given up all their moisture and the mixture is quite dry. Season to taste with salt and pepper and use as directed in recipes.

M A K E S about 1 cup.

TO CLARIFY BUTTER

❖ ❖ ❖

Clarified butter does not burn at as low a temperature as ordinary butter, so it is used whenever high heat is needed. This is useful when the addition of oil to prevent the butter from burning would alter the flavor of a dish.

Cut the butter into pieces and put it into a small heavy saucepan over low heat. Skim off the white froth as it rises. When the butter has melted, let it stand for 2 to 3 minutes. There will be a milky residue on the bottom of the pan. Strain the clear yellow liquid into a bowl. The residue can be added to soups, stews or sauces to enrich them.

Unsalted or sweet butter is more satisfactory to use when clarifying butter. The amount of salt in salted butters varies a great deal, making it hard to judge the saltiness of dishes. Unsalted butter has a more delicate flavor and is best used for all cooking.

PUFF PASTRY

❖ ❖ ❖

This elegant pastry, though not difficult to make, is time-consuming. However, it has a great many uses, often turning an ordinary dish into a special one. It is sometimes available in supermarkets and specialty shops frozen, and is quite satisfactory. The British kitchen has a simpler pastry, Rough Puff Pastry, that is very useful and easier to make than classic puff pastry.

2 cups bread flour or all-purpose
   flour
½ teaspoon salt
2 tablespoons unsalted butter, cut
   into bits

1 teaspoon lemon juice
½ cup ice water, approximately
½ pound (2 sticks) unsalted
   butter

Sift the flour and salt together into a large bowl. Work the 2 tablespoons butter bits into the flour with the fingertips until the mixture resembles coarse meal. Make a well in the center and add the lemon juice and water. Still using the hands, work the mixture into a fairly stiff, smooth dough, adding a little more water if necessary. Form the dough into a ball, sprinkle lightly with flour, put into a plastic bag, and refrigerate for about 1 hour.

While the dough is chilling, work the butter into a square. Put it between 2 sheets of wax paper and roll it out with a rolling pin to make a 4-inch square. Peel off the wax paper, sprinkle butter lightly with flour, wrap up in fresh paper, and refrigerate until butter is firm.

On a lightly floured board roll out the dough to a 7-inch square and put the butter diagonally in the center. Fold the dough over the butter as if making an envelope. Make sure the butter is completely sealed in. Turn the package over. Dust the board and the dough lightly with flour and roll out the dough gently and evenly into a rectangle 6 by 10 inches. Fold the top over all but the bottom third of the rectangle. Fold the bottom third over the top to make a square of 3 overlapping layers. This is the first fold. The process will be repeated, making 5 folds in all.

Turn the dough so that one of the open ends faces you. Always turn the dough in the same direction. Roll the dough, gently and evenly, once more into a 6- by 10-inch rectangle. Do not roll right to the edges. Stop about ½ inch before the edge so as not to force the butter out of the paste. Fold up the dough once more into 3 overlapping layers. This is the second fold. Wrap the dough in wax paper and refrigerate for 30 minutes. It is a good idea to mark the dough by pressing it lightly with a finger so that it can be turned from the correct position. Always have an open end facing you when rolling out the dough.

Continue to turn roll out, and fold the dough, refrigerating it if it seems to be getting the least warm and sticky, until it has been rolled

(recipe continues)

out and folded 5 times in all. Chill the dough, wrapped in wax paper, for at least 30 minutes after the last fold. It is now ready to be used.

The dough will keep, refrigerated, for about a week. Wrapped in foil, it will keep in the freezer for up to 6 months.

M A K E S 1 pound.

ROUGH PUFF PASTRY

❖   ❖   ❖

2 cups bread flour or all-purpose flour
½ teaspoon salt
¼ pound (1 stick) unsalted butter, cut into bits

¼ cup (4 tablespoons) lard, cut into bits
6 tablespoons ice water, approximately

Sift the flour and salt into a large bowl. Work the butter and lard into the flour with the fingertips until the mixture resembles coarse meal. Pour 4 tablespoons of the ice water into the dough, mix with the hands, and form into a ball. Add more water, if necessary. Wrap the ball of dough in wax paper, or put it in a plastic bag, and refrigerate for 30 minutes.

Follow the same procedure as for puff pastry: roll out the dough into a rectangle and fold it up into a 3-layered package. Turn, roll out, and fold 4 times in all. Wrap the dough in wax paper, or put it in a plastic bag, and refrigerate it for at least 30 minutes. It is now ready to be used.

M A K E S about 1 pound.

VOL-AU-VENT

❖   ❖   ❖

Carême is credited with inventing these very useful pastry cases, using the puff pastry that is generally credited to the French landscape painter, Claude Lorrain, who lived from 1600-1682. Vol-au-vent are sometimes available ready made, needing only to be thawed and baked, or they can be made from frozen puff pastry also available from supermarkets or specialty shops, if kitchen time is short. When I have time

I much prefer to make my own puff pastry and use it for *vol-au-vent* as well as other things.

1 recipe Puff Pastry (see Index)   1 teaspoon water or heavy cream
1 large egg yolk

Roll out the pastry to ½-inch thickness. Using a scalloped 3-inch pastry cutter, cut the pastry into rounds. Choose a slightly smaller plain cutter and carefully press it into the center of each round down to about two thirds of the thickness of the dough. Chill for 30 minutes.

Mix the egg yolk and water or cream in a small bowl. Arrange the pastry cases on an ungreased baking sheet and brush the tops with the egg-yolk mixture. Bake in a preheated moderate oven (350°F.) for 40 to 45 minutes, or until the pastry is well risen and golden brown. Using a small sharp knife remove the center rounds. With a small spoon scoop out any soft pastry from the shells. Fill the cases and replace the center circle as a lid.

SHORT-CRUST PASTRY

❖   ❖   ❖

2 cups all-purpose flour
½ teaspoon salt
6 tablespoons chilled unsalted
  butter, cut into bits
2 tablespoons chilled lard, cut
  into bits, or vegetable
  shortening

1 egg yolk
3 tablespoons ice water,
  approximately

Sift the flour and salt together into a large bowl. Toss in the butter and lard bits to coat them with flour, then rub them into the flour with the fingertips until the mixture resembles coarse meal. Mix the egg yolk with the water. Add it to the flour mixture all at once and quickly mix together. If the dough crumbles, add a little more ice water. Form the dough into a ball, wrap it in wax paper or put it into a plastic bag, and refrigerate it for at least 1 hour before using.

For sweet pastry add 1 tablespoon of sugar to the dough and reduce the amount of salt to ¼ teaspoon.

M A K E S enough for a 10- to 11-inch pie shell.

CHOUX PASTRY

❖   ❖   ❖

1 cup water
½ teaspoon salt
¼ pound (1 stick) unsalted butter

1 cup all-purpose flour
4 large eggs

Combine the water, salt and butter in a medium-size saucepan. Bring to a boil over moderate heat, stirring once or twice. When the water boils, add the flour, all at once, stirring vigorously with a wooden spoon until the batter draws away from the sides of the pan and forms a compact ball. This takes less than 1 minute. Remove the dough from the heat and let it stand for 2 to 3 minutes. Beat in the eggs one by one until the batter is smooth and shiny. The pastry is now ready to be used.

For sweet puffs add 1 tablespoon of sugar to the water, salt and butter mixture.

M A K E S about 2 cups, enough for about 40 small puffs, 1½ inches in diameter.

TO MAKE PUFF SHELLS

❖   ❖   ❖

Make 1 recipe choux pastry. For puff shells about 1½ inches in diameter, use a pastry bag with ½-inch round tube and pipe circles of dough about 1 inch around and ½ inch high onto a baking sheet, 2 inches apart, or drop by teaspoons onto the sheet. Brush with egg wash made with 1 egg yolk beaten with 1 teaspoon water. Slightly flatten the puffs. Bake in a preheated hot oven (425°F.) for 15 to 20 minutes.

Remove the puffs from the oven and pierce the sides with the point of a small sharp knife. Return the puffs to the turned-off oven and leave for 10 minutes, with the oven door ajar. Take out and cool on racks.

Use a pastry bag with a ¼-inch opening for tiny puffs, and a ¾-inch round tube opening for larger puffs.

BRIOCHE BREAD

❖   ❖   ❖

I have been using this recipe for years, at least since the mid-seventies. I asked my dear mentor and friend Jim (James Andrews) Beard for a simpler brioche recipe when I just wanted to make brioche toast. He gave me this recipe, which is reproduced here with only the most minor changes. It appears in *How to Eat Better for Less Money* by James Beard and Sam Aaron, a wonderfully useful book. I miss Jim, as indeed I think the whole world of cooks does, and it makes me happy to be able to remember him when I knead this delicious, easy, quick and wonderful bread.

*5 teaspoons (two ¼-ounce
    packages) active dry yeast
¼ cup lukewarm water (110° to
    115°F.)
1¼ cups warm milk
2 large eggs, lightly beaten
6 ounces (1½ sticks) butter,
    softened at room temperature*

*¼ cup sugar
2 teaspoons baking powder
2 teaspoons salt
5 to 5½ cups bread flour or all-
    purpose flour*

In a large bowl soften the yeast in the warm water. Add the milk, eggs, butter, sugar, baking powder, salt and 5 cups of the flour. Mix thoroughly, using a wooden spoon and the hands. Turn out on a lightly floured surface and knead until smooth, about 10 minutes, adding remaining ½ cup flour as needed.

Oil or butter two baking pans, each 9 by 5 inches, and fit the dough into them. Cover and set in a warm, draft-free place to rise until doubled in bulk, about 1 hour.

Bake in a preheated moderate oven (350°F.) for 45 minutes, or until golden brown. The recipe can be halved.

M A K E S 2 loaves.

OATCAKES

❖   ❖   ❖

Oatcakes are a Scots tradition. They make a pleasantly crunchy accompaniment to pâtés, terrines or cheese, or are delicious just by themselves with butter. The catering staff at Hopetoun House near Edinburgh gave me this recipe when I told them how much I enjoyed their oatcakes.

½ pound fine oatmeal (rolled
    oats)
½ cup all-purpose flour
1½ teaspoons double-acting
    baking powder

Pinch each of salt and sugar
2 ounces (4 tablespoons) lard,
    butter or vegetable shortening
Milk

Put the oatmeal into a large bowl. Sift in the flour, baking powder, salt and sugar. Rub in the lard or other shortening with the fingertips to form a coarse meal. Add enough milk to make a fairly stiff dough. Form the dough into 18 patties about 2 inches in diameter, and flatten them slightly. Arrange the patties on a greased baking sheet and bake in a preheated moderate oven (375°F.) for 15 to 20 minutes. Allow to cool before storing.

M A K E S 18 oatcakes.

CRÊPES
(Pancakes)

❖   ❖   ❖

This is a basic batter for any savory crêpe. For dessert pancakes add sugar, or any other ingredients as indicated in the recipe.

1½ cups all-purpose flour
½ teaspoon salt
4 large eggs, lightly beaten
4 egg yolks

1 cup milk
1 tablespoon melted butter or
    vegetable oil

Sift the flour and salt into a large bowl. Add the whole eggs and egg yolks; stir to mix. Add the milk and melted butter or vegetable oil and beat with a balloon whisk until the mixture is very smooth. Or combine all the ingredients in a food processor and process until the mixture is smooth and silky. It should be like heavy cream. Refrigerate the batter for 2 hours before using.

To make the pancakes, have a nonstick skillet with a 6-inch diameter at the bottom. Brush the pan with vegetable oil, or crumple a piece of wax paper, rub it over some butter, and grease the pan with it. Set the pan over moderately high heat and when it is almost hot enough to smoke, pour in ¼ cup of batter. A ladle or a measuring cup is best to use. Quickly tilt the pan so that the batter covers the whole surface. Cook for about 1 minute. Lift the edge of the pancake to see if it is done. It should be very lightly browned. Turn with a spatula or the fingers, or flip over by tossing up in the pan. Cook the other side for about ½ minute. Grease the skillet for each pancake.

Stack the finished pancakes until ready to use. They can be kept warm by wrapping them lightly in aluminum foil and putting them into a warm oven, or by setting them on a plate, covered, over simmering water in a saucepan. They can be made ahead of time and reheated when ready to use.

M A K E S about twelve 6-inch pancakes.

A NOTE ON CRAYFISH

❖   ❖   ❖

The crayfish called for in British recipes are not the spiny or rock lobster, which are as large as lobsters but lack the lobster's large claws and have the meat in the tail. They are a much smaller shellfish, *Nephrops norvegicus*, the Norway lobster or Dublin Bay prawn. They are also known by their Italian name, *scampi*. They are widely available in Britain cleaned, shelled and frozen, but are also available fresh, unshelled. Use lobsterettes, crayfish or frozen langoustines instead. Jumbo prawns are always an acceptable substitute.

TO WASH LEEKS

❖   ❖   ❖

Leeks need thorough washing to remove any dirt or sand between the outer layers of the leaves. To clean leeks trim the root end and remove any wilted leaves. Trim the tough tops, then slit the leeks lengthwise in two places almost to the white part. Wash thoroughly under cold running water, pulling the leaves apart to rinse away sand or dirt.

If recipes call for using the white part only, use the green parts for making soups or stocks. The leeks are now ready to be cooked.

SHALLOTS

❖   ❖   ❖

Shallots (*Allium ascalonicum*) are members of the onion family, small round bulbs with a brownish-purple skin. Their flavor is mild and delicate, reminiscent of both onion and garlic. They are much used in sauces. If they are not obtainable, use the white part of scallions.

YOGURT CHEESE

❖   ❖   ❖

This is the easiest of all the fresh cheeses to make. It is attractive with fresh fruit or other desserts instead of cream, perhaps with a little sugar.

4 cups plain or low-fat yogurt   Pinch of salt

Line a large sieve with a double layer of dampened cheesecloth and pour in the yogurt mixed with the salt. Set over a deep bowl and let the whey drain out until the cheese is firm, about 6 hours. Put into a covered container and refrigerate. Will keep for 2 to 3 days.

M A K E S about 2 cups.

STABILIZED YOGURT

❖　　　❖　　　❖

4 cups yogurt　　　　　*1 tablespoon cornstarch*
½ teaspoon salt

Pour the yogurt into a large saucepan and mix with the salt. Mix the cornstarch with a little water and stir into the yogurt. Bring to a simmer over very low heat, stirring frequently with a wooden spoon. Cook, uncovered, over the lowest possible heat, below a simmer, for about 10 minutes or until thickened. If it is at all grainy transfer to a blender or food processor and process for about 30 seconds. The yogurt can now be used in cooking without curdling. To keep, pour into a container and refrigerate.

FRESH WHITE CHEESE

❖　　　❖　　　❖

This is based on Michel Guérard's *fromage blanc* and I have used it very satisfactorily in sauces, and in poultry and seafood dishes. It should be heated very gently and not allowed to boil.

1½ cups low-fat ricotta cheese　　*4 tablespoons plain yogurt*
¼ teaspoon salt

In a blender or food processor combine all the ingredients and process until very smooth. Transfer to a covered container and refrigerate for 12 hours before using.

If a sauce calls for reducing a mixture with cream, omit this step. Add fresh white cheese and simply warm it through without reduction.

JUNKET CHEESE

❖   ❖   ❖

This easy-to-make fresh cheese, when made with whole milk, is an admirable substitute for cream in many recipes, with desserts, or added to soups and sauces at the last minute. When made with skim milk, it is an easy and attractive way to reduce the amount of fat in the diet. Anton Mosimann, the famed Maître Chef des Cuisines of London's Dorchester Hotel, and the creator of *cuisine naturelle*, makes a junket cheese with skim milk that has an exceptionally good texture. He lets the milk and junket mixture stand for 24 hours instead of the usually much shorter time, just until set.

4 cups whole or skim milk   *1 junket tablet, or 2 teaspoons*
Pinch of salt   *rennet essence*

In a saucepan heat the milk to lukewarm (110°F.). Pour into a bowl. Add salt. Crush the junket tablet with a little water and stir it quickly into the milk, or stir in the rennet essence. Cover the bowl and let it stand for 24 hours, or until set.

Pour the mixture carefully into a sieve lined with a double thickness of dampened cheesecloth set over a large deep bowl, and leave until the cheese is firm, about 45 minutes. Pour off and discard the whey. Put the cheese into a container and refrigerate until ready to use. It will keep, refrigerated, for 3 to 4 days.

M A K E S about 1½ cups.

APPETIZERS

❖   ❖   ❖

Appetizers, called "starters," in Britain, and a favorite
course there, are among the most original and innovative
dishes to come out of the cooking renaissance, with new
flavor affinities and contrasting textures. Chefs have taken advantage of the era of cooking liberation and have used their
unfettered imaginations to create dishes that whet the appetite
without overwhelming it, and thus entice the diner into the rest
of the meal. They also beguile the eye, making unfussy edible
pictures on the plate. They use tableware with great flair, bor-
rowing ideas from the Japanese in the use of multishaped china
to show food off to its best advantage.

Many of the appetizers, when served in larger portions, make
superb lunch or supper main courses, while an array of them
makes a fine buffet for a party. A smaller selection is ideal to
serve when friends drop by for drinks. They are extremely versatile.

Today's chefs care about healthy as well as enjoyable eating.
Sauces are no longer thickened with butter and flour, just reduced to concentrate flavor and lightly thickened with a little
butter and cream, just enough to give a good texture. They are
rich so chefs serve them in small quantities to balance taste with
health. However, many of us today want to avoid even a small
amount of cream when cooking at home, except perhaps for
special occasions.

I have found that the fresh cheeses, which can substitute for
cream, provide an answer. They are usually known by their
French name, *fromage blanc*, since France is where they originated. Anton Mosimann, the Maître Chef des Cuisines at London's Dorchester Hotel, in his book *Cuisine Naturelle* (recipes
without fat or cream) has a good one—Junket Cheese, which
is easy to make with either junket tablets or rennet essence.
There is also a simple Yogurt Cheese, and Stabilized Yogurt that

does not curdle when heated and is therefore good in soups. Yet another, and one I find very satisfactory in cooking, is Michel Guérard's version made with low-fat ricotta cheese. There are recipes for all of these in the Basic Recipes section.

In this section there are some elegant dishes that are worth spending time on for a celebratory meal, others that can be made ahead of time, and still others that are quick and simple to make.

Salads are also very popular as appetizers. These new salads use a wide variety of salad greens and may include game, poultry, meat, fish or shellfish. Many of them are served warm. A selection of these can be found in the Vegetables and Salads section.

SWEET RED PEPPER MOUSSE WITH FRESH TOMATO PURÉE

❖   ❖   ❖

Raymond Blanc, the young chef-patron of Le Manoir aux Quat'
Saisons at Great Milton, Oxfordshire, a lovely Cotswold-stone Tudor
manor house now a very elegant country house hotel, has extraordinary
talent. He has had no formal training but his genius in the kitchen
has been widely recognized. This simplest and freshest of appetizers is
a delight, like all his creations.

Mousse

¾ pound ripe red bell peppers
Vegetable oil
1 medium-size ripe tomato, about
   ¼ pound, peeled, seeded and
   chopped
¼ cup sugar

¼ cup red-wine vinegar
1 teaspoon unflavored gelatin
Salt, freshly ground pepper
½ teaspoon cayenne pepper
½ cup heavy cream, whipped

Fresh Tomato Purée

3 medium-size tomatoes, about
   ¾ pound, peeled, seeded and
   chopped
3 tablespoons red-wine vinegar

Salt, freshly ground pepper
3 tablespoons olive oil
1 teaspoon sugar (optional)

Halve the peppers and remove the stems, ribs and seeds. Lightly oil
a baking sheet and arrange the peppers on it. Bake in a preheated hot
oven (450°F.) for 15 minutes. Cool slightly, then peel. Chop coarsely
and set aside with the tomato.

Put the sugar into a small, heavy saucepan over moderate heat. Stir
with a wooden spoon from time to time until the sugar caramelizes
and is golden brown. Add the vinegar and continue to cook until the
caramel dissolves in the vinegar. Reduce the mixture to half, still over
moderate heat. Set aside.

Pour ¼ cup cold water into a small saucepan and sprinkle on the
gelatin. When it has softened, dissolve the gelatin over low heat,
stirring.

(recipe continues)

In a blender or food processor combine the peppers and tomato and process to a purée. Pour into a saucepan and simmer over moderate heat to reduce excess liquid. When the mixture has thickened slightly add the gelatin and the sugar and vinegar mixture. Season with salt, pepper and cayenne and chill lightly. Fold in the cream, transfer to a bowl, and refrigerate until set, about 3 hours.

While the mousse is setting, make the fresh tomato purée. In a blender or food processor combine the tomatoes with the vinegar. Season with salt, pepper and, if liked, the sugar, and process until smooth. With the machine running gradually pour in the oil.

Pour the purée over 6 chilled plates. Using 2 spoons, shape the pepper mousse into quenelles (ovals) and place on top of the purée.

S E R V E S 6. Do not serve wine with this.

SMOKED SALMON AND AVOCADO SOUFFLÉ

❖   ❖   ❖

Murdo MacSween, a nephew of the famed author Sir Compton Mackenzie, is a passionate cook devoted to excellence. A founding member of Country Chefs Seven, the group of young British chefs in country house hotels who banded together to help each other, help raise cooking standards, and invent new and original dishes, he created this inspired but simple dish. Murdo is now head chef at Oakley Court, a Victorian mansion now a country house hotel on the banks of the Thames at Windsor, Berkshire. Serve with a white Chiltern Valley wine.

3 tablespoons butter, plus butter
  for molds
3 tablespoons all-purpose flour
Salt, freshly ground pepper
1 cup milk, boiling
4 egg yolks
5 egg whites

¾ cup grated Swiss cheese
¼ pound smoked salmon,
  chopped
1 medium-size avocado, peeled,
  pitted and chopped
1 teaspoon green peppercorns

If serving as a main course, butter a 6-cup soufflé mold generously with melted butter, or butter eight ¼-cup soufflé molds. Refrigerate until the butter is set.

Heat 3 tablespoons butter in a medium-size heavy saucepan and stir in the flour. Cook over low heat, stirring with a wooden spoon, for 2 minutes without letting the flour color. Season to taste with salt and pepper, remove from the heat, and pour in the boiling milk all at once, stirring until the mixture is smooth and well blended. Return to the heat and cook, stirring, for 2 minutes longer.

Off the heat beat in the egg yolks, one by one. Beat the egg whites with a pinch of salt until they stand in firm peaks. Stir about one quarter of the whites into the soufflé mixture, then gently but thoroughly stir in remaining whites, the cheese, smoked salmon, avocado and green peppercorns. Spoon the soufflé mixture into the large soufflé mold, or into the 8 small ones. Bake in a preheated moderate oven (350°F.) for 10 minutes for the small soufflés, 25 to 30 minutes for the large one.

S E R V E S 4 as a main course, 8 as an appetizer.

V A R I A T I O N : Christopher Grist, chef de cuisine as he prefers to be called, at Great Fosters in Egham, Surrey, has an interesting variation on Murdo's Smoked Salmon and Avocado theme. He adds a generous pinch of nutmeg and ½ cup snipped chives to the soufflé mixture and serves it with a Black-Currant and Sorrel Sauce, using black-currant vinegar. If this is hard to get, raspberry vinegar is a good substitute.

To make the sauce pour ¼ cup black-currant or raspberry vinegar into a small saucepan and let it reduce over moderate heat, uncovered, to about 1 tablespoon. Cut the coarse ribs and stems from the sorrel and shred it fine. Add 1 cup firmly packed sorrel to the saucepan. Stir in ¼ cup heavy cream or use Fresh White Cheese (see Index). Season with salt and pepper, stir, and simmer for 1 minute. Pour the sauce onto the plate on which the soufflé is to be unmolded, or serve separately.

PASTA WITH MIXED MUSHROOMS

❖   ❖   ❖

Robert Jones was born in Newmarket, Suffolk, son of the famous jockey R. A. (Bobby) Jones who won every classic race except the Derby. His son took to cookery and is now head chef at Ston Easton Park, in Somerset, near Bath in Avon. He believes that food should foster good health, but be attractive to look at and good to eat. He keeps away from too-rich sauces and wants to cook dishes that are modern and also essentially British. This pasta dish is a fine example of his point of view. It is light and unusual. Serve with a white Palatinate wine.

2 ounces dried French morel
   mushrooms
3 ounces dried Chinese
   mushrooms
Whiskey, preferably Irish
1 medium-size onion, chopped
   fine
1 tablespoon chopped fresh herbs
   (parsley, mint, chervil, etc.)

2 tablespoons butter
2 cups sliced fresh mushrooms
1 cup heavy cream, or Fresh
   White Cheese (see Index)
Salt, freshly ground pepper
8 ounces fresh pasta

Combine the morels and Chinese mushrooms in a bowl and pour over enough whiskey barely to cover. Leave to soak for about an hour, or until soft. Lift out and slice. Reserve the soaking liquid.

Sauté the onion and herbs in the butter in a skillet until the onion is soft but not browned. Add the sliced dried mushrooms and the sliced fresh mushrooms and sauté for 3 or 4 minutes. Add the reserved soaking liquid (whiskey) and the cream. Simmer until the sauce thickens slightly. Season to taste with salt and pepper and keep warm. The sauce should be thick enough to coat the back of a spoon. If using fresh white cheese, just heat through.

Drop the pasta into a large saucepan of briskly boiling salted water and cook for 2 to 3 minutes. Drain. Add the mushroom sauce and heat through. Serve in shallow bowls.

S E R V E S 4.

This makes a good main course for a simple lunch for 2. Serve with a green salad, fruit and cheese for lunch.

BRIE FAVORS

❖   ❖   ❖

Willie MacPherson, when he was chef of The Feathers in Wood-stock, near Oxford, says that Michael Smith, the great expert on English cookery, first suggested this eighteenth-century recipe to him. He has given it his own special touch turning it into a modern dish and adding the fresh herbs he loves to use. The favors are delicious with predinner drinks, or as a first course. In the nineteenth century they were served as a savory at the end of the meal, a course that has largely disappeared. Serve with a white Burgundy wine.

½ pound ripe Brie cheese, rind
   left on, cut into ¼-inch cubes
¼ cup olive oil
¼ cup fresh herbs, a mixture of
   any of the following: parsley,
   thyme, rosemary, basil, mint,
   tarragon, chervil

1 garlic clove, crushed
½ pound Puff Pastry (see Index)
1 egg yolk
Vegetable oil for deep-frying
Garnish: salad greens and lemon
   wedges

In a bowl combine the cubes of Brie with the oil, herbs and garlic and leave at room temperature, turning cubes over from time to time with a wooden spoon, for 4 hours.

Roll out the pastry to about ⅛-inch thickness and cut it into 24 rounds, using a 2-inch cutter. Beat the egg yolk lightly with a teaspoon of water and brush half of the pastry circles with the egg wash. Drain the oil from the cheese cubes and distribute them, with any herbs and garlic, among the egg-washed pastry circles. Top with remaining pastry circles and press to seal the edges firmly. Arrange on a tray or flat dish and refrigerate for 20 to 30 minutes to rest the pastry.

Deep-fry the pastry circles in the vegetable oil until they are golden brown on both sides and puffed up. Drain on paper towels.

Serve hot, garnished with salad greens and lemon wedges, two per person as an appetizer; or serve with predinner drinks on a plate lined with paper napkins.

S E R V E S 6 as an appetizer.

LEEK SOUFFLÉ

❖   ❖   ❖

This lovely beginning to a meal is another of Willie MacPherson's appetizers. He uses the fruits of the earth with charming simplicity, and cooks with meticulous care. Serve with a Pouilly-Fuissé.

3 medium-size leeks, trimmed and washed	Salt, freshly ground pepper
2 tablespoons butter, plus butter for mold	2 egg yolks
	3 egg whites
¼ cup all-purpose flour, plus flour for mold	6 tablespoons heavy cream, or Stabilized Yogurt (see Index)
1 cup milk, warm	¼ cup dry white wine

Chop two of the leeks coarse, put into a blender or food processor and process to a purée. If necessary, add a little water or stock. Cut the third leek into julienne strips and set aside.

In a small heavy saucepan melt a little butter. Brush a 6-cup mold generously on bottom and sides with the butter. Refrigerate the mold until the butter has set, then brush it again with butter and lightly dust with flour, shaking out excess flour. Refrigerate again until the butter has set. The mold is now ready to use.

In a medium-size saucepan heat the 2 tablespoons butter and stir in the ¼ cup flour. Stir constantly with a wooden spoon over very low heat for 5 minutes without letting the flour mixture color. Remove from the heat and gradually stir in the warm milk. Return to heat and cook, stirring, for another 5 minutes. The sauce should be very thick and smooth. Season it to taste with salt and pepper. Off the heat beat in the egg yolks, one by one. Add two thirds of the leek purée. In a large bowl beat the egg whites until they stand in peaks. Stir 2 tablespoons of the whites into the soufflé mixture, then gently but thoroughly fold in the rest. Pour the soufflé into the prepared mold and run under a broiler to brown the top. Put the soufflé into a baking pan with water to come about halfway up, and bake in a preheated moderate oven (375°F.) for 25 minutes, or until well risen.

While the soufflé is cooking combine the rest of the leek purée, the cream, white wine and julienne of leek in a saucepan and simmer until lightly thickened. Season with salt and pepper and serve as a sauce with the soufflé.

The soufflé can also be made in individual dishes. It will take only 15 minutes to cook.

SERVES 4.

WATERCRESS MOUSSE

❖   ❖   ❖

When watercress is at its crisp, fresh green best I like to make this mousse, created by John Hornsby when he was head chef at the Castle Hotel in Taunton, Somerset. It demonstrates this chef's originality and his love of simple, natural ingredients. Serve with a light Moselle.

Mousse

3 bunches of watercress, stems
  discarded (4 cups leaves)
¾ cup heavy cream
5 large eggs

1 garlic clove, chopped
Salt, freshly ground pepper
Freshly grated nutmeg
Butter for molds

Sauce

1 small carrot, cut into julienne
  strips
1 small celery rib, cut into
  julienne strips
White part of 1 small leek, cut
  into julienne strips

1 tablespoon butter
⅓ cup chicken stock
⅓ cup dry white wine
¾ cup heavy cream, or Fresh
  White Cheese (see Index)

In a blender or food processor purée the watercress, add the cream, and blend to mix. Transfer the mixture to a bowl and whisk in the eggs, one by one. Add the garlic, salt and pepper to taste and nutmeg to taste. Pour the mixture into 6 buttered ½-cup ramekins. Bake in a preheated moderate oven (350°F.) for 30 minutes, or until the ramekins are puffed and golden and a knife inserted into the center comes out clean. Stand on a rack for 5 minutes.

While the ramekins are baking make the sauce. In a heavy skillet sauté the carrot, celery and leek in the butter over low heat until vegetables are soft. Transfer vegetables to a bowl. Pour the chicken stock and wine into the skillet and reduce the liquid over high heat to ⅓ cup. Add the cream and vegetables and cook, stirring, for a few minutes until the sauce is slightly thickened. Season to taste with salt and pepper.

Spoon the sauce onto 6 warmed plates. Run a knife round the edge of each ramekin and unmold the soufflés onto the plates.

S E R V E S 6.

TERRINE OF VEGETABLES AND CREAM CHEESE

❖ ❖ ❖

Philip Burgess, chef of the Arundell Arms in Lifton, Devon, has an inspired way with simple ingredients. This terrine could not be easier to make and is a perfect first course for an elegant lunch or dinner. I find it makes a good main course for lunch when accompanied with a little cold meat or poultry or seafood such as crab and a green salad, or sliced tomatoes drizzled with oil and sprinkled with chopped basil or chervil. Serve with a Muscadet.

1 recipe Crêpes (Pancakes) (see Index)
3 egg yolks
1 whole egg
4 ounces cream cheese
½ cup heavy cream
2 teaspoons grated Parmesan cheese
1 garlic clove, crushed
1 tablespoon chopped fresh tarragon, or 1 teaspoon dried
Salt, freshly ground pepper
12 whole green peppercorns, or ½ teaspoon cayenne pepper (optional)

1 small zucchini, cut into thin 2-inch strips
1 medium-size carrot, scraped and cut into thin 2-inch strips
1 medium-size leek, cut into strips ½ inch by 2 inches
1 cup cauliflowerets
5 tiny Brussels sprouts, left whole, or larger ones halved
2 button mushrooms, cut into thick slices
2 tablespoons butter, approximately, for the terrine

Make the crêpes (pancakes) and set aside. In a bowl combine the egg yolks, whole egg, cream cheese, cream, Parmesan cheese, garlic, tarragon, and salt and pepper to taste. If liked add the green peppercorns or cayenne. Whisk the ingredients together until the mixture is smooth.

To assemble the terrine, generously butter a loaf pan 9 by 5 inches and line it with the crêpes, reserving two or three to top the terrine. Put half of the vegetables into the loaf pan and cover with half of the cheese mixture. Top with remaining vegetables and cover with rest of the cheese mixture. Fold the crêpes over the terrine and cover with the reserved crêpes. Cover with buttered wax paper and aluminum foil and place in a baking pan with water to come about halfway up the terrine. Bake in a preheated moderate oven (375°F.) for 1¼ to 2 hours. Remove from the oven, cool, and refrigerate for several hours or overnight.

To unmold stand the terrine very briefly in warm water. Cut into 6 slices and serve garnished with lettuce leaves.

S E R V E S 6.

CRAYFISH TAILS
WITH CURRY SPICES

❖   ❖   ❖

Mark Napper, a young English chef, was in charge of the kitchen at Cromlix House in Dunblane, Central Region, Scotland, when I met him and enjoyed this attractive dish. The curry spices make a reticent appearance in the sauce, adding to its subtlety.

½ red bell pepper, seeded and cut into thin strips
½ green bell pepper, seeded and cut into thin strips
Salt
12 large crayfish tails or langoustines or jumbo shrimps, shelled

1 cup heavy cream, or Fresh White Cheese (see Index)
1 teaspoon mixed curry spices (turmeric, garam masala, cuminseed, coriander), or use curry powder with a little extra ground coriander
Freshly ground pepper

Drop the pepper strips into a large saucepan of briskly boiling salted water and simmer for 3 minutes. Drain, rinse immediately in cold water, drain, and set aside.

Combine the crayfish tails, langoustines or jumbo shrimps, cream and curry spices or powder in a medium-size saucepan and bring to a simmer. Cover and simmer for 2 to 3 minutes. Take out the shellfish and keep them warm. Reduce the cream over moderately high heat until it is of coating consistency. Taste for seasoning and add salt and pepper as necessary. If using fresh white cheese, simply add it without reducing.

Have ready 4 warmed plates. Place 3 shellfish on each plate and coat with the sauce. Arrange 2 piles, one red, one green, of pepper strips on each side of the shellfish. Serve immediately.

S E R V E S 4.

CRAYFISH TAILS IN PUFF PASTRY

❖　　　❖　　　❖

Paul Vidic, head chef of Michael's Nook at Grasmere, Cumbria, in the Lake District, likes uncomplicated presentation without a medley of colors on the plate. This simple dish meets that requirement. It tastes wonderful, with an understated balance of flavors. The crayfish used in the recipe are usually called scampi or Dublin Bay prawns in Britain. Langoustines or jumbo shrimps make a good substitute. Serve with a Sauvignon Blanc.

4 Puff Pastry rectangles, 3 by 2 inches (see Index)
18 crayfish tails, or 12 jumbo shrimps or langoustines
½ cup strong Fish Stock (see Index)
1 cup dry vermouth, preferably Noilly Prat
1 cup heavy cream

½ teaspoon chopped fresh tarragon leaves, or ¼ teaspoon crumbled dried tarragon
Salt, freshly ground pepper
⅓ cup each of julienne of leek, celery and carrot
2 tablespoons butter
1 squeeze of lemon juice

Bake the puff pastry rectangles. Set aside, but keep them warm.

If using fresh crayfish, snap off the ridged tail, then either break the tail shell in half with the fingers, or snip it with a pair of scissors. Remove the meat from the tail shell. Keep the shells for making shellfish stock. If using jumbo shrimps, remove the heads and shell the shrimps. Keep the heads and shells for making shellfish stock. In both cases the shells can be frozen until ready to be used.

In a small heavy saucepan heat the fish stock and the vermouth and simmer for a minute or two. Add the crayfish tails, jumbo shrimps or langoustines and simmer, covered, for 1 minute. Remove shellfish from the pan and keep warm, covered. Over brisk heat reduce the liquid in the saucepan until syrupy. Add the cream and tarragon, season with salt and pepper, and reduce until the sauce coats the back of a spoon.

Meanwhile cook the vegetables separately in salted water until crisp. Drain, combine, and add to the sauce. Add the butter, shaking the saucepan over moderate heat until the butter has melted. Taste for seasoning, adding salt and pepper if necessary. Squeeze in the lemon juice. Add the shellfish and warm through. Serve immediately on the bottom half of the puff pastry, split in two, and top with the other half.

S E R V E S 4.

SMOKED SALMON AND CRAB MOUSSE

❖   ❖   ❖

Melvin Jordan, head chef of Pool Court restaurant, at Pool-in-Wharfe-dale in West Yorkshire, has devised a most attractive first course in this dish. It shows his talent for creating dishes that look as good as they taste. Serve with a Chardonnay.

½ pound fresh crab meat, picked over to remove any cartilage
1 tablespoon grated Parmesan cheese
¼ cup heavy cream, or Fresh White Cheese (see Index)
Salt, freshly ground pepper
⅛ teaspoon cayenne pepper
½ teaspoon paprika
2 tablespoons lemon juice
1 tablespoon mayonnaise (optional)

1 envelope unflavored gelatin (7 grams)
Butter for molds
½ pound thin-sliced smoked salmon
2 egg whites
Garnish: lemon wedges and parsley sprigs, or endive and hazelnut (filbert) salad, tossed in vinaigrette dressing

In a blender or food processor combine the crab meat, cheese and cream and process to a smooth purée. Season with salt and pepper to taste, cayenne, paprika, lemon juice, and mayonnaise if using it. Soften the gelatin in ¼ cup cold water. Pour it into a small saucepan and stir over very low heat until the gelatin has dissolved. Let it cool, then stir it into the crab mixture. Set aside.

Butter 4 small soufflé dishes or ramekins, ¾- to 1-cup size, and line them with the smoked salmon strips, letting the excess hang over the edges. In a bowl beat the egg whites until frothy but not dry and fold them into the crab mixture. Spoon the mixture into the ramekins and cover with the overhanging salmon. Refrigerate for at least 3 hours, or until firmly set.

To unmold stand ramekins in hot water for a few seconds to loosen the salmon, then turn out onto 4 plates. Garnish with sprigs of parsley and lemon wedges, or serve with a small salad of endive and hazelnuts.

S E R V E S 4.

N O T E : Lining the molds can be tricky. If liked, omit the smoked salmon until the crab mousse has been unmolded, then carefully cover it with smoked salmon, tucking the ends under. This will require less salmon.

DEVILED CRAB AND SHRIMPS

❖   ❖   ❖

This light, attractive appetizer is a good example of Alain Dubois' talent for making new combinations of fresh ingredients, keeping all their flavor. He is head chef at the sixteenth-century Cotswold Inn, The Lygon Arms in Broadway, Hereford and Worcester, now a country house hotel with twentieth-century comforts and a twentieth-century approach to food. This is especially delicious for a summer meal. Serve with a Muscadet.

2 tablespoons butter, plus butter
   for molds
1 red bell pepper, seeded and
   chopped fine
1 green bell pepper, seeded and
   chopped fine
1 small onion, chopped fine
1 cup bread crumbs, made with
   day-old bread

Salt, freshly ground pepper
1 teaspoon English dry mustard
2 teaspoons Worcestershire sauce
⅛ teaspoon Tabasco
1 cup crab meat, picked over and
   any cartilage removed
½ cup heavy cream, or Fresh
   White Cheese (see Index)
1 cup small shrimps

In a medium-size heavy saucepan or casserole heat the butter and sauté the red and green bell peppers and the onion until the vegetables are tender, without letting them brown. Transfer to a bowl and add the bread crumbs, salt and pepper to taste, mustard, Worcestershire sauce and Tabasco, tossing lightly to mix. Fold in the crab meat, then stir in the cream or fresh white cheese.

Butter four 1-cup ramekins and arrange the shrimps on the bottom. Cover with the crab mixture. Bake in a preheated moderate oven (350°F.) for 15 minutes, or until heated through.

S E R V E S   4.

MOUSSE OF SMOKED TROUT

❖   ❖   ❖

This is a very light and pleasant beginning to a meal. Martin Bredda, who is chef to the Earl and Countess of Normanton, cooks a lot of game from the estate at Somerley, in Ringwood, Hampshire. The venison dish he gave me is one of the best I have ever had, but it isn't, by its nature, light. Martin feels that getting the right balance in a meal is as important as good cooking and presentation. Serve with a Pouilly-Fuissé.

1 smoked trout, about 10 ounces
⅛ teaspoon grated nutmeg
Generous pinch of saffron
1 egg
1 egg white

Salt, freshly ground pepper
½ cup heavy cream
Butter
Tomato Sauce (see Index)

Bone the trout and put the flesh into a food processor or blender with the nutmeg, saffron, whole egg, egg white, and salt and pepper to taste. Process until the mixture is smooth. Scrape the mixture out of the machine and rub it through a fine sieve into a bowl. Beat in the cream with a wooden spoon and pour the mousse into a buttered 1½-pint soufflé dish. Bake in a preheated moderate oven (350°F.) for 15 to 20 minutes, or until a knife inserted into the mousse comes out clean. Serve with tomato sauce.

S E R V E S 4 to 6.

POTTED SALMON AND SOLE

❖   ❖   ❖

Stephen Ross and Antony Pitt of Homewood Park country house hotel at Hinton Charterhouse, Freshford, near Bath in Avon, are keen on fish and shellfish dishes and have a special delivery each week from the Cornish coast, giving them 15 to 20 different varieties. This simple appetizer was invented to make use of two types of fish when they were abundant. Other fish can be substituted. Serve with a Riesling from Alsace.

¾ pound fresh salmon, skinned
  and boned
¾ pound fillet of sole
1 tablespoon lemon juice
Dry white wine or dry cider
Salt, freshly ground pepper

1 teaspoon chopped fresh dill
Pinch of grated nutmeg
1 teaspoon minced parsley
2 hard-cooked eggs, chopped fine
1 lemon segment
Clarified butter

Poach the fish in a heavy saucepan or skillet with the lemon juice and enough dry white wine or cider barely to cover, about 8 to 10 minutes. Cool, then flake into a serving bowl just large enough to hold the flaked fish comfortably with room for the other ingredients. Season with salt and pepper.

In a small bowl mix together the dill, nutmeg and parsley. Cover the fish with a layer of chopped egg, place the lemon segment on top and sprinkle the mixed flavorings over. Chill lightly, then cover with a layer of clarified butter and refrigerate until ready to serve.

Serve with toast and, if liked, a little chopped cucumber tossed in oil and vinegar or oil and lemon-juice dressing.

S E R V E S 6 to 8.

SALMON AND PRAWN TERRINE

❖   ❖   ❖

Sheena Buchanan-Smith, chef-patronne of the Isle of Eriskay Hotel and Restaurant, at Ledaig in Strathclyde, Scotland, enjoys cooking

and enjoys pleasing people with what she cooks. Widely traveled, she
has come to believe very strongly that Scots cooks, especially in country house hotels like Eriskay, should maintain the traditions of Scottish
cooking by using what are some of the very best raw ingredients in
the world. This delicious recipe demonstrates her point of view very
well. It is interestingly different from chef Melvin Jordan's Smoked
Salmon and Crab Mousse. Serve with a Sancerre.

½ pound smoked salmon, sliced
  thin in long strips
½ pound cooked shelled medium
  or small shrimps
3 tablespoons lemon juice
Freshly ground pepper
1 cup Mayonnaise, using lemon
  juice (see Index)
1 cup heavy cream, or Fresh
  White Cheese or Junket
  Cheese or Yogurt Cheese (see
  Index)

Salt
1 envelope unflavored gelatin (7
  grams)
Garnish: lettuce leaves and lemon
  wedges

Line an oiled terrine, about 9 by 5 inches, with the salmon strips,
letting the excess hang over the edges. A long narrow terrine is best.

In a food processor or blender combine the shrimps, any bits of
salmon left over, the lemon juice, pepper and mayonnaise. Process to
a smooth purée. Add the cream or fresh cheese and process for 30
seconds longer. Taste for seasoning and add a little salt if necessary.

Pour ¼ cup cold water into a small heavy saucepan. Sprinkle the
gelatin on the water to soften it. Set the saucepan over the lowest
possible heat and stir until the gelatin has dissolved. When it is cool,
pour it into the food processor or blender and process just long enough
to mix thoroughly. Pour the mixture into the terrine and cover it with
the overhanging salmon strips. Cover the terrine with aluminum foil,
weight lightly, and refrigerate overnight.

To unmold, stand the terrine in hot water for a few seconds to
loosen the salmon, then invert it onto a flat serving platter. Slice and
serve on plates garnished, if liked, with lettuce leaves and lemon
wedges.

S E R V E S 6.

MARINATED SALMON

❖   ❖   ❖

Scotland has very fine salmon, a challenge to chefs looking for new ways to use it without destroying the integrity of its flavor and texture. I found three dishes I particularly liked, one from England, two from Scotland, which show the chefs' ingenuity. Each different, each good. This recipe from Kenneth Bell, M.B.E., a Scot who owns and runs the sixteenth-century Thornbury Castle restaurant and hotel near Bristol, Avon, is classical in its simplicity. Serve with a Pouilly-Fuissé.

1½ pounds center cut of salmon	⅓ cup orange juice
¾ cup dry white wine	1 small onion, chopped fine
1 teaspoon salt	1 garlic clove, minced
¼ teaspoon freshly ground pepper	4 tablespoons olive oil
4 tablespoons lemon juice	

Cut the salmon horizontally into halves and remove all skin and bones, leaving 2 fillets. Cut each fillet into 3 little steaks, each weighing 2 to 3 ounces.

In a bowl whisk together all the ingredients for the marinade. Add the salmon pieces to the marinade, and refrigerate. Turn the salmon pieces from time to time to make sure they are all covered by the marinade. The salmon is ready after 6 hours, but it is at its best after 24 to 48 hours. Serve with a little salad at the side of the plate.

S E R V E S   6.

V A R I A T I O N   I :   Denis Woodtli, head chef at Lochalsh Hotel, Kyle of Lochalsh, Highland, Scotland, is also a hunter and fisherman. He created this recipe for the salmon he loves to catch.

½ pound fresh salmon, skinned and boned, and cut into strips ¼ by ½ inch	2 teaspoons chopped parsley
	1 tablespoon green peppercorns
½ cup lemon juice	¼ cup olive oil
	Salt, freshly ground black pepper

Combine all the ingredients in a bowl and refrigerate for 4 to 6 hours. Stir with a wooden spoon from time to time to make sure all the pieces are well covered by the marinade. Serve on a bed of shredded lettuce.

S E R V E S 2.

Chef Woodtli sometimes omits the green peppercorns and adds 1 tablespoon chopped shallots and 1 tablespoon freshly grated ginger-root.

V A R I A T I O N I I : Michael Collom, the young head chef at the Priory Hotel in Bath, sees cooks as artists who orchestrate their dishes to create the right harmony of flavors. His marinated salmon is interestingly different from the other two.

2-pound piece of fresh salmon from tail section	1 cup coarse-chopped fresh dill
	½ cup brandy
¼ cup coarse sea salt	1 teaspoon English dry mustard
Freshly ground pepper	

Prepare the salmon one day in advance. Ask the fishmonger to skin and fillet the salmon and remove all the small bones. Sprinkle the fillets with the sea salt. Do not use ordinary salt as this dissolves too quickly. Press the salt firmly into the fish on both sides and wrap in aluminum foil. Refrigerate for 24 hours.

Unwrap the salmon and brush away any salt that has not dissolved. The fish should be firm to the touch. Season generously with pepper then sprinkle with the dill, pressing it down firmly. Sprinkle with the brandy. Using a fine sieve, shake the mustard over the fish. Rewrap in foil, and refrigerate for 3 to 4 hours before serving.

Cut the salmon into thin slices and serve with mayonnaise mixed with a little snipped chives and dill.

S E R V E S 6.

BRANDADE OF SMOKED MACKEREL IN PASTRY

❖   ❖   ❖

This is an interesting putting together of ideas, and it demonstrates George Perry-Smith's philosophy of letting ingredients combine as naturally as possible. George, who now is chef-patron of the Riverside Restaurant at Helford in Cornwall, helped spark the renaissance of British cooking, training many of today's innovative young chefs. Serve with a Muscadet or Sancerre.

2 large garlic cloves
Salt
½ pound smoked mackerel,
    skinned and boned
6 tablespoons olive oil, warmed
6 tablespoons milk, warmed

Freshly ground pepper
2 teaspoons lemon juice
2 recipes of Puff Pastry (see
    Index)
1 egg yolk

Pound the garlic in a mortar with a little salt. In a food processor or blender purée the mackerel with the garlic until it is very light, or pound it in a mortar with the garlic. Put the purée in the top pan of a double boiler over warm water. It is important that the purée should be warm, not hot. Pour the oil and milk into 2 small jugs and add them to the mackerel alternately, a little at a time, beating with a wooden spoon. Keep the mixture light and soft, not sloppy. When the mackerel has absorbed all the oil and milk it will take without becoming runny, season it with pepper and lemon juice and a little salt, if necessary. Chill in the refrigerator.

Roll out the pastry fairly thin and cut into twenty-four 3-inch circles. Put a heaping teaspoon of mackerel mixture in the center of each, fold over and seal. Refrigerate for at least 1 hour.

Mix the egg yolk with 1 teaspoon of cold water and brush the turnovers with it. Bake them in a preheated hot oven (400°F.) for about 12 minutes, or until they are puffed and golden. Serve three per serving with a choice of sauces—Dill Cream or Cucumber Sambal.

SERVES 8.

Dill Cream

½ cup heavy cream, or Fresh
    White Cheese (see Index)
Salt, freshly ground pepper

1 teaspoon lemon juice
1 tablespoon ground dill seed

Whip the cream until it stands in soft peaks, then season with salt, pepper and lemon juice and fold in the dill seed. If using fresh white cheese, simply combine the ingredients.

Cucumber Sambal

1 cucumber, peeled and diced
   fine
Salt
1 tablespoon minced onion
1 tablespoon minced celery
½ to 1 teaspoon cayenne pepper,
   according to taste, or 1 fresh
   hot red chili pepper, seeded and
   chopped

Freshly ground black pepper
1 tablespoon minced parsley or
   fresh coriander
2 tablespoons Oil and Vinegar
   Dressing (see Index), made
   with lemon juice

Put the cucumber in a bowl and sprinkle it lightly with salt. Let it stand for 15 minutes, then rinse and drain thoroughly. Add the onion, celery, cayenne or chili pepper, freshly ground black pepper to taste and parsley or coriander. Mix well, then toss with the oil and lemon-juice dressing.

FRESH CRAB, SORREL AND TOMATO TART

❖   ❖   ❖

David Harding, head chef at Bodysgallen Hall, Llandudno, Gwynedd, in North Wales, has had his training in Wales and the North of England. His point of view is very British, but he also wants his cooking to suit the atmosphere of Bodysgallen, a great country house, mainly seventeenth century, now a small hotel. The result is exciting. His dishes are all highly original, though based firmly on tradition. Serve with a Pouilly-Fuissé.

½ recipe Short-Crust Pastry (see Index)
1 cup crab meat, picked over and any cartilage removed
1 cup heavy cream, or Fresh White Cheese (see Index)
1 medium-size tomato, peeled, seeded and chopped

½ cup fine-chopped sorrel leaves
Salt, freshly ground pepper
½ cup Hollandaise Sauce (optional) (see Index)
Watercress

Make the short-crust pastry and refrigerate until ready to use.

In a bowl combine the crab meat, cream, tomato, sorrel and salt and pepper to taste. Line four 3-inch soufflé dishes or ramekins with short-crust pastry and fill with the crab mixture. Bake in a preheated moderate oven (350°F.) for about 10 minutes, or until lightly set.

Pour 2 tablespoons of hollandaise sauce, if using it, onto each of 4 warmed plates. Unmold the crab tarts on each and garnish with a little watercress.

SERVES 4.

GRATINÉE OF FRESH CRAB

❖   ❖   ❖

Thérèse A. Boswell, better known as Terry Boswell, is the chef in her restaurant at Combe House Hotel at Gittisham, in Devon. Her life has involved lots of travel, teaching her much that she has added to her formal training in cooking. She has a simple philosophy in the kitchen, namely that shopping is an art, that only the best ingredients are good enough, and that it is a good idea to have an herb garden if you can, as fresh herbs add that little extra something. Serve with a Chardonnay.

½ recipe of Béchamel Sauce (see Index)
1 teaspoon Dijon mustard
⅛ teaspoon ground mace
Freshly ground black pepper
⅛ teaspoon paprika
6 anchovy fillets, pounded to a paste
2 tablespoons dry sherry

Salt
1 pound fresh crab meat, picked over to remove any cartilage
2 tablespoons minced scallions
1 cup fresh white bread crumbs
½ cup grated Parmesan or Gruyère cheese
1 tablespoon butter

Make the béchamel sauce. Stir in the Dijon mustard, mace, black pepper to taste, paprika, pounded anchovies and sherry. Taste for seasoning and add salt if necessary. Stir in the crab meat and the scallions and spoon into 6 buttered ¾-cup ramekins. Sprinkle with bread crumbs and cheese and dot with butter. Bake in a preheated hot oven (425°F.) for 15 minutes, or until the top is golden and crunchy.

SERVES 6.

POACHED EGGS AND SHRIMPS IN TARTLET SHELLS

❖   ❖   ❖

In this recipe David Harding has created an appetizer with a lovely mix of flavors and contrasting textures, crisp pastry in contrast with the unctuous smoothness of egg yolk, and herbs blending with spinach in hollandaise sauce. It is a complicated, though not a difficult dish, and is well worth the trouble. I find this a great luncheon dish if double portions are served. If it is served as an appetizer course, follow it with a very plain main course like broiled lamb chops. Serve with a Chardonnay.

6 ounces unpeeled medium raw
   shrimps
2 tablespoons butter
1 cup Fish Stock (see Index) or
   water
½ cup dry white wine
1 sprig each of thyme and parsley
1 tablespoon all-purpose flour
Salt, freshly ground pepper
1 teaspoon tomato purée
   (optional)
1 cup Hollandaise Sauce (see
   Index)

1 tablespoon heavy cream
½ cup mixed fresh herbs such as
   parsley, tarragon, thyme, basil
   and marjoram, puréed
½ cup puréed cooked spinach
Eight 3-inch Short-Crust Pastry
   tart shells (see Index)
½ recipe Duxelles (see Index)
8 large eggs, poached
Garnish: watercress sprigs and
   chopped peeled tomato

Peel the shrimps and set them aside. In a small saucepan heat 1 tablespoon of the butter and toss the shells in the butter over moderate heat until they turn pink. Pour in the fish stock or water and the dry white wine and add the thyme and parsley sprigs. Simmer, covered, for 15 minutes. Strain, pressing down hard on the shells to extract all the flavor. Measure the liquid and reduce to 1 cup over moderately high heat. Rinse out and dry the saucepan.

Heat remaining tablespoon of butter in the pan, stir in the flour, and cook over very low heat for 2 minutes without letting the mixture color. Off the heat gradually stir in the shrimp stock until the mixture is smooth, then simmer over low heat until the sauce is reduced to about ½ cup. Season with salt and pepper. If liked, a teaspoon of tomato purée may be added to enhance the color. Stir in the cream and set the sauce aside.

Pour the hollandaise sauce into another small saucepan and stir in the puréed herbs and spinach. Set the saucepan in a larger pan of warm water to keep it warm without curdling.

Warm the tartlets and half-fill them with the duxelles. Put a poached egg into each and spoon the hollandaise sauce over them. Arrange them on a baking sheet and glaze quickly under the broiler.

Add the shrimps to the shrimp sauce and simmer for about 2 minutes to cook the shrimps.

Pour the sauce over 8 warmed plates and place a tartlet on each. Garnish with watercress sprigs and chopped tomato and serve as an appetizer. For a main course arrange 2 tartlets on each of 4 warmed plates.

S E R V E S 8 or 4.

TARTE AUX FROMAGES BLANC

❖   ❖   ❖

This is another of Terry Boswell's favorite appetizers. It is a wonderful way to use leftover cheese. She usually has a mixture of Cheddar and Brie with a little Stilton or other blue cheese. It demonstrates another aspect of her kitchen philosophy, which is a detestation of waste, a point of view shared by many of her fellow chefs. Serve with a Chardonnay.

1 recipe Short-Crust Pastry (see Index), with 1 tablespoon paprika added to the flour	5 large egg yolks
	¼ cup snipped chives or minced scallions
1 pound mixed grated cheeses such as Cheddar, Stilton or other blue, Muenster, etc.	¼ cup minced parsley
	Salt, freshly ground pepper
	⅛ teaspoon freshly grated nutmeg

Make the pastry, adding the paprika to the flour. Line an 8-inch flan case, fill it half full of dried beans or rice, and bake in a preheated hot oven (425°F.) for 8 minutes until set. Remove the dried beans or rice and keep them for using again. The flan case should be firm on the bottom. If necessary, return it to the oven for 2 or 3 minutes.

In a bowl mix remaining ingredients together. Pour the filling into the flan ring and bake in a preheated oven (350°F.) until it is firm to the touch and golden, 30 to 40 minutes. If the cheese mixture seems at all dry, add a tablespoon or two of light cream. Serve warm or cold.

S E R V E S 8.

STILTON AND PEAR MOUSSE

❖   ❖   ❖

Sheena Buchanan-Smith has a special talent with appetizers, and I find this as attractive as her salmon and prawn terrine. She has an abundance of fresh pears from her garden in the season and invented this dish to take advantage of them. Serve with a Riesling from Alsace.

Vegetable oil
2 large, very slightly underripe pears
2 envelopes gelatin (7 grams each)
½ cup Tawny Port wine

¾ pound Stilton or other blue cheese, chopped coarse
1½ cups cream cheese (½ pound)
1 cup Mayonnaise (see Index)
Salt, freshly ground pepper

Brush a terrine 9 by 5 inches with oil and set it aside.

Peel and core the pears. Cut into quarters, and poach in water to cover over low heat for 8 minutes. Drain, cool, and chop coarse.

Pour ½ cup cold water into a small heavy saucepan and sprinkle on the gelatin to soften it. When it has softened, set the saucepan over low heat, add the Port wine and cook, stirring, until the gelatin has dissolved. Cool.

In a food processor or blender combine the blue cheese, cream cheese and mayonnaise and process to a smooth purée. Pour in the gelatin mixture and process to mix. Transfer to a bowl, season to taste with salt and pepper, and stir in the chopped pear. Pour into the oiled terrine and chill until set.

Slice and serve with brioche toast or other toast as a first course.

S E R V E S 6.

To serve with drinks, accompanied by cheese biscuits, pour the mixture from the food processor or blender into a serving bowl, add salt and pepper and the chopped pear, and refrigerate until set.

TERRINE OF FRESH CRAB

❖   ❖   ❖

Baba Hine, chef-patronne of Corse Lawn House, Corse Lawn, Gloucestershire, has a natural flair for cooking and the sort of feeling for food that is born, not made. She has no formal training but comes from a family deeply interested in good food. She is an unfussy cook, her technique a nice mix of traditional and modern with an emphasis on lighter dishes. Serve with a Sancerre.

Butter
Six 6-inch Crêpes (see Index)
12 ounces monkfish or similar
    nonoily white fish
3 egg whites
½ cup snipped chives
½ cup chopped parsley
Salt, freshly ground pepper

⅛ teaspoon grated nutmeg
6 tablespoons heavy cream
½ pound each of white and
    brown crab meat, or all white
    meat
Beurre Blanc (see Index)
    (optional)

Lightly coat a terrine 9 by 5 inches with butter. Line the terrine with the crêpes, letting them hang over the sides of the terrine so they can be folded over the fish and crab meat.

Have the monkfish, egg whites, herbs and cream thoroughly chilled. In a blender or food processor process the monkfish to a purée. Add the egg whites and process again until the mixture is light and smooth. Add the herbs, salt and pepper to taste and nutmeg. Process for a few seconds to mix, then with the machine running, slowly pour in the cream.

Pour one third of the puréed mixture into the crêpes-lined terrine. Top with the white crab meat, another third of the mixture, the brown crab meat (or white if using all white crab meat), and the remaining third of the mixture. Fold the crêpes over to cover the terrine. Set the terrine in a baking pan with water to come about halfway up the sides. Cover and bake in a preheated hot oven (425°F.) for 50 minutes. Allow to cool, then refrigerate, weighted, for several hours.

Make 1 recipe of Beurre Blanc if using it, with tarragon vinegar instead of white-wine vinegar.

To serve pour a little beurre blanc onto the serving plates and top with slices of the terrine. The plate may be garnished, if liked, with sprigs of any fresh herb.

S E R V E S 6.

POTTED GAME

❖ ❖ ❖

This is another of Baba Hine's very good appetizers. More traditional than her terrine of crab, she has used the past to create something beautifully simple. It could make the main part of a salady summer lunch. Serve with a white Rhône wine or a Hermitage Blanc.

4 tablespoons butter
1 pound boneless game (wild duck, venison, hare, etc.), cut into 1-inch cubes
1 teaspoon minced marjoram
1 teaspoon minced parsley
6 bay leaves
Salt, freshly ground pepper

½ teaspoon paprika
2½ cups rich Game Stock (see Index), or use beef or chicken
1¼ cups Tawny Port wine
½ cup concentrated calf's foot jelly, or Aspic (see Index), or ½ cup rich stock plus 1 envelope unflavored gelatin

In a heavy casserole melt the butter, add the game, and sauté until the meat is browned all over. Stir in the marjoram and parsley, add the bay leaves, salt and pepper to taste and paprika. Stir to mix. Pour in the stock and Port, cover and simmer until the meat is tender, about 2 hours. Add the jelly or aspic. If using gelatin, soften it in ¼ cup water. Pour the stock into a small saucepan, add the softened gelatin, and simmer over low heat until the gelatin is completely dissolved. Add to the casserole. Allow to cool slightly, then pour into an earthenware or other container and refrigerate until set.

To serve, unmold and slice, or spoon directly from the container. Serve with any fruit chutney, such as tomato, apple or mango. If, like Baba Hine, you make your own fruit chutneys, use them.

S E R V E S 6 to 8.

GÂTEAUX OF TOMATOES
WITH SCALLOP SAUCE

❖ ❖ ❖

W. John Dicken, the head chef at Longueville Manor, St. Saviour, in Jersey (the Channel Islands), never wanted to do anything but cook. Now, fully trained but still very young, he feels the same way. He takes infinite pains, insists on having superb ingredients and, in this appetizer, has created an unusually appealing dish. Serve with a Moselle or white wine from the Palatinate.

5 tablespoons butter
2 medium-size onions, chopped fine
1 garlic clove, minced
1 pound tomatoes, peeled, seeded and chopped

1 teaspoon minced fresh basil
2 teaspoons tomato purée
Salt, freshly ground pepper
2 large eggs
1 egg yolk
3 tablespoons heavy cream

Scallop Sauce

1 cup Fish Stock (see Index), or clam juice
¼ cup dry vermouth, preferably Noilly Prat
8 large scallops, each cut into 3 slices

½ cup light cream, or Junket Cheese or Fresh White Cheese (see Index)
4 tablespoons (½ stick) butter, cut into bits

Using 1 tablespoon of the butter, prepare four ½-cup ramekins or small soufflé dishes. Melt the butter, brush the insides of the ramekins generously, and refrigerate them until the butter has set.

Heat the rest of the butter in a medium-size heavy saucepan, add the onions and garlic, cover, and cook over very low heat for about 10 minutes. Do not let the onions brown. Add the tomatoes, basil, tomato purée and salt and pepper to taste. Cook, covered, still over very low heat for 15 minutes. Pour through a very fine strainer to get rid of surplus liquid, or cook uncovered for the last 5 minutes of cooking to evaporate excess liquid. Transfer to a food processor or blender and process until smooth. In a bowl beat the whole eggs and egg yolk together; beat in the cream and stir in the tomato mixture. Check the seasoning and add more salt and pepper if necessary. Pour the mixture into the prepared ramekins. Cover with aluminum foil, set into a baking pan with water to come halfway up, and bake in a preheated slow oven (300°F.) for about 20 minutes, or until the gâteaux are firm to the touch when the foil is removed. Allow to rest for 2 to 3 minutes before unmolding. To unmold, slide a knife around the inside edge of the ramekins, then invert onto 4 warmed plates.

While the tomato gâteaux are cooking, make the sauce. In a saucepan combine the fish stock and vermouth and the scallops. Simmer the scallops for 1 minute; lift them out and keep warm. It is important not to overcook them. Over brisk heat reduce the fish stock mixture to half. Pour in the cream and bring to a simmer. Whisk in bits of

(recipe continues)

the butter, one at a time, adding a new bit as the last one is absorbed. If using junket or fresh white cheese, simply whisk it into the reduced fish stock mixture and heat gently through. Do not reduce it. Omit the butter.

To serve, garnish the tomato gâteaux with the scallop sauce, pouring it over and around the gâteaux. Make sure each plate gets 6 slices of scallop in the sauce.

S E R V E S 4.

SCALLOPS AND CRAYFISH TAILS WITH MUSHROOMS AND CHIVES

❖   ❖   ❖

When I am feeling self-indulgent I cook this Michael Croft dish just for myself. It is delicate with a lovely mix of flavors. Michael uses wild mushrooms, much more flavorful than cultivated ones, though these will do quite well if wild ones are not available. Serve with a white Rioja.

5 tablespoons butter
3 baby scallops, halved
   horizontally
Salt, freshly ground pepper
4 lobsterette, langoustine or
   crayfish tails or jumbo shrimps
1 cup wild mushrooms or tiny
   button mushrooms

1 ounce dry vermouth
½ cup strong Fish Stock (see
   Index)
2 tablespoons reduced Shellfish
   Stock (if available) (see Index)
2 tablespoons snipped chives

Melt 1 tablespoon of the butter in a small skillet. Season the scallops lightly with salt and pepper and toss them in the butter. Lift out and set aside. Season the lobsterette, langoustine or crayfish tails or shrimps and toss in the butter. Add to the scallops. Add the wild mushrooms or tiny button mushrooms to the pan and cook over moderately high heat for 3 minutes. Add to the scallops. Pour the vermouth into the skillet, then add the fish stock and shellfish stock, if using it. Reduce the mixture to 4 tablespoons. Pour in any liquid that has collected with the shellfish, then whisk in remaining butter, cut into small pieces. Add the chives and shellfish and warm through over low heat. Arrange on a warmed plate at random.

S E R V E S 1.

SCRAMBLED QUAIL EGGS
WITH TRUFFLES

❖   ❖   ❖

Michael Croft, head chef at the Royal Crescent Hotel in Bath, Avon, who was Michael Quinn's *sous-chef* at the Ritz in London, matches the luxury of the hotel with his cooking. He has an especially imaginative way with appetizers. This one would make a late Sunday breakfast into an occasion, or start a celebratory dinner on a festive note. Michael keeps his quail eggs in a container with 2 or 3 fresh truffles for 24 hours to truffle-scent the eggs before using them, an impractical suggestion for most of us. Even without truffle-scented eggs and a fresh truffle, the dish has great charm. Serve with a white Burgundy, Chardonnay or Chablis.

6 tablespoons butter	2 ounces Cognac or other brandy
1/4 cup very fine-diced carrot	2 cups Veal Stock (see Index)
1/4 cup very fine-diced celery	20 quail eggs
1/4 cup very fine-diced onion	1 tablespoon heavy cream
1 small fresh truffle, brushed and washed, or 1 small canned truffle	Salt, freshly ground pepper
	4 rectangles, 2 by 3 inches, of cooked Puff Pastry (see Index)
2 ounces dry Madeira wine	

In a medium-size casserole heat 1 tablespoon of the butter. Add the carrot, celery and onion, cover, and cook over very low heat without letting the vegetables color. Add the truffle, Madeira and Cognac and enough of the veal stock barely to cover the truffle. Simmer, covered, over low heat for 30 minutes. Lift out the truffle, let it cool and cut it into 1/4-inch dice. Set aside. Reduce the liquid to half and beat in 3 tablespoons of the butter, cut into bits, adding each piece as the previous one is incorporated into the sauce. Set aside in a warm place.

Break the quail eggs into a bowl and season with salt and pepper. Fold in the heavy cream. Heat remaining 2 tablespoons of butter in a skillet, add the egg mixture, and gently stir with a wooden spoon or spatula. While eggs are still soft and runny, fold in the truffle dice and remove from the heat. Have ready the puff-pastry rectangles, split horizontally and warmed. Put the bottom halves of the pastry on 4 warmed dessert-size plates and top with the scrambled quail eggs. Put the pastry tops on the eggs and pour some of the sauce to one side of each plate.

SERVES 4.

FRESH ASPARAGUS MOUSSE WITH CARROT SAUCE

❖   ❖   ❖

This is another of Michael Croft's elegant inventions. Serve with a Moselle.

Carrot Sauce

1½ pounds tender young carrots, scraped and sliced
Chicken stock
4 tablespoons Noilly Prat or other very dry vermouth

¼ pound (1 stick) butter, cut into bits
Salt, freshly ground pepper

Asparagus Mousse

2 pounds asparagus, preferably green
Salt, freshly ground pepper
3 egg yolks

1 whole egg
¾ cup heavy cream
Garnish: fresh chervil sprigs

Put the carrots in a saucepan with enough chicken stock barely to cover. Cover and cook over moderate heat until carrots are tender. Pour off and reserve the cooking liquid. In a food processor or blender purée the carrots until very smooth, using a little of the reserved liquid if necessary. Transfer carrot purée to a sieve, set it over a bowl and let it drain, pressing down on the solids to extract all the liquid. Set the purée aside for another use. In a saucepan combine the carrot juice with the reserved cooking liquid and the vermouth and reduce over moderately high heat until the liquid reaches coating consistency. Beat in the butter bit by bit until the sauce is creamy and thick. Season to taste with salt and pepper.

Meanwhile peel the asparagus with a small sharp knife to remove any inedible parts. Tie asparagus in bundles of about 8 spears and put into a large saucepan or oval casserole of briskly boiling salted water. Bring the water back to a boil, lower the heat to a simmer and cook the asparagus, uncovered, for 15 minutes. Drain, cool, untie, and purée in a blender or food processor. Season with salt and pepper, add the egg yolks and whole egg, and process to mix. Add the cream and process for a few seconds longer. Pour mousse into 4 buttered

1-cup ramekins and set them in a baking pan with water to come about halfway up the ramekins. Bake in a moderate oven (375°F.) for 15 minutes, or until the mousse is firm.

To serve, unmold the asparagus mousse onto 4 warmed dessert-size plates and pour a circle of carrot sauce round each one. Garnish with sprigs of chervil.

SERVES 4.

CHICKEN LIVER TERRINE WITH MARSALA GLAZE

❖   ❖   ❖

The versatile chicken liver is used here with great simplicity by Eamonn Webster, head chef of Balcraig House, near Scone, in Perthshire, Scotland. The Marsala glaze makes an interesting contrast to the smooth richness of the liver pâté, while the mango accompaniment is an unusual and delicious addition. The terrine is even richer in flavor when made with duck livers. Serve with a Burgundy wine.

Butter	Salt, freshly ground pepper
½ pound chicken livers	½ cup Marsala wine
2 eggs	1 ripe mango, peeled and diced

Butter three 3-inch ramekins or small soufflé dishes and set them aside. Pat the livers dry and cut them into halves. Put them into a blender or food processor with the eggs and salt and pepper to taste, and process to a smooth purée. For a very fine purée push this mixture through a fine sieve set over a bowl. Spoon the purée into the ramekins or small soufflé dishes and set them in a baking pan with water to come about halfway up. Bake in a preheated slow oven (300°F.) for about 1½ hours, or until the liver mixture is firm to the touch.

While the livers are baking pour the Marsala into a small heavy saucepan and reduce it over moderate heat to coating consistency. Glaze the ramekins with the reduced wine when they are done. Cool, and chill lightly in the refrigerator. Garnish with mango and serve with fresh whole-wheat bread.

SERVES 4.

Duck livers may also be used for the terrine.

CHICKEN LIVERS WITH MARJORAM

❖　　　❖　　　❖

This is one of Francis Coulson's deceptively simple dishes. It was inspired by the herb garden at Sharrow Bay, a beautiful antique-filled country house hotel in Dooley Bridge at the edge of Lake Ullswater in the English Lake District, Cumbria, owned and run by Francis Coulson and Brian Sack. Establishing an herb garden was an early priority for Francis, who feels that fresh herbs add immeasurably to the flavor of dishes. One of the pioneers of the renaissance of British cooking, he is now world famous not just for his cooking, but for the warm hospitality that greets the traveler. Serve with a Pouilly-Fuissé.

3 tablespoons bacon fat or butter
1 medium-size onion, chopped
　fine
2 slices of bacon, chopped fine
1 garlic clove, chopped (optional)
½ pound chicken livers, cut into
　½-inch pieces
2 tablespoons fresh marjoram
　leaves, chopped, or 1
　tablespoon crumbled dried
　marjoram

6 medium-size mushrooms, sliced
　thin
1 tablespoon all-purpose flour
½ cup light cream
⅓ cup Chicken Stock (see Index)
Salt, freshly ground pepper
2 tablespoons minced parsley

Heat the bacon fat or butter in a skillet and sauté the onion and bacon over moderate heat until onion is soft. Add the garlic, if liked, and sauté for 1 minute longer. Lift vegetables and bacon out with a slotted spoon to a bowl and keep warm.

In the fat remaining in the skillet, adding a little more if necessary, sauté the chicken livers with the marjoram over moderately high heat for about 4 minutes, or until livers are lightly browned on the outside but still pink inside. Lift out with a slotted spoon and add to the onion and bacon mixture. Add the mushrooms to the skillet and sauté, still over moderately high heat, until the mushrooms have given up all their liquid. Add to the other cooked ingredients.

Stir in the flour and cook over low heat, stirring, for about 1 minute. Stir in the cream and chicken stock to make a smooth sauce. Season to taste with salt and pepper, stir in all the reserved ingredients, and cook just long enough to heat them through. Spoon into small individual dishes and sprinkle with parsley.

S E R V E S 4.

CHICKEN LIVER PÂTÉ

❖ ❖ ❖

Chicken livers are infinitely useful, as well as being inexpensive and always available, so I was delighted to find this chicken liver pâté, the creation of Brian Prideaux-Brune, the chef at Plumber Manor in Sturminster Newton in Dorset, the seventeenth-century home of the Prideaux-Brune family which they have turned into a restaurant with rooms. It is simple to make and has just that touch of originality that makes it different from the usual pâté, while still refreshingly uncomplicated. Serve with a Burgundy wine.

¾ pound unsmoked bacon, sliced
2 teaspoons vegetable oil
1 small onion, minced
2 garlic cloves, minced
4 tablespoons butter
1¼ pounds chicken livers, halved and patted dry
1 tablespoon fresh thyme leaves, chopped

2 teaspoons black peppercorns, crushed
3 ounces brandy
3 ounces dry Madeira wine
⅔ cup heavy cream, or Fresh White Cheese (see Index)
Salt
Clarified butter (see Index)

In a heavy skillet sauté the bacon in the vegetable oil until it is crisp. Drain on paper towels and crumble, or chop it fine.

Wipe out the skillet and sauté the onion and garlic in the butter until the onion is soft. Add the chicken livers and sauté until they are lightly browned on the outside but still pink inside. Add the crumbled bacon, the thyme and peppercorns to the skillet, stir to mix, then scrape the contents into a food processor or blender and reduce to a coarse purée. The mixture should not be smooth. Return the purée to the skillet and stir in the brandy, Madeira, cream and salt to taste. Heat the mixture through until it is just under the boiling point. Pour into a terrine and cool. Cover with a layer of clarified butter and refrigerate. Serve with toast strips.

S E R V E S 6 to 8.

CHICKEN LIVERS
WITH PINE KERNELS

❖   ❖   ❖

Martin Rowbotham, head chef at Huntstrete House, Huntstrete, near Bath, Avon, did not start off intending to be a chef. He fell in love with cooking at college, and deciding that blending ingredients was like Beethoven creating a symphony, set out to learn all he could. His dishes are never ordinary or routine but demonstrate his natural inventiveness. Serve with a Burgundy wine.

3 tablespoons butter
8 large chicken livers, halved
1 cup pine kernels (pine nuts)
1 garlic clove, crushed
⅔ cup dry Madeira wine
⅔ cup Veal or Chicken Stock
   (see Index)

Escarole leaves
1 cup Garlic Croutons (see
   Index)
Salt, freshly ground pepper

Heat 2 tablespoons of the butter in a skillet and sauté the chicken livers over moderate heat until they are browned outside but still pink inside, about 6 minutes. Lift out the chicken livers into a bowl. Add the pine kernels and sauté for a minute or two, until they are lightly browned. Lift out and add to the chicken livers. Add the garlic to the skillet and sauté for about 30 seconds. Pour in the Madeira and reduce to ½ cup. Pour in the stock, stir to scrape up any brown bits, and reduce to about ⅓ cup. Leave the sauce in the skillet.

On 4 warmed salad or dessert plates arrange some escarole leaves. Arrange 2 chicken livers in the center of each plate with pine kernels and garlic croutons on top. Add remaining tablespoon of butter to the sauce in the skillet and simmer over low heat just long enough to warm it through. Season to taste with salt and pepper and pour the sauce over the chicken livers.

S E R V E S 4.

QUAIL BREASTS
WITH HERB DUMPLINGS

❖   ❖   ❖

Alan Vikops, young head chef at the County Hotel in Canterbury, Kent, says that food should be prepared and presented with a feeling that comes from the heart. Expertise is not enough, though he has plenty of that, having worked under Anton Mosimann of the Dorchester and Michael Quinn when he was at the Ritz. This rather grand dish is not as difficult to make as it sounds. It is, in fact, quite simple as the choux pastry used for the dumplings is the easiest of all pastries to make. The juxtaposition of quail breasts and herb dumplings is deliciously unusual and makes the perfect beginning to a meal with fish as the main course. Serve with a white wine from the Rheinhessen region.

4 quail
5 tablespoons butter
1 tablespoon vegetable oil
3 cups Veal or Chicken Stock
    (see Index)
½ cup dry Madeira wine

Salt, freshly ground pepper
4 tablespoons chopped mixed
    herbs—chives, parsley,
    tarragon
½ recipe Choux Pastry (see
    Index)

Using a small, sharp knife cut and pull the breasts from the quail, or have your butcher do it. Chop the carcasses with the legs and wings. Heat 1 tablespoon of the butter and the tablespoon of oil in a large heavy skillet and brown the bones in the mixture. Transfer to a saucepan, pour in 1½ cups of the stock, and simmer until the liquid is reduced to ½ cup. Add the Madeira and reduce to ¼ cup. Strain, pressing down hard on the bones to extract all the flavor. Season to taste. Set aside.

Pour remaining stock into a large shallow saucepan and bring to a simmer. Mix the herbs into the choux pastry. Using 2 teaspoons, shape the pastry into quenelles and drop into the simmering stock. Simmer for approximately 5 minutes or until they have risen to the surface. Lift them out with a slotted spoon and keep them warm.

Heat 2 tablespoons of the butter in a skillet large enough to hold all the quail breasts in a single layer. Add the breasts and sauté over moderate heat until they are lightly browned on both sides but still pink inside, about 4 minutes.

(recipe continues)

Heat the reserved sauce in a small saucepan and whisk in the remaining butter, cut into bits, over moderate heat.

Arrange the quail breasts on 4 warmed plates. Surround with the herbed dumplings. Pour the sauce over the quail breasts. Serve immediately.

SERVES 4.

HARE PÂTÉ WITH GREENGAGE PLUM RELISH

❖   ❖   ❖

Graham Flanagan, head chef of the Cottage in the Wood, Malvern Wells, in Hereford and Worcester, has a great feeling for traditional British cooking, which he produces with great flair and with his own transforming touches. This pâté is good enough to make it worth the trouble of bespeaking a hare from a specialty butcher. Serve with a white Hermitage.

Pâté

1 young hare, about 3 pounds,
  boned, with bones reserved
Liver of hare, chopped
½ pound pork fatback, chopped
¼ pound pork liver, chopped
2 medium eggs

2 tablespoons all-purpose flour
2 tablespoons Cognac or other
  brandy
Salt, freshly ground pepper
½ teaspoon crumbled dried thyme
1 bay leaf

Marinade

2 cups dry white wine
1 tablespoon white-wine vinegar
2 tablespoons olive or vegetable
  oil
1 medium-size onion, chopped
1 medium-size carrot, chopped
1 celery rib, chopped

1 garlic clove, chopped
1 tablespoon minced parsley
2 cloves
1 teaspoon black peppercorns,
  lightly crushed
½ teaspoon salt

To prepare the pâté, there should be about 2 pounds of hare meat. Chop the meat coarse and transfer it to a food processor or blender with the hare liver, pork fatback and pork liver and process it to a coarse purée. Set it aside and make the marinade.

To make the marinade, combine the reserved hare bones with the marinade ingredients in a large saucepan. Bring to a simmer over low heat, cover, and cook for 1 hour. Cool, strain, and discard the bones and solids. Put the pâté into a large bowl and pour the marinade over it. Cover, and refrigerate overnight.

Pour off and reserve the marinade. Combine the pâté with the eggs, flour, Cognac or other brandy, salt and pepper to taste, thyme and 2 tablespoons of the reserved marinade.

Oil a 6-cup terrine and spoon in the hare mixture. Press the bay leaf on top. Cover the terrine with foil, then with a lid. Bake in a preheated moderate oven (375°F.) for 2 hours. Cool, chill lightly, and unmold. Serve sliced, with Greengage Plum Relish.

S E R V E S 8 to 10.

Greengage Plum Relish

2 tablespoons salt
1 teaspoon ground cloves
1 teaspoon ground ginger
1 teaspoon ground allspice
2¼ cups vinegar, preferably malt vinegar
1 cup Demerara or brown sugar
2 pounds greengage plums, pitted and quartered

½ pound tart green apples, peeled, cored and chopped
3 medium-size onions, chopped
1 medium-size carrot, scraped and sliced thin
¾ cup seedless raisins

In a small bowl combine the salt, cloves, ginger and allspice with enough of the vinegar to make a paste. In a large stainless-steel or enameled saucepan combine the rest of the vinegar with the sugar and bring it to a boil over low heat. Stir in the spice mixture, the plums, apples, onions, carrot and raisins. Simmer, uncovered, stirring from time to time, until the mixture is well blended and thick, about 45 minutes. Cool, spoon into a glass container, and chill lightly until ready to serve.

M A K E S about 8 cups.

POTTED SWEETBREADS
AND MUSHROOMS

❖   ❖   ❖

This is a most delicate and subtle terrine given me by Scots chef
Alan Casey when he was at Culloden House in Inverness, Highland,
Scotland. Now a country house hotel converted from a Jacobean
castle, it was once the headquarters of Bonnie Prince Charlie. Alan's
aim is to keep the flavors of the foods he cooks as pure and direct as
possible and, in the interests of good nutrition, to avoid the pitfalls
of too much butter, cream and eggs. He succeeds admirably here.
Serve with a light, red Bordeaux.

2 pounds veal sweetbreads
½ pound medium-size mushrooms
4 cups Veal or Chicken Stock
    (see Index)
½ cup dry white wine
Salt, freshly ground pepper
⅛ teaspoon ground mace
1 onion, chopped fine
1 medium-size carrot, scraped
    and chopped

1 celery rib, chopped
1 sprig each of parsley and thyme
1 bay leaf
½ cup minced parsley
2 teaspoons unflavored gelatin
2 tablespoons dry Madeira or
    Tawny Port wine

Rinse the sweetbreads, then put them into a bowl with cold water to
cover and soak, changing the water 2 or 3 times, for 2 hours. Drain
and pull away the skin that covers them. Put into a saucepan or
casserole with the mushrooms, stock, wine, salt and pepper to taste,
mace, onion, carrot, celery, parsley, thyme and bay leaf. Simmer,
covered, over low heat for 30 to 45 minutes, or until the sweetbreads
are tender. Cool slightly, then lift the sweetbreads and mushrooms to
a chopping board and chop fine. Mix with the minced parsley and
season to taste with salt and pepper. Pack into a terrine.

Strain the stock and discard the solids. Measure 1 cup into a small
saucepan and sprinkle the gelatin over it. When gelatin has softened,
simmer stock over low heat, stirring, until gelatin has dissolved. Stir
in the Madeira or Tawny Port. Pour the mixture into the terrine. Let
it cool, then cover with aluminum foil and weight it. Refrigerate for
several hours or overnight.

Unmold and serve sliced, with lettuce leaves, sliced tomatoes and
cucumber, or any vegetable garnish such as asparagus.

S E R V E S 6 to 8.

VARIATION : If veal sweetbreads are not available, lamb sweetbreads can be used. These will need a shorter soaking and cooking time.

VENISON LIVER WITH ORANGE AND JUNIPER BERRY SAUCE

❖ ❖ ❖

This is a most exciting appetizer course although it is not always easy to find venison liver. I tried it with calf's liver; though it lacks the special flavor of venison liver, it is very good indeed. The sauce is quite superb. It is the creation of chef John McGeever of Congham Hall in Grimston, near King's Lynn, Norfolk, who has a special gift for using local produce to its best advantage. Serve with a white wine from the Loire or a Côte du Rhône.

4 seedless oranges, peeled and
  segmented
⅓ cup Mandarin liqueur
¼ cup brandy
1¼ pounds venison or calf's
  liver, sliced thin

All-purpose flour
Salt, freshly ground pepper
½ pound (2 sticks) butter
1½ teaspoons juniper berries,
  crushed

In a bowl combine the orange segments, Mandarin liqueur and brandy and set aside to macerate.

Dip the liver slices into flour seasoned with salt and pepper. In a skillet heat 4 tablespoons of the butter and sauté the liver slices over moderately high heat for about 1 minute a side. Transfer to a plate and keep warm.

Lift out the orange segments from the liqueur and brandy and set aside. Pour the liquid into the skillet, add the juniper berries, and season to taste with salt and pepper. Whisk in remaining butter, cut into bits, adding a new piece as the previous one is absorbed into the sauce.

Arrange the liver slices on 4 warmed plates, garnish with the orange segments, and pour the sauce over the liver.

SERVES 4.

VENISON PÂTÉ

❖   ❖   ❖

I very much enjoyed this venison pâté developed by David Moir when he was head chef at Gleddoch House at Langbank, near Greenock, Strathclyde. It is time-consuming to make and I had to search out venison, but it was worth it. I agree with David that oatcakes with butter are far better than ordinary toast especially since they are very easy to make and keep well. Serve with a Chardonnay.

1 pound venison, chopped fine
1 garlic clove
¼ cup diced pork fat
1 large egg
Salt, freshly ground pepper
3 tablespoons Tawny Port wine
6 tablespoons butter, melted and
  cooled
½ cup heavy cream
1 large tart apple, peeled, cored
  and chopped coarse

Butter
4 mushrooms, sliced
½ medium-size onion, chopped
  fine
¼ cup blanched pistachio nuts
¾ cup raisins
12 juniper berries, crushed
½ cup Aspic (see Index) or
  gelatin dissolved in chicken
  stock

Put the venison and garlic with the pork fat into a food processor or blender and process until smooth. Add the egg, salt and pepper to taste, and the Port, and process to mix. With the machine running, slowly pour in the melted butter and the cream. Transfer the mixture to a large bowl.

Mix in the apple. In a small skillet heat a tablespoon of butter and sauté the mushrooms and onion over moderate heat, covered, for 5 minutes. Add the pistachio nuts, raisins and juniper berries, sauté for 1 or 2 minutes, then add to the venison mixture.

Generously butter a terrine 9 by 5 inches and pack the venison mixture into it. Cover with foil and set in a baking pan with water to come about halfway up. Bake in a preheated slow oven (300°F.) for about 2 hours, or until the terrine feels firm to the touch. Remove from the oven and cool. While it is still slightly warm, pour the melted aspic over it. Cool and refrigerate for at least 12 hours before unmolding and serving.

When sliced the terrine should be marbled with apples, nuts and raisins. Serve sliced accompanied by oatcakes and butter, and Cumberland Sauce (recipe follows).

S E R V E S 6 to 8.

CUMBERLAND SAUCE

❖ ❖ ❖

This traditional sauce is served with cold meats, veal and ham pie, ham, venison, and this venison pâté. Tart yet richly flavored, it will keep for several weeks refrigerated. This is David Moir's own version of the sauce and one I find particularly appealing.

1 cup red-currant jelly
¼ cup Tawny Port wine
1 teaspoon juice squeezed from
  grated fresh gingerroot
¼ cup lemon juice

¼ cup orange juice
Rind of 1 lemon, cut into
  julienne strips
Rind of 1 orange, cut into
  julienne strips

Combine the red-currant jelly, Port wine, ginger juice, and orange and lemon juice in a small saucepan and bring to a simmer over low heat. Add the lemon and orange rind, which should be cut into very fine strips. Bring back to a simmer, remove from the heat, and cool. Pour into a glass container and refrigerate until ready to use.

M A K E S about 1¾ cups.

SOUPS

❖   ❖   ❖

Soup, LIGHT and delicate or robust and hearty, is one of the most delightful products of the kitchen. It is usually economical, and with blenders and food processors, simple to make. Homemade stocks are very little trouble as they simmer for hours, needing almost no attention. Excellent canned stocks are available when it is impractical to make stock at home, and good stock cubes can be used as enrichments. I was happy to find that today's chefs share my enthusiasm for soup. They delight in inventing new soups and transforming traditional ones.

A lightly chilled soup makes a perfect beginning to a party dinner or lunch, and since it is made ahead and chilled it makes kitchen planning and timing easier. Hot soups take little more trouble. A really hearty soup is wonderfully restorative for a quick lunch at home, or as the main part of a simple supper. A most versatile dish, soup can be elegant or a standby family favorite.

The recipes here have all been given me by chefs and tested by me at home. Any changes that have been made in the recipes are purely practical ones, translating a restaurant recipe into a domestic kitchen one. I have also suggested ways to avoid using cream for those who find this desirable.

BEET SOUP WITH TOMATO AND BASIL SORBET

❖ ❖ ❖

John Hornsby created this soup when he was head chef at the Castle Hotel in Taunton, Somerset. Before that he was *sous-chef* to Anton Mosimann at the Dorchester. A farmer's son from Norfolk with a mother who was an excellent cook, he learned from childhood to recognize quality in all types of food. He achieves original dishes from unexotic, often quite ordinary ingredients, as this demonstrates. It is the freshest-tasting beet soup I've ever had.

Beet Soup

6 cups chicken broth
3 pounds beets, trimmed,
  scrubbed and sliced
1 bay leaf
6 peppercorns

2 egg whites, lightly beaten
2 egg shells, crushed
Salt
2 envelopes unflavored gelatin
  (7 grams each)

Sorbet

¾ cup tomato juice
1 teaspoon Worcestershire sauce
1 teaspoon lemon juice
1 tablespoon minced fresh basil
  leaves

Garnish: fresh chervil leaves
  (optional)

In a large saucepan combine the chicken broth, beets, bay leaf and peppercorns. Bring to a simmer and cook, covered, for 1½ hours. Strain the mixture through a fine sieve into a bowl. Discard the solids. Measure the liquid and add enough water to bring it up to 6 cups, if necessary. Return the mixture to the saucepan and add the egg whites and shells. Whisk over very low heat until the liquid comes to a simmer. Simmer without stirring for 20 minutes. Strain through a fine sieve lined with a double layer of dampened, squeezed-out cheesecloth into a bowl. Rinse out and dry the saucepan and return the soup to it. Season to taste with salt.

Sprinkle the gelatin into ½ cup water in a small bowl and let it soften for about 5 minutes. Add it to the soup and simmer, whisking, over low heat until the gelatin has dissolved. Cool the soup, then refrigerate it until lightly set, about 2 hours.

To make the sorbet combine the tomato juice, Worcestershire sauce, lemon juice and fresh basil leaves in a small metal bowl or in an ice-cube tray without the dividers. Freeze the mixture, stirring every 15 minutes, for 1 hour, until the sorbet is firm but not hard.

Spoon the jellied soup into bowls. Put a spoonful of the sorbet in the center and decorate the rims of the bowls with chervil leaves, if liked.

SERVES 6.

TOMATO AND FENNEL SOUP

❖ ❖ ❖

I was impressed with the cooking of young Scots chef Alan Casey, whom I first met at Culloden House in Inverness. His philosophy is a forthright one. He seeks to maintain the integrity of the raw materials he cooks with, and he is in favor of modern trends toward better nutrition and lighter foods that retain their natural flavor.

4 fennel bulbs, trimmed and cut
  into thin slices
2 tablespoons butter
2 ounces dry vermouth
2 pounds tomatoes, about 8
  medium-size, peeled, seeded
  and chopped
1 small garlic clove, minced

1 bouquet garni: parsley, thyme
  and bay leaf
5 cups Chicken or Veal Stock
  (see Index)
Salt
1 cup light cream, or Fresh
  White Cheese (see Index)
1 teaspoon Worcestershire sauce

In a large saucepan sweat the fennel in the butter, covered, over very low heat for about 10 minutes. Add the vermouth, tomatoes, garlic, bouquet garni, stock, and salt if necessary. Simmer, covered, for 30 minutes, or until the fennel is soft. Remove and discard the bouquet garni. Reduce the solids to a purée in a blender or food processor and return the purée to the liquid. Stir in the cream and Worcestershire sauce and heat the soup through. Garnish with a sprig of fennel and, if liked, with a teaspoon of whipped cream.

SERVES 4.

JERUSALEM ARTICHOKE SOUP

❖   ❖   ❖

Jerusalem artichokes, sometimes marketed as "sunchokes," are small edible tubers indigenous to North America, and unknown to the Old World until the Pilgrim Fathers arrived. Members of the Daisy Family, they are closely related to the sunflower, another North American indigene. The name is an amusing corruption of *girasole*, the Italian for sunflower. I choose the larger tubers, as it is easier to scrape the light brown skin from them, an allowable form of kitchen laziness.

Nicholas Gill, the gifted young chef in charge of the kitchen at Hambleton Hall in Oakham, Leicestershire, created this as a winter soup. It has an exquisite flavor, but it is one of the easiest things I know to make. This says a good deal about Nick Gill's special talent —he delights in creating dishes that will give pleasure, some of them elaborate, some simple, but all as near perfection as he can make them. I find the soup good even without its butter and cream enrichment.

1 pound Jerusalem artichokes,
  scraped and chopped coarse
4 cups Chicken Stock (see Index)
Salt, freshly ground pepper

1 tablespoon unsalted butter
½ cup heavy cream
Garnish: ¼ cup heavy cream,
  pinch of ground saffron

Combine the artichokes and stock in a large saucepan, cover, and simmer over moderate heat until artichokes are tender, about 20 minutes. Strain the soup through a sieve into a bowl; keep the solids. Rinse out and dry the saucepan and pour in the strained soup. Purée the solids in a blender or food processor, then put through a sieve so that any bits of skin from the artichokes can easily be discarded. Add to the saucepan. Season to taste with salt and pepper. Heat the soup and stir in the butter and cream. Pour into 4 warmed soup bowls.

For the garnish, mix the saffron into the cream and whip the cream. Make a cone with wax paper and fill it with the cream. Pipe a thin spiral of the cream mixture on top of the soup, then draw a knife through it to cut it into quarters. If this is too difficult or seems too elaborate for family dining, put a small spoonful of cream in the center of each bowl of soup. The delicate yellow of the saffron in the cream makes an attractive contrast to the creamy white of the soup.

SERVES 4.

LETTUCE SOUP, ROY RICHARDS

❖   ❖   ❖

I first met Roy Richards when he and his wife Veronica, who does the desserts, were running the Lake Isle restaurant in Uppingham, Leicestershire before they moved to their present restaurant Manor House at Pickworth, in Lincolnshire. Roy came late to cooking. He first taught English, then did a stint in business, but the kitchen captured him and he got his training with the Savoy Group, then went to Thornbury Castle to work with Kenneth Bell. He has a very decided philosophy. He hates pretentious food and cares most for what he calls "family cooking"—simple food carefully prepared from the best ingredients. He will only use exotic ingredients when they belong in a dish naturally. This is my favorite lettuce soup. It is simplicity itself, wonderfully fresh and summery.

3 heads of Boston lettuce
4 tablespoons butter
1 small onion, chopped fine
2 tablespoons all-purpose flour
2½ cups Chicken Stock (see
Index)

½ cup milk
½ cup heavy cream
Salt, freshly ground pepper
Pinch of grated nutmeg

Separate the lettuces into leaves and discard any wilted ones. Rinse, spin dry, and chop coarse. Drop the chopped lettuce into a large saucepan of briskly boiling salted water and blanch for 5 minutes. Drain thoroughly, then purée in a blender or food processor.

Heat the butter in a saucepan and sauté the onion until soft. Remove from the heat and stir in the flour. Return to low heat and cook, stirring, for 2 minutes. Gradually stir in the chicken stock and milk. Bring the liquid to a boil and simmer, stirring, for 5 minutes. Stir in the lettuce purée and the cream. Season to taste with salt, pepper and nutmeg. Heat the soup through without letting it boil.

S E R V E S 4.

LETTUCE, SORREL, MINT AND YOGURT SOUP

❖   ❖   ❖

Eamonn Webster followed his journalist father's footsteps at the beginning of his career but was lured into food by sheer interest. He found his way into the kitchen of the famed Royal Crescent Hotel in Bath and from there worked with such gifted chefs as Shaun Hill, now of Gidleigh Park, Chagford, in Devon. As head chef at Balcraig House near Scone in Perthshire, Scotland, Eamonn is able to express his philosophy that cooking starts in the sea and the ground, not in the pot. This soup demonstrates that philosophy in a very light and delicious way, lovely for summer.

1 head of Boston lettuce, washed and dried	2½ cups plain yogurt
1 tablespoon minced fresh mint	1 tablespoon lemon juice
1 cup firmly packed sorrel leaves	Salt, freshly ground pepper
	2 tablespoons snipped chives

Chop the lettuce very fine and put it into a bowl. Add the mint. Wash the sorrel leaves and shake to remove excess moisture. Cut away and discard the stems and center veins of the leaves. Stack, roll them up, and slice very fine. Drop the sorrel into a saucepan of briskly boiling salted water for 30 seconds, drain, plunge into cold water, and drain at once. Purée the sorrel in a blender or food processor. It almost purées itself.

Add the sorrel purée to the lettuce and mint mixture and stir in the yogurt. Add the lemon juice and season with salt and pepper to taste; mix well. Chill the soup in the refrigerator for several hours.

Serve the soup garnished with snipped chives. Other garnishes may be added, if liked. Shredded carrot, radish, cucumber or diced strawberries may be served in small bowls as accompaniments.

SERVES 4.

MINT SOUP

❖   ❖   ❖

Chef François Huguet of Inverlochy Castle, a romantic Victorian Castle now a luxurious hotel at Fort William in Scotland's Highland Region, loves to use fresh things from the herb and kitchen gardens at the castle when they are at their best. He says mint is best from April through July and certainly this refreshing soup is perfect for spring and summer.

4 tablespoons (½ stick) butter	Salt, freshly ground pepper
½ cup all-purpose flour	6 tablespoons light cream
6 cups Chicken Stock (see Index)	Garnish: whipped cream and
2 cups loosely packed young mint leaves	mint sprigs

In a saucepan heat the butter and stir in the flour. Cook, stirring with a wooden spoon, over low heat for about 2 minutes without letting the mixture color. Off the heat stir in the chicken stock. Return the saucepan to the heat and simmer, stirring from time to time, for 30 minutes.

Pick over and wash the mint. Chop it coarse and add it to the saucepan. Simmer for 5 minutes. Lift mint from liquid and in a blender or food processor reduce to a purée, using a little of the soup. Strain the purée through a fine sieve into the soup. Season to taste with salt and pepper, stir in the cream, and heat through.

Serve in bouillon cups. Garnish, if liked, with a teaspoon of whipped cream and a sprig of mint.

S E R V E S 6.

V A R I A T I O N S : This soup is very refreshing served chilled. Yogurt or sour cream can be used instead of light cream, also for the garnish.

Chef Huguet also makes a rosemary-flavored consommé in which sprigs of fresh rosemary are simmered in a very rich clear chicken consommé, then strained out and discarded, leaving just a delicate rosemary flavor.

BRAZIL NUT AND LEMON SOUP

❖   ❖   ❖

Joyce Molyneux, the brilliant chef who runs the Carved Angel restaurant in Dartmouth, Devon, created this soup to use up an excess of Brazil nuts. It is delicious either hot or cold, and illustrates her creative approach to cooking.

1½ cups chopped onions
2 tablespoons butter
5 cups Chicken or Veal Stock
   (see Index)
1 cup shelled Brazil nuts, peeled
   and chopped coarse

Rind of 2 lemons, in thin strips
Salt, freshly ground pepper
¼ cup heavy cream

In a large saucepan cook the onions in the butter, covered, over very low heat until soft. Do not let them brown. Add the stock, nuts, lemon rind, and salt and pepper to taste. Simmer gently, covered, for 20 minutes.

Remove the solids from the soup and purée them in a blender or food processor, using a little of the soup if necessary. The purée should be very smooth. Return the purée to the liquid, stir in the cream, and heat through.

S E R V E S 4.

FENNEL AND GREEN BELL PEPPER SOUP

❖   ❖   ❖

Brian Prideaux-Brune, who is chef at the family's Dorset home, Plumber Manor, which they run as a restaurant with rooms, has produced an entirely different fennel soup from Alan Casey's, though both are inspired by the subtle flavor of the vegetable. Brian, whose training has not been formal, is an excitingly original cook, creating new dishes from everyday foods.

4 fennel bulbs, trimmed, peeled and sliced

4 green bell peppers, seeded and chopped coarse

2 leeks, trimmed, thoroughly washed and chopped coarse

1 medium-size potato, peeled and sliced

6 cups Chicken Stock (see Index)

Salt, freshly ground pepper

½ cup heavy cream (optional)

Combine all the vegetables with the chicken stock in a large saucepan and simmer, covered, over moderate heat until the vegetables are tender, about 20 minutes. Remove the solids from the soup and purée them in a blender or food processor. Return the purée to the liquid and season to taste with salt and pepper. Stir in the cream, if liked, and heat the soup through. If the soup is too thick, add a little more chicken stock.

S E R V E S 6 to 8.

TURNIP AND FRESH GINGER SOUP

❖   ❖   ❖

This is a most unusual soup from young Nigel Lambert of the Elms in Abberley, near Worcester, who describes his cooking as English country cooking with modern influences, an intriguing combination. The soup is easy to make and as delicious as it is easy.

¼ pound (1 stick) butter

1 pound small white turnips, peeled and diced

½ cup coarse-grated fresh gingerroot

1 small onion, chopped fine

1 garlic clove, crushed

5 cups Chicken Stock (see Index)

Salt, freshly ground pepper

½ cup heavy cream

Heat the butter in a large saucepan, add the turnips, gingerroot and onion, cover, and cook over very low heat for about 20 minutes. Add the crushed garlic, stir to mix, and pour in the stock. Simmer, covered, until the vegetables are tender, about 30 minutes.

In a blender or food processor reduce the solids to a purée. Return the purée to the saucepan, season to taste with salt and pepper, and heat the soup through. Add the cream and cook just long enough to heat the soup without letting it boil.

S E R V E S 6.

WATERCRESS SOUP

❖   ❖   ❖

For years I searched for the perfect watercress soup, now found. Head chef Melvin Jordan of Pool Court Restaurant with Rooms, at Pool-in-Wharfedale, West Yorkshire, was equally unsatisfied with the versions he encountered and set about experimenting until he achieved a soup that pleased him. It is typical of his approach to food that he will take so much trouble over a very simple, ordinary-seeming dish. He originally specialized in *pâtisserie*, a most exacting art. It may explain his meticulous approach to food, and his talent for beautiful presentation.

2 tablespoons butter
1 medium-size onion, peeled and
  chopped
1 small garlic clove, crushed
2 tablespoons mild white vinegar
2 tablespoons dry white wine
4 cups Chicken Stock (see Index)

½ cup light cream
3 bunches watercress, about 6
  ounces, washed and trimmed
2 teaspoons cornstarch
Salt, freshly ground pepper
Garnish: watercress leaves, 4
  tablespoons heavy cream

Melt the butter in a saucepan and sauté the onion and garlic until onion is soft. Add the vinegar and wine and simmer until the liquid is reduced by half. Add the chicken stock, cover, and simmer over low heat for 30 minutes. Stir in the cream and bring the liquid back to a simmer. Add the watercress, stir to mix, and immediately remove from the heat. Purée the solids in a blender or food processor, then push through a sieve set over a bowl. Return the purée to the saucepan. Mix the cornstarch with a little cold water and stir it into the soup. Bring the soup to a simmer over moderate heat, stirring once or twice. Season to taste with salt and pepper. It is important not to cook the soup for long once the watercress has been added as this tends to make the soup bitter.

Serve in bowls with a spoonful of cream floated on top, and a watercress leaf placed on top of the cream.

SERVES 4.

CREAM OF CARROT SOUP

❖   ❖   ❖

Philip Burgess grew up in kitchens. His father was chef to the Earl of Morley, and by the time he was six Philip knew he wanted to be a cook. He trained in England, France and Switzerland and now is head chef at the Arundell Arms in Lifton, Devon. He respects food and does not like to see natural flavors disguised by heavy sauces and garnishes. This delicious carrot soup is a good example of his point of view.

4 tablespoons butter
1 pound carrots, scraped and
    chopped coarse
1 large onion, chopped
1 leek, thoroughly washed and
    chopped
1 bay leaf
½ teaspoon sugar

6 bacon rinds
5 cups Chicken Stock (see Index)
Salt, freshly ground pepper
½ cup heavy cream, or Fresh
    White Cheese (see Index)
Garnish: 1 tablespoon chopped
    parsley, whipped cream
    (optional)

In a large saucepan heat 3 tablespoons of the butter and sauté the carrots, onion and leek until vegetables are soft. Add the bay leaf, sugar and bacon rinds and stir to mix. Pour in the stock, cover, and simmer until carrots are very tender, 20 to 30 minutes. Remove and discard the bay leaf and bacon rinds. Strain the soup into a bowl. Purée the solids in a blender or food processor and return both liquid and purée to the saucepan. Heat the soup, stir in the cream and remaining tablespoon of butter, and simmer just until the soup is heated through.

Serve garnished with parsley and, if liked, a teaspoon of whipped cream.

S E R V E S 6.

V A R I A T I O N : The soup can be served chilled; in that case omit the last tablespoon of butter and the whipped cream garnish. If liked, omit the cream or fresh white cheese and, when the soup is chilled, stir in ½ cup plain yogurt.

PARSNIP AND ORANGE SOUP

❖   ❖   ❖

Young Pierre Chevillard, head chef at Chewton Glen Hotel, once an eighteenth-century mansion, now a deluxe country house hotel at New Milton, Hampshire, on the fringe of the New Forest, has a subtle approach to food. He combines English tradition and his own innovative ideas in this soup with unexpected and delicious results.

1 small onion, chopped
1 medium-size potato, peeled and
   diced
3 pounds parsnips, peeled and
   diced
3 tablespoons butter
5 cups Chicken Stock (see Index)

⅔ cup orange juice
Rind of 1 orange, cut into wide
   strips
Salt, freshly ground pepper
1 cup heavy cream (optional)
Garnish: 1 orange, sectioned
   (optional)

In a large saucepan cook the onion, potato and parsnips in 2 tablespoons of the butter over very low heat, covered, until the vegetables are softened, about 10 minutes. Add the chicken stock, orange juice and rind. Season to taste with salt and pepper, cover, and simmer for 30 minutes. Purée the solids in a blender or food processor, then push through a sieve for a finer texture. Return the purée to the saucepan with the liquid. Stir in the cream. Heat through and stir in the remaining tablespoon of butter.

Serve in soup bowls garnished, if liked, with orange segments.

S E R V E S 6.

V A R I A T I O N : If not using the cream, add an extra cup of chicken stock or use one of the fresh cheeses in the Basic Recipes section (see Index).

TOMATO, ORANGE AND GINGER BROTH

❖   ❖   ❖

Martin Lam, the young chef from Bristol who created this soup, had to struggle for the right to cook. His Welsh mother, a splendid cook, had the kitchen all week. On Sundays his father, an importer of fine foods, took over. All the frustrated small boy was allowed to do was make the gravy. Undeterred, he went on to become head chef at L'Escargot in Soho in London, after working at the English House Restaurant, where his special interest in English food was encouraged by co-owner Michael Smith, the author of authoritative books on English cooking. This soup is from his English House period.

5 cups Chicken Stock (see Index)
1 cup orange juice
Rind of 1 orange, cut into
  julienne strips
2 tablespoons drained ginger in
  syrup, cut into julienne strips
1 tablespoon tomato purée
1 pound tomatoes, about 4
  medium-size, peeled, seeded
  and chopped

Salt, freshly ground pepper
Garnish: 2 tablespoons chopped
  fresh mint, 1 thin-sliced
  unpeeled orange, seeds
  removed

In a large saucepan combine the chicken stock, orange juice, orange rind, ginger and tomato purée. Simmer, covered, over low heat for 5 minutes. Add the tomatoes and salt and pepper to taste. Bring back to a simmer and cook for 5 minutes longer.

Serve in soup bowls with a garnish of mint and orange slices.

S E R V E S   6.

CHILLED CUCUMBER SOUP

❖   ❖   ❖

Enlivened by a touch of vinegar and mint, this cucumber soup is not only perfect for summer but makes an attractive beginning to lunch or dinner at any season. It is a good example of the culinary point of view of its inventor, Christopher Pitman, head chef at the George of Stamford in Lincolnshire. He combines ordinary ingredients in an unordinary way.

2 hothouse or seedless cucumbers
3 tablespoons butter
2 medium-size onions, chopped
 fine
4 sprigs of fresh mint, or 1 sprig
 of dried mint
¼ cup all-purpose flour
4 cups Chicken Stock (see Index)

2 cups light cream, or Fresh
 White Cheese or Yogurt
 Cheese (see Index)
2 tablespoons mild white vinegar
Salt, freshly ground white pepper
Garnish: julienne strips of
 cucumber peel

Peel the cucumbers and chop to coarse pieces. Cut one quarter of the peel into julienne strips and set aside for the garnish. Heat the butter in a large saucepan, add the cucumbers, onions and mint, and cook until onions are soft. Remove and discard the mint. Stir in the flour and cook, stirring, for 2 minutes. Off the heat gradually stir in the chicken stock. Return the saucepan to the heat and simmer, covered, for 20 minutes. Purée the mixture in a blender or a food processor and pour it into a bowl or jug. When it is cool, stir in the cream and vinegar. Season to taste with salt and pepper. Refrigerate the soup until thoroughly chilled, about 4 hours.

Serve in soup bowls, garnished with the julienne strips of cucumber peel.

S E R V E S 6.

TOMATO, APPLE AND CELERY SOUP

❖   ❖   ❖

John Evans, chef-patron of a small hotel and restaurant, Meadow-sweet, in Llanrwst, Gwynedd, Wales, took this traditional soup and created his own version. It is an example of the inventiveness of today's British chefs who not only create new dishes, but revamp old ones. It is good hot, and makes a refreshing summer soup when served chilled.

4 tablespoons butter
1 medium-size onion, chopped
1 pound tomatoes, about 4
    medium-size, unpeeled,
    quartered
1 pound celery, including leaves,
    chopped coarse
4 tart green apples, unpeeled,
    uncored and chopped coarse

4 tablespoons dry sherry wine
    (optional)
4 cups Chicken Stock (see Index)
Salt, freshly ground pepper
1 tablespoon lemon juice
Garnish: chopped chervil

Heat the butter in a saucepan and sauté the onion until soft. Add the tomatoes, celery, apples, and sherry if using it. Cover and cook over very low heat for 5 minutes. Add the chicken stock and simmer, covered, for 45 minutes. Cool.

Purée the solids in a food processor or blender, then put through a sieve. Return the purée to the saucepan with the stock. Season with salt and pepper to taste and add lemon juice. If the soup is to be served hot, heat it through. If it is to be served cold, chill it lightly.

Serve garnished with a little chopped chervil. The soup may also be garnished with a teaspoon of salted whipped cream and a little chopped apple.

S E R V E S 4 to 6.

STILTON SOUP, ARDSHEAL HOUSE

❖   ❖   ❖

Robert Gardiner was encouraged in the kitchen by Bob Taylor, owner of Ardsheal House Hotel, Kentallen, Highland, in Scotland, and himself an enthusiastic amateur cook. I was surprised when Robert told me he used a whole pound of Stilton cheese in the soup, which I had found light and delicate. He was right as I discovered when I cooked it for myself. If Stilton isn't available, other blue cheeses can be used instead.

4 tablespoons (½ stick) butter
1 small onion, chopped fine
1 garlic clove, minced
1 pound Stilton cheese, rind
 removed, grated
½ cup all-purpose flour
4 cups Chicken Stock (see Index)
½ cup dry white wine

1 bay leaf
Salt, freshly ground pepper
1 cup light cream, or Fresh
 White Cheese or Junket
 Cheese (see Index)
Garnish: snipped chives or black
 pepper

Heat the butter in a saucepan and cook the onion until soft. Add the garlic and cook for about a minute longer. Stir in the cheese and flour and continue to cook over low heat until the mixture is well blended, about 3 minutes. Stir in the stock and wine, add the bay leaf and bring to a simmer, whisking from time to time, for 15 minutes. Remove the bay leaf. Season to taste with salt and pepper. Add the cream or fresh cheese and cook just long enough to heat the soup through.

Garnish with snipped chives, or with a generous grinding of black pepper.

SERVES 6.

CHILLED STILTON SOUP WITH ALMOND GARNISH

❖   ❖   ❖

Anthony Blake, chef de cuisine at Eastwell Manor, a country house hotel set in private parkland in Ashford, Kent, has created a subtly flavored, chilled summer soup with an interesting garnish. It is smooth and delicate and can be prepared well ahead of time for a lunch or dinner party.

2 celery ribs, chopped fine
½ medium-size onion, chopped fine
1 leek, white part only, well washed, chopped fine
4 tablespoons butter
Salt, freshly ground pepper
1 bay leaf

¼ cup dry white wine
½ cup all-purpose flour
5 cups Chicken Stock (see Index)
¾ cup grated Stilton or other blue cheese
¼ cup light cream

Almond Cream Garnish

½ cup heavy cream
2 tablespoons ground almonds

⅛ teaspoon almond extract
4 sprigs of chervil

In a saucepan cook the celery, onion and leek in the butter over low heat until vegetables are soft, 10 to 15 minutes. Do not let them color. Season with salt and pepper, add the bay leaf and white wine, and simmer for 3 to 4 minutes. Stir in the flour and cook, stirring, for 5 minutes without letting the flour color. Off the heat gradually stir in the chicken stock. The mixture should be smooth. Return the saucepan to low heat, cover, and cook at a bare simmer for 1 hour.

Remove and discard the bay leaf. Add the Stilton cheese and the light cream, stir to mix, and add salt and pepper if necessary. Simmer, uncovered, for 6 minutes. Remove from the heat, cool slightly, then pour into a blender or food processor and process until very smooth. Transfer to a jug or other container and chill thoroughly in the refrigerator for 2 to 3 hours.

In a bowl whip the heavy cream until it stands in peaks. Fold in the almonds and almond extract. When ready to serve, pour the soup into 4 lightly chilled bowls. Using 2 teaspoons, make quenelles with the cream and gently place on top of the soup, 2 quenelles to each bowl. Garnish with the chervil sprigs.

SERVES 4.

BRIE AND SCALLION SOUP

❖   ❖   ❖

This is a rich, delicate and unusual soup created by Campbell Cameron, the enthusiastic young chef at Culloden House in Inverness, Scotland. It makes a fine prelude to a simple main course.

1½ pounds Brie cheese, chopped
   coarse
4 cups Chicken Stock (see Index)
⅔ cup fine-chopped trimmed
   scallions, using some of the
   green part

2 cups light cream
6 egg yolks
Salt, freshly ground white pepper
Garnish: ½ cup fine-chopped
   scallions

Combine the Brie and chicken stock in a saucepan and melt the cheese over very low heat, stirring from time to time. Add the scallions and cook for 10 minutes, or until scallions are very soft. Strain the soup through a sieve into a bowl. Return the liquid to the saucepan and purée the solids in a blender or food processor. Add the purée to the liquid.

In another saucepan bring the cream almost to boiling point. Have the egg yolks in a bowl and whisk the hot cream into them. Reheat the soup and whisk in the egg-yolk and cream mixture, taking care not to let the soup boil. Season to taste with salt and pepper.

Garnish soup with scallions and serve in bouillon cups. If soup seems too thick, thin with a little hot chicken stock.

SERVES 6.

JOHN DORY AND OYSTER SOUP

❖   ❖   ❖

John Dory, Saint-Pierre in France, so-called for the "thumbprints," dark round marks on each side of the fish said to have been imprinted by Peter the Fisherman, is no beauty as fish go. However, it has firm, white, bone-free fillets. Either sole or flounder makes an admirable substitute. Christopher Oakes, head chef at the Castle Hotel in Taunton, Somerset, created this very elegant fish soup. It isn't difficult to cook. Although the ingredients list looks rather long, nothing is exotic and only the oysters make this a luxury dish, lovely for a party. The home cook need not trim the carrots and zucchini into neat ovals, but may just leave the vegetables plainly sliced, and may use mussels or clams instead of oysters.

16 slices of young carrot, 1 inch thick, trimmed into ovals

16 slices of young zucchini, 1 inch thick, trimmed into ovals

6 tablespoons butter

12 ounces skinned and boned John Dory or sole or flounder fillets, cut at an angle into 8 slices

2 cups Fish Stock (see Index)

1 small leek, white part only, trimmed, thoroughly washed, and cut into julienne strips

2 tablespoons minced shallots

⅛ teaspoon saffron threads, ground

1 garlic clove, crushed

2 tablespoons brown lentils, soaked

1 cup dry white wine

¼ cup diced, peeled and seeded tomato

1½ cups rich Chicken Stock (see Index)

Salt, freshly ground pepper

16 oysters

Fresh thyme leaves, about 8

Cook the carrots and zucchini in boiling salted water in separate saucepans until tender but still crisp. Drain and set aside.

Heat 2 tablespoons of the butter in a skillet and cook the fish, turning once, over low heat for about 1 minute on each side. Heat the fish stock separately.

Heat the rest of the butter in a saucepan, add the leek, and cook over low heat for about 3 minutes. Add the shallots, saffron, garlic and lentils and cook for 2 minutes longer. Add 1½ cups of the warmed fish stock, and the chicken stock. Season to taste with salt and pepper and skim, if necessary. Bring the liquid to a simmer, add the fish, oysters, thyme leaves, carrots and zucchini. Just before the soup comes to a full simmer, remove it from the heat, and serve.

S E R V E S 4.

V A R I A T I O N : If oysters are not available, substitute mussels, cooked in a little white wine just until they open. Clams can also be used.

COCK-A-LEEKIE

❖   ❖   ❖

Scots chefs have a great deal of respect for their traditional dishes, and an even greater respect for fine fresh ingredients, so I was pleased when Ken Stott of Kildrummy Castle Hotel, Kildrummy, Grampian, and David Moir of Gleddoch House, Langbank, both in Scotland, gave me recipes for Cock-a-Leekie soup, a chicken and leek soup with prunes, that is hearty enough for a main course. Both chefs are keenly interested in new developments in food, especially some of the innovative starters, but do not wish to lose the good things of the past. The recipes, which are traditional, are very similar, so I am giving only one of them. Both are simpler to cook than older versions which call for boiling fowls rather than stock.

2 tablespoons butter
4 leeks, trimmed, thoroughly
    washed and cut into ¼-inch
    slices
8 cups rich Chicken Stock (see
    Index)

¼ cup long-grain rice
6 ounces pitted prunes, about 1
    cup, halved
½ pound cooked chicken breast,
    cut into ½-inch pieces
Salt, freshly ground pepper

Heat the butter in a skillet and sauté the leeks over moderate heat until they are soft without letting them color. Set aside.

Pour the chicken stock into a large saucepan, add the rice and simmer, covered, until rice is cooked, about 15 minutes. Add the leeks, prunes and chicken, and season to taste with salt and pepper. Simmer over low heat for 5 minutes to blend the flavors.

S E R V E S 6 to 8.

MUSHROOM AND MUSTARD SOUP

❖   ❖   ❖

This is Stephen Frost's version of a traditional English soup. An Englishman from Cambridge, he is head chef at Cromlix House, Dunblane, in Perthshire, Scotland, the family home of the Edens and now a luxury country house hotel set in a 5,000-acre estate, which includes a grouse moor. He is also the youngest of the Scottish Master Chefs. The soup is wonderful on a chilly day, and also makes a good beginning to a salad lunch. It is typical of today's young chefs that they not only create new dishes, but recreate old ones.

2 tablespoons butter
1 medium-size onion, chopped
1 medium-size leek, chopped; if not available, then 2 medium-size onions
2 celery ribs, chopped
1 medium-size carrot, scraped and chopped

2 cups chopped mushrooms
3 cups Chicken Stock (see Index), approximately
½ teaspoon English dry mustard, or 1 tablespoon prepared Dijon mustard
Salt, freshly ground pepper
¼ cup dry sherry wine

Heat the butter in a saucepan and add the onion, leek, celery, carrot and mushrooms. Cook over very low heat until vegetables are softened, about 5 minutes; do not let them brown. Add the chicken stock, bring to a simmer, cover, and cook until vegetables are very tender, about 30 minutes. Lift out the solids and transfer to a food processor or blender. Add the mustard and process to a purée, adding a little of the stock if necessary. Return the purée to the saucepan and season with salt and pepper. If the soup seems very thick, add more stock. Pour in the sherry and heat through.

If liked stir in a little cream, or Fresh White Cheese (see Index), just before serving.

S E R V E S 4.

V A R I A T I O N : Chef Frost, an enthusiastic who cherishes simplicity in cooking and dislikes too many contrasting flavors in a dish, seeks to look at food from a new perspective. An example is his Tomato and Orange Soup, another traditional soup brought skillfully up-to-date and simplified. Omit the carrot, mushrooms, sherry and mustard in the recipe and substitute 1 cup chopped, peeled and seeded tomatoes, ½ cup orange juice and the grated rind of 1 orange. Cook as in the basic recipe. The soup could not be simpler to make, is good hot, and lovely chilled in summer.

S E R V E S 4.

CREAM OF MUSSEL SOUP

❖   ❖   ❖

This is another soup from Philip Burgess of the Arundell Arms, Lifton, Devon. It is hearty enough to make a light main course when served in generous portions. Cider is an old Devonshire tradition and gives this soup its distinctive flavor.

3 dozen large fresh mussels	¼ cup flour
1 large onion, chopped fine	5 cups Fish Stock (see Index)
½ cup dry cider	½ cup heavy cream, or use Fresh
2 tablespoons butter	White Cheese or Yogurt
2 leeks, thoroughly washed and	Cheese (see Index)
chopped fine	Salt, freshly ground pepper
1 celery rib, chopped fine	1 tablespoon chopped parsley
1 garlic clove, crushed	

Scrape the mussels and with a sharp knife remove the beards. Wash the mussels thoroughly, changing the water several times until it is clear of sand. Let the mussels soak for an hour or two in fresh clean water to disgorge any sand. Discard any that are open. Put the mussels in a large pan with the onion and cider. Cover and steam over low heat until the mussels open, about 5 minutes. Discard any unopened ones. Remove mussels from the pan, take them out of the shells, and set aside. Discard the shells. Strain the liquid through a fine sieve lined with a double layer of dampened cheesecloth, and set it aside.

In a saucepan melt the butter; add the leeks, celery and garlic and cook over low heat until vegetables are soft. Stir in the flour and continue to cook, still over low heat, stirring from time to time, for about 5 minutes. Do not let the flour brown. In another saucepan bring the fish stock to a boil and pour it, all at once, into the saucepan with the flour and vegetable mixture. Stir to mix, then simmer covered for 15 minutes, stirring occasionally. Add the strained liquid from the mussels, the cream, salt and pepper to taste, and the mussels and heat through.

Serve immediately, garnished with chopped parsley. Serve with crusty bread.

S E R V E S 4 as a main course, 6 as a soup.

SCALLOP CHOWDER

❖ ❖ ❖

This is another of chef Martin Lam's soups, created by him at L'Escargot restaurant in London's Soho. It has his pleasantly innovative touch. When I cook it, I serve double portions and make it a main course as it is so appetizing I always want more than just a soup serving.

8 ounces salt pork
1 medium-size onion, sliced thin
1 carrot, scraped and diced
1 small parsnip, peeled and diced
1 medium-size green bell pepper,
    seeded and cut into julienne
    strips
2 celery ribs, diced
2½ cups milk

½ cup orange juice
Salt, freshly ground pepper
1 tablespoon all-purpose flour
1 tablespoon butter
1 pound scallops
2 tablespoons lemon juice
2 cups Fish Stock (see Index)
Garnish: 4 tablespoons heavy
    cream, paprika (optional)

Drop the salt pork into boiling water and blanch for a minute or two. Drain, pat dry with paper towels, and cut into ¼-inch dice. Sauté the pork in a saucepan over low heat until the fat runs out. Lift out the pieces with a slotted spoon and drain on paper towels. Add the onion to the saucepan and sauté in the pork fat until soft. Add the carrot, parsnip, green bell pepper and celery, and stir to mix. Add the milk, orange juice, diced pork, salt and pepper to taste; simmer, uncovered, until vegetables are soft.

In a small bowl mix the flour and butter together with a fork. Set aside. While the vegetables are cooking, toss the scallops with the lemon juice and let them stand for 5 minutes. If they are large, cut them into quarters; if small, leave whole. When the vegetables are soft, add the scallops and any juice to the saucepan with the fish stock. Stir to mix. Stir in the flour and butter mixture (beurre manié) bit by bit and simmer just until the soup is lightly thickened.

Serve at once. Garnish, if liked, with 2 teaspoons of heavy cream and a little paprika on each soup bowl.

S E R V E S 6 as a soup, 4 as a main course.

CONSOMMÉ OF THE FRUITS OF SEA AND EARTH

❖   ❖   ❖

Lyn Hall, who runs La Petite Cuisine School of Cooking in London, is a perfectionist with a great understanding of the importance of technique. She believes one can never take too much trouble when cooking with love. All the same this is not a difficult or time-consuming dish, and other fish can be used instead of trout and salmon. It makes a satisfying main course for two.

½ pound fillet of trout, skinned and boned
½ pound salmon fillet, skinned and boned
½ pound mixed fresh vegetables —zucchini, carrots, celery ribs, button mushrooms, small white onions, small new potatoes

3 cups Clarified Fish Stock (see Index)
1 cup dry white wine
Salt, freshly ground pepper
3 sprigs of fresh dill

Cut the fish into ½-inch cubes and set aside. Cut the zucchini into diagonal slices, slice the carrots and celery into equal-size pieces, and cut the mushrooms into quarters. Peel the onions and scrape the new potatoes. Cook the vegetables separately in a large saucepan of briskly boiling salted water until they are tender. Refresh them quickly under cold water and set aside.

In a saucepan heat 2 cups of the stock with the wine. Bring to a boil and simmer for 4 minutes, skimming off any froth from the surface. Cover, reduce the heat as low as possible, and keep hot. Pour remaining cup of stock into a saucepan. Season the fish with salt and pepper and add it to the stock with the vegetables. Simmer for 1 minute to cook the fish and heat the vegetables through. Pour into a warmed tureen. Pour the hot stock from the other saucepan into the tureen. Float the dill on top and serve immediately.

S E R V E S 3 or 4, or 2 as a main course.

SALMON BISQUE

❖ ❖ ❖

Scottish salmon is magnificent and so was this bisque, which I enjoyed on a trip to Scotland. It was created by Raymond Baudon, then executive head chef at Johnstounburn House, Humbie, in Lothian, near Edinburgh. He has a passion for cooking and a great appreciation of Scottish fish whose excellence stimulates his inventiveness.

2 pounds salmon tail in one piece
4 tablespoons butter
1 medium-size onion, chopped
  fine
2 medium-size carrots, scraped
  and diced
2 garlic cloves, minced
1 celery rib, diced
1 small leek, trimmed, thoroughly
  washed, and sliced
1 bay leaf

1 thyme sprig
10 tarragon leaves
1 tablespoon tomato purée
1 tablespoon all-purpose flour
4 tablespoons Armagnac or other
  brandy
1 cup dry white wine
6 cups Fish Stock (see Index)
Salt, freshly ground pepper
½ cup heavy cream (optional)

Measure the salmon at the thickest part. The cooking time will be 10 minutes for each inch.

In a large saucepan melt the butter; add the onion, carrots, garlic, celery, leek, bay leaf, thyme and tarragon. Cook over very low heat until vegetables are soft. Stir in the tomato purée and the flour, mixing well. Add the salmon, flame with the Armagnac, then pour in the white wine. Bring to a simmer and cook over low heat for a minute or two. Add the fish stock and salt and pepper to taste, cover, and simmer for 10 minutes for each inch the salmon measures at its thickest part. At the end of the time, carefully lift out the salmon, and remove the skin and bones. Flake the salmon and set it aside.

Set a fine sieve over a bowl and strain the bisque through it, pressing down hard on the solids to extract all the juices. Discard solids. Rinse out and dry the saucepan. Return the bisque to the saucepan, add the salmon, and stir in the cream if using. Heat the soup through over moderate heat, taste for seasoning, and add salt and pepper if necessary. Serve with crusty bread.

S E R V E S 6.

HOTPOT OF SCALLOPS, CRAYFISH TAILS AND MUSSELS

❖   ❖   ❖

Julian Waterer knew from a very early age that he wanted to cook, and he was lucky enough to be living near Le Talbooth Restaurant at Dedham, near Colchester, Essex. His father was a friend of owner Gerald Milsom and eventually he was allowed, after school, to help with the dishes. Later he worked there as an apprentice under chef-patron Sam Chalmers, rising to *sous-chef*. I met him when he was the very young head chef at Greywalls, an Edwardian country house designed by Lutyens and now a country house hotel, at Gullane, near Edinburgh, Scotland. He is now at the Salisbury restaurant at Old Hatfield in Hertfordshire. Cooking is not just his profession, it is his passion. He loves to play variations on a theme. This one is derived from Paul Bocuse's idea of topping soups with pastry. Julian calls his soups hotpots. He varies the fillings according to the season and what is best in the market. I have enjoyed two of them. They invite one's own experimentation. Julian suggests sometimes using a 1-quart soufflé dish instead of 6 individual dishes, as the pastry topping looks very impressive brought to the table, a golden dome.

2 tablespoons minced shallots
2½ cups Fish Stock (see Index)
1 cup dry white wine
2 cups heavy cream
1 teaspoon lemon juice
Salt, freshly ground pepper
12 large scallops

18 shelled mussels
12 shelled crayfish tails or jumbo
  shrimps
1½ pounds Puff Pastry (see
  Index)
2 egg yolks

In a heavy saucepan combine the shallots, fish stock and dry white wine and simmer over moderate heat, uncovered, until the liquid is reduced to just over ½ cup. Add the cream and lemon juice and continue to simmer until the liquid is reduced to 2 cups. Season this sauce to taste with salt and pepper. Cool slightly.

Have ready six 1-cup soufflé dishes or ramekins, or small ovenproof soup bowls. Slice scallops into thirds, and distribute among the bowls, two to each bowl. Add the mussels and top with the crayfish tails or jumbo shrimps, halved. Cover with the sauce and set aside.

Roll out the pastry about ⅛ inch thick and cut it into six 5-inch circles. Beat the egg yolks with 1 teaspoon cold water and brush the rims of the circles with the mixture. Drape the circles of puff pastry, brushed sides down, over the pots with the hands. Do not press down hard on the rims. Brush the tops with more of the egg yolk and refrigerate for 20 minutes. Bake in a preheated hot oven (425°F.) for about 15 minutes, or until the pastry is puffed and golden.

Using a spatula, slide the bowls onto plates and serve. To eat, break the crust into the soup.

S E R V E S 6.

V A R I A T I O N : Instead of the crayfish tails, scallops and mussels, use 1 pound fresh salmon fillets, skinned, boned and cut into 1-inch pieces, 18 crayfish tails or jumbo shrimps, halved, and/or 18 oysters.

V A R I A T I O N I : Pierre Chevillard of Chewton Glen has his own version of this dish. He calls it Little Surprise Pots as he never knows what is going to be the best fish and shellfish available in the market. He uses sole, salmon, scallops—whatever is best—and adds to the ramekin a julienne of carrots, fennel, celery and leeks tossed in butter, a small amount of chopped truffle and a julienne of raw white mushrooms.

V A R I A T I O N I I : Sam Chalmers of Le Talbooth restaurant in Dedham has his own special way with the dish. He adds a little saffron to the sauce and uses assorted fish mixed with sliced mushrooms—¼ pound mushrooms to 1 pound fish. He makes a bed of washed, drained and finely chopped spinach at the bottom of each ramekin, using ½ pound spinach for 8 pots.

SCALLOP SOUP

❖   ❖   ❖

Peter Jackson is a Scottish chef whom I first met in Wales when he was chef de cuisine at Bodysgallen Hall Hotel, Llandudno, and later at Eastwell Manor, Ashford, Kent, in England, when he was head chef there. His dishes are fresh and natural as this soup shows. I have had it without the garlic, paprika and egg-yolk thickening, as well as with it, and enjoyed this extremely delicate soup both ways. Peter is now chef-patron of The Colonial Restaurant in Glasgow, Strathclyde, Scotland.

4 tablespoons (½ stick) butter
4 tablespoons shallots, sliced thin
1 medium-size carrot, scraped
and cut into julienne strips
1 celery rib, cut into julienne
strips
1 inch slice of fennel, cut into
julienne strips
1 leek, white part only, cut into
julienne strips
4 medium-size tomatoes, about
1 pound, peeled, seeded and
chopped

2 tablespoons Pernod liqueur
¼ cup dry white wine
4 cups Fish Stock (see Index)
1 garlic clove
1 teaspoon paprika
2 egg yolks
½ pound scallops, sliced if large,
halved if small
Salt, freshly ground pepper

In a large saucepan heat the butter and sweat the shallots, carrot, celery, fennel and leek over low heat until vegetables are soft. Add the tomatoes and cook for 3 or 4 minutes longer. Pour in the Pernod and white wine; stir to mix. Add the fish stock and simmer, covered, over low heat for 15 minutes.

Pound the garlic, paprika and egg yolks in a mortar with a pestle, or crush the garlic in a garlic press and mix it with the paprika and egg yolks. Set aside.

Add the scallops to the soup and simmer for ½ minute. Stir in the egg-yolk mixture, whisking for about 1 minute, or just long enough to thicken the soup lightly. It is important not to overcook the scallops as they toughen very quickly and lose their texture and flavor. Season with salt and pepper to taste.

SERVES 4.

CABBAGE AND OYSTER SOUP WITH SAFFRON

❖ ❖ ❖

I love what Paul Gayler, the young head chef at the Inigo Jones restaurant in London, has done with cabbage soup. He has put together ingredients that do not usually find themselves in the same dish. Although his training has been quite formal, his cooking is modern, his dishes light.

4 tablespoons butter
2½ cups chopped white cabbage
1 teaspoon whole cuminseed
⅛ teaspoon saffron threads
4 cups Chicken Stock (see Index)

4 egg yolks
½ cup heavy cream
Salt, freshly ground pepper
12 fresh oysters and their liquor

Heat 2 tablespoons of the butter in a large saucepan. Add the cabbage, cover, and cook over very low heat until the cabbage is soft, about 5 minutes; do not let cabbage brown. Stir in the cuminseed. Grind the saffron threads in a mortar and add to the chicken stock. Pour the stock into the saucepan with the cabbage, stir and simmer, covered, over low heat for 15 minutes.

In a bowl beat the egg yolks into the cream. Pour ½ cup of the soup into the egg-yolk mixture, stirring well, then pour it into the soup and cook over very low heat, stirring, until the soup has thickened lightly. Season to taste with salt and pepper. Strain the oyster liquor and stir it into the soup, then stir in the remaining 2 tablespoons butter. Divide the oysters among 4 bowls and pour in the hot soup. Serve immediately.

S E R V E S 4.

CREAM OF SEAFOOD SOUP

❖ ❖ ❖

This is one of Lyn Hall's special fish soups. It has a delicious flavor and looks very pretty with the pink fish and shrimps surrounded by the creamy white soup. It makes an elegant beginning to an important lunch or dinner. I find I can use Fresh White Cheese (see Index) when I am running away from 2 cups of heavy cream without losing the velvety richness of the soup. Instead of reducing the stock and cheese over brisk heat, I do it gently, and if it is at all grainy I whirl it briefly in a blender.

12 large shrimps, unpeeled	¼ pound skinned and boned
8 cups Fish Stock (see Index)	halibut, cut into 1-inch pieces
2 cups dry white wine	¼ pound skinned and boned
2 cups heavy cream	salmon, cut into 1-inch pieces
½ pound scallops	Salt, freshly ground pepper

In a large saucepan simmer the shrimps in the fish stock for 2 minutes. Lift out, allow to cool, shell, and set aside.

Pour the wine into the saucepan with the fish stock and reduce over brisk heat to half, 5 cups. Pour in the cream and still over brisk heat reduce again to 5 cups. If the scallops are large, cut them into 1-inch pieces; if small leave whole. Add the fish and scallops to the soup and cook for a few seconds. Add the shrimps and cook just to reheat them. Season the soup to taste with salt and pepper. Have ready 6 warmed soup bowls.

Lift out the seafood with a slotted spoon and pile it in a mound in the center of each bowl, putting 2 shrimps on top in each bowl. Pour the soup around the seafood and serve immediately.

S E R V E S 6.

CULLEN SKINK
(Smoked Haddock Soup)

❖ ❖ ❖

Chef Ken Stott of Kildrummy Castle Hotel, who comes from Findochty, a village near Cullen, Grampian, in Scotland, claims he was weaned on this soup. Cullen is a fishing village and "skink" is the old

Scots name for broth. It is a splendid soup, just right for wintry weather, especially in this modern version.

1 pound potatoes, peeled and cut
    into ½-inch dice
1 large onion, chopped fine
1 pound smoked haddock fillets,
    skinned, boned and chopped
    coarse

2 cups milk
¼ pound (1 stick) butter, diced
Salt, freshly ground black pepper

Put the potatoes and onion into a large saucepan with 4 cups cold water. Bring to a simmer and cook, covered, over moderate heat until the potatoes are tender, about 10 minutes. Add the haddock, milk and butter, stir to mix, and simmer for 5 minutes longer. Add salt, if necessary. Season generously with black pepper.

S E R V E S 6.

SMOKED HADDOCK AND LEEK SOUP

❖   ❖   ❖

Christopher Oakes, head chef of the Castle Hotel in Taunton, Somerset, has put together two traditional Scots soups, Cullen Skink (Smoked Haddock) and Cock-a-Leekie (Chicken Soup), to produce an interesting new soup. The prunes add a delicious sweet-sour touch.

1 pound smoked haddock fillets
1 leek, trimmed, thoroughly
    washed and cut into julienne
    strips
5 cups rich Chicken Stock (see
    Index)

4 pitted prunes, cut into julienne
    strips
Salt, freshly ground pepper

Skin and bone the haddock fillets. Combine the haddock, leek and chicken stock in a large saucepan and simmer for 1 minute. Add the prunes and simmer just long enough to heat them through. Season to taste with salt, if necessary, and a generous amount of pepper.

S E R V E S 4 to 6.

MIXED SHELLFISH CONSOMMÉ

❖ ❖ ❖

This exceptionally light, attractive shellfish soup is the creation of Gunther Schlender, the young head chef at Rue St. Jacques restaurant in London. He believes in the light touch with food and in mixing different cooking styles to create new dishes.

½ medium-size onion, diced
½ medium-size carrot, scraped
  and diced
1 medium-size leek, white part
  only, well washed and chopped
2 medium-size celery ribs,
  chopped
2 juniper berries
1 small bay leaf
½ pound any nonoily white fish,
  chopped

1 small tomato, peeled and
  chopped
1 sprig each of fennel, dill,
  parsley and fresh coriander
1 pinch of saffron threads,
  crumbled
6 cups Fish Stock (see Index)
Salt, freshly ground pepper

Garnish

8 crayfish tails or medium
  shrimps
4 slices of lobster

4 large scallops, halved
  horizontally
12 coriander leaves

Combine all the ingredients for the consommé in a large casserole or saucepan. Mix well and simmer, covered, for 45 minutes. Strain the soup through a sieve lined with a double layer of dampened cheesecloth. Rinse out and dry the casserole and return the strained soup to it. Season to taste with salt and pepper, and heat through.

In a small saucepan combine all the ingredients for the garnish except the coriander leaves. Pour in just enough of the consommé to cover and simmer until the shellfish is done, 1 or 2 minutes.

Arrange the shellfish garnish in 4 heated soup bowls and pour in the hot soup at the table. Float 3 coriander leaves on each bowl.

SERVES 4.

FISH
AND
SHELLFISH

❖ ❖ ❖

B RITISH CHEFS have come up with wonderfully innovative recipes for fish and shellfish, and in this they have been greatly helped by the marketing revolution which has brought back to the fishmongers a great many fish and shellfish not seen for years, as well as types not previously sold there. Fishmonger, still used in Britain, simply means "one who deals in fish." It has been used since 1464, a truly venerable expression. Sometimes fish on the Eastern side of the Atlantic do not swim in American waters, but close, often nearly identical, substitutes can be found in fish markets, and I have given these equivalents in recipes. Seafood has the great advantage of taking little time to prepare and cook; it is appetizing, attractive to look at, and good for us.

SOLE BAKED IN HERBED CUSTARD

❖　　　❖　　　❖

This is a quick, simple and easy recipe made special by the fresh herbs which head chef Graham Flanagan of Cottage in the Wood, a small secluded Georgian hotel at Malvern Wells, Hereford and Worcester, likes to use. His cooking is an interesting blend of traditional and modern. Serve with a Pouilly-Fuissé.

4 skinned and boned fillets of sole
　or flounder, each 6 ounces
Salt, freshly ground pepper
Butter
2 tablespoons lemon juice
3 large eggs

¾ cup light cream
Pinch of cayenne pepper
2 tablespoons minced mixed
　herbs, such as parsley, chives,
　tarragon, basil and chervil

Season the fish with salt and pepper and roll the fillets up. Secure with a toothpick if necessary. Generously butter a shallow ovenproof baking dish large enough to hold the fish in a single layer. Add the fish. Sprinkle with the lemon juice.

Beat the eggs in a bowl with the cream; add salt to taste and the cayenne pepper. Fold in the herbs and pour the mixture over the fish. Cover the dish with foil and bake in a preheated moderate oven (350°F.) for 25 to 30 minutes, or until the fish is done. The custard will be very lightly set, more like a sauce. Serve immediately.

S E R V E S　4.

POACHED FILLETS OF SOLE WITH ORANGE SAUCE

❖　　　❖　　　❖

This turns fillet of sole into something special, and is easy and quick to cook. Nigel Lambert, head chef at the Elms, a Queen Anne house now a country house hotel at Abberley in Worcester, who created this dish, describes his cooking as English country cooking. His aim is to produce unpretentious honest food that is also original and interesting. Serve with a Chardonnay.

2 pounds skinned and boned sole
　or flounder fillets, cut into 8
　pieces
Salt, freshly ground pepper
¼ pound (1 stick) butter, plus
　butter for pan
1 tablespoon chopped shallot
1 cup fresh orange juice
4 tablespoons lemon juice

½ cup heavy cream
¼ cup Grand Marnier or other
　orange liqueur
1 orange, peeled and separated
　into segments
2 tablespoons chopped parsley
Puff Pastry shapes (see Index)
　(optional)

Season the fish with salt and pepper and fold the fillets in half. Lightly butter an ovenproof dish large enough to hold the fish in a single layer. Sprinkle dish with the shallot and arrange the fish on top. Pour in the orange and lemon juice, cover with buttered paper or foil, and cook in a preheated moderate oven (350°F.) for about 10 minutes. Lift out the fillets to a warmed dish, cover, and keep warm.

Strain the cooking liquid from the pan into a saucepan and reduce over fairly high heat to about ¼ cup. It should be very concentrated. Pour in the cream and continue to reduce until the sauce reaches coating consistency. Off the heat stir in the Grand Marnier and beat in ¼ pound butter, cut into bits, until it is all incorporated.

Arrange the fish on 4 warmed plates and coat with the sauce. Garnish with the orange segments and parsley, and the puff pastry shapes if liked.

SERVES 4.

VARIATION: If I want to cut down on butter and cream, I stir in ½ cup Fresh White Cheese or Yogurt Cheese (see Index) instead of the cream and just heat it through, then stir in the Grand Marnier and leave out the butter.

STUFFED POACHED FILLETS OF SOLE

❖   ❖   ❖

I admire the forthright approach of young John Martin Grimsey of the White Hart Hotel, a hostelry since 1489 in Coggeshall, Essex. He cares deeply for traditional British cooking but recognizes the need for change. He feels this dish meets his requirements, and says of it that he particularly enjoys the subtle blend of flavors and textures. I agree. The true sole is not an American fish and though many flat fish are called sole, they should more properly be called flounder. Winter flounder, gray sole or lemon sole are good substitutes. Serve with a Pouilly-Fuissé.

*2 large lemon or gray sole or
    winter flounder*
¼ pound (1 stick) unsalted butter
Salt, freshly ground pepper
*1 ounce smoked salmon, about 4
    slices*

*1 medium-size avocado, peeled,
    pitted and sliced*
*Hollandaise Sauce (see Index)
    (optional)*

Have a fishmonger skin the sole and remove a whole fillet from each side, giving 4 large fillets. Keep the bones for making stock, if liked.

Melt the butter in a small saucepan over low heat. Generously brush an ovenproof dish, large enough to hold the fish when folded into envelopes, with the melted butter. Put the fillets on a board and season with salt and pepper. Brush with melted butter and top with the smoked salmon slices. Brush the salmon with melted butter and top with the sliced avocado. Fold the fish over the filling to make an envelope. Brush with butter and press down lightly to seal. Arrange in the buttered dish. Bake in a preheated moderate oven (350°F.) for about 15 minutes, or until done.

Arrange the fish on 4 warmed plates and pour the hollandaise sauce, if using it, over them. Garnish, if liked, with tomato roses, puff pastry cut into tiny fish shapes, or sprigs of fresh chervil or parsley. Serve with new potatoes and an assortment of fresh green vegetables, such as green peas, snow peas, zucchini or green beans, arranged on small separate plates.

S E R V E S 4.

FILETS DE SOLE AU BEURRE D'AVOCAT ET BASILIC
(Fillets of Sole with Avocado and Basil)

❖   ❖   ❖

John Armstrong, head chef at Martin's restaurant in London, unlike many of today's chefs, prefers to use French when describing his dishes. French, he feels, is the language of the kitchen, with neat poetic terms that can become clumsy in English. His food, however, is very English, is poetic, and is never at all clumsy. He cares about presentation, and even more about flavor. In addition he is a true original. Serve with a Sauvignon Blanc.

5 tablespoons butter
4 tablespoons chopped shallots
12 fillets of Dover sole, or similar
  fish, each about 4 ounces
Salt, freshly ground pepper
2 cups Fish Stock (see Index)

½ cup light cream
2 large ripe avocados
1 tablespoon chopped basil leaves
1 tomato, about 6 ounces, seeded
  and diced
6 small sprigs of chervil

Butter an ovenproof baking dish, about 6 by 9 inches, with 1 table-spoon of the butter. Sprinkle with the chopped shallots. Season the fish with salt and pepper. Lightly flatten the fillets and tie each into a loose knot, or fold over to make triangles. Arrange in the baking dish. Bring the stock to a simmer and pour over the fish. Cover the dish with aluminum foil and bake in a preheated moderately hot oven (400°F.) until firm to the touch, about 8 to 12 minutes. Lift out the fillets to a warmed dish and keep warm.

Pour the cooking liquid into a saucepan and reduce to 1 cup over moderately high heat. Add the cream and reduce again to 1 cup. Pour liquid into a food processor or blender, add one of the avocados, diced, and the basil leaves and process to a purée. Cut remaining butter into bits. With the machine running add the butter, a piece at a time, until it has all been incorporated. Season to taste with salt and pepper. For a very fine sauce, put through a strainer.

Peel remaining avocado and cut into slices. Arrange a fan of avocado on each of 6 warmed plates. Arrange 2 fillets on each plate and coat with the sauce. Garnish with tomato dice and chervil sprigs.

S E R V E S 6.

FILLET OF SOLE WITH SMOKED SALMON

❖   ❖   ❖

Ken Stott, head chef of Kildrummy Castle Hotel, a country house hotel in Scotland, is himself a Scot who has always worked in the northeast of his own country. He believes in using the produce for which Scotland is famed and applying his skills and ideas to create appetizing new dishes which will give pleasure to those who eat them. I found this utterly delicious. Serve with a Chardonnay.

2 teaspoons butter, plus 2 tablespoons butter, cut into bits
2 teaspoons all-purpose flour
½ cup Fish Stock (see Index)
8 large fillets of sole or flounder, each about 6 ounces

4 ounces smoked salmon, about 8 slices
½ cup dry white wine
½ cup light cream
Salt, freshly ground pepper

Heat the 2 teaspoons butter in a small saucepan and stir in the flour. Cook, stirring, over low heat for 1 minute. Off the heat whisk in the fish stock, return the saucepan to the heat and cook, stirring or whisking, until the sauce is smooth and lightly thickened. Set aside.

Put the fillets of sole on a board and flatten them slightly. Top each with a slice of smoked salmon and roll them up. If necessary secure each roll with a toothpick. Arrange the fish in a single layer in a large skillet with a lid. Mix the sauce, wine and cream together and pour over the fish. Bring to just under a simmer, cover, and poach the fish until done, about 8 minutes. Lift out the fish and keep warm. Reduce the sauce over fairly brisk heat to 1 cup. Lower the heat and whisk in the pieces of butter one by one. Taste for seasoning and add salt and pepper if necessary.

Have ready 8 warmed plates. Cut each fillet though the middle and arrange on the plate cut side up so that the pink of the salmon can be seen. Pour the sauce round the fish. Serve immediately, with new potatoes and a green vegetable or two, such as snow peas or green beans, on small separate plates.

S E R V E S 8.

The recipe can easily be halved.

FILLETS OF SOLE WITH SCALLOPS

❖   ❖   ❖

This is one of Raymond Baudon's attractive, easy-to-cook fish dishes, which I enjoyed when he was head chef at Johnstounburn House, at Humble in Scotland. Serve with a Chardonnay.

8 large scallops, with roe if
  possible
8 fillets of sole or flounder, each
  about 6 ounces
½ cup Fish Stock (see Index)
½ cup dry sherry wine
4 medium-size mushrooms, sliced
  thin

Salt, freshly ground pepper
½ cup heavy cream, or Fresh
  White Cheese, Junket Cheese
  or Yogurt Cheese (see Index)
1 tablespoon butter
Garnish: sprigs of dill

Using a small sharp knife, cut the coral from the scallops and reserve it. Cut each scallop into 3 slices. Lightly flatten the fish and place 3 slices of scallop on each of the sole or flounder fillets. Carefully roll up the fillets and secure each with a toothpick.

Pour the fish stock and sherry into a flameproof dish large enough to hold the fish in a single layer. Add the mushrooms, the rolled-up fish and salt and pepper to taste. Top each fillet with a scallop roe. Bring the liquid to a simmer over moderate heat, cover the pan with wax paper and a lid, or with aluminum foil, and cook in a preheated moderately hot oven (400°F.) for 5 minutes. Lift out the fish to a serving dish, cover, and keep warm.

Pour the liquid from the pan into a saucepan and reduce it to half its volume over moderate heat. Add the cream, simmer for 2 to 3 minutes, and stir in the butter.

Pour the sauce around the sole, not over it. Garnish with sprigs of dill. Serve with new potatoes and a green vegetable or two such as peas, snow peas, baby carrots or zucchini, served separately.

S E R V E S 8.

V A R I A T I O N: The sauce can be made, if liked, with fresh white cheese or junket or yogurt cheese, simply stirred in and gently warmed through. Omit the butter.

SALMON WITH HERBED VANILLA DRESSING

❖   ❖   ❖

Anthony Blake, head chef at Eastwell Manor, now a country house hotel of considerable elegance at Ashford in Kent, first began cooking at the age of 13 when he opted out of a woodworking class in favor of food, a decision he has never regretted. I first met him when he was *sous-chef* to Christopher Oakes at the Castle Hotel at Taunton, Somerset, an important experience for his career. He is a highly creative cook who likes his dishes to be simple and light. This one is very adventurous. Serve with a Chardonnay.

Vanilla and Lemon Balm Dressing

1 vanilla bean
1¼ cups vegetable oil
1 tablespoon lemon juice

2 tablespoons white-wine vinegar
Salt, freshly ground pepper
½ cup lemon balm leaves

Salmon

4 slices of skinned and boned
   fillet of salmon, each about 7
   ounces
Salt, freshly ground pepper
Butter

¼ cup dry white wine
½ pound spinach, washed and
   trimmed, about 3 cups loosely
   packed
Grated rind of lemon

In a jar soak the vanilla bean in the oil for 24 to 36 hours. In a bowl whisk the lemon juice with the vinegar and salt and pepper to taste. Add the oil, the vanilla bean and the lemon balm leaves, and bottle until ready to use.

Season the salmon fillets with salt and pepper. Butter a large, shallow ovenproof dish and arrange the salmon fillets in the dish. Pour half of the reserved vanilla dressing over the salmon, and put 2 lemon balm leaves on top of each fillet. Pour in the white wine and cover with buttered paper. Put into a preheated moderate oven (350°F.) for 10 to 12 minutes, or until the salmon is just cooked. Remove from the oven and keep warm.

Cook the spinach in a large saucepan of briskly boiling salted water for 4 minutes. Drain, refresh in cold water and drain thoroughly, squeezing out as much liquid as possible. Return to the saucepan with a tablespoon of butter; season with salt and pepper.

To serve, put spinach on each of 4 heated plates and top with a salmon fillet. Strain the dressing, whisk, and pour over the salmon. Garnish with the grated lemon rind.

S E R V E S 4.

SALMON IN RED WINE

❖ ❖ ❖

This was cooked for me by Alan Casey when he was head chef at Culloden House, Inverness, in Scotland. It is extremely simple and very flavorful. There are not a great many fish recipes using red wine, and this has become one of my favorites.

4 slices of salmon fillet, each 6 ounces, cut on the slant
Salt, freshly ground pepper
Flour
4 tablespoons butter
12 white onions, about 1 inch in diameter, peeled
12 button mushrooms

2 cups dry red wine
1 bay leaf
½ teaspoon dried thyme
½ cup heavy cream
1 teaspoon lemon juice
½ teaspoon Worcestershire sauce
2 tablespoons minced parsley

Season the salmon with salt and pepper and dredge with flour, shaking to remove excess flour. Heat the butter in a skillet with a lid and seal the salmon steaks quickly on both sides. Lift out and set aside, covered. In the butter remaining in the pan lightly brown the onions and mushrooms. Pour in the wine, add the bay leaf and thyme, and bring to a simmer. Return the salmon and any juices that may have collected to the pan, cover, and simmer just until the salmon is tender, about 10 minutes. Remove the fish to a warmed serving dish and keep warm.

Remove and discard the bay leaf and thyme. Add the cream and reduce the sauce to coating consistency over fairly high heat. Add the lemon juice and Worcestershire sauce. Pour the sauce over the salmon and sprinkle with the parsley. Serve with boiled new potatoes.

S E R V E S 4.

SALMON FILLETS WITH LEEK AND SPINACH SAUCE

❖   ❖   ❖

This is an attractive, easy-to-cook dish given me by Peter Jackson when he was head chef at Bodysgallen Hall, Llandudno, Wales. I have cooked it very happily with sea (salmon) trout and other fish and always enjoy its simple fresh taste. Peter is now chef-patron at the Colonial Restaurant in Glasgow, Scotland. Serve with a Chardonnay.

2 cups loosely packed fresh
    spinach leaves
4 slices of salmon fillet, boned
    and skinned, each 5 to 6
    ounces
Flour
Salt, freshly ground pepper
4 tablespoons butter
2 medium-size leeks, thoroughly
    washed and cut into julienne
    strips, white part only

¼ cup strong Fish Stock (see
    Index)
¼ cup dry vermouth
½ cup heavy cream, or ¼ cup
    Fresh White Cheese (see
    Index)

Drop the spinach into a saucepan of briskly boiling water and cook for 4 minutes. Drain, refresh in cold water, then drain thoroughly, pressing out as much water as possible. Rolling the spinach up in a bamboo mat and squeezing it is the easiest way. Purée the spinach in a blender or food processor and set aside.

Dredge the salmon with flour, shaking to remove excess flour. Season the fish with salt and pepper. Heat half of the butter in a skillet large enough to hold the fish in a single layer and sauté the fillets, turning once, for about 6 minutes, or until done. Lift fillets out of the skillet to a warmed plate, cover, and keep warm.

Add the rest of the butter and the leeks to the skillet and cook, stirring, over low heat for 2 to 3 minutes, until leeks are tender. Add the fish stock and vermouth and simmer, uncovered, until the liquid is reduced to about half. Add the cream and reduce until the sauce is of coating consistency. Stir in the spinach and add salt and pepper if necessary. Spoon the sauce onto 4 heated plates and put a salmon fillet on top.

SERVES 4.

If liked, omit the cream and stir in the fresh white cheese and warm it through.

SALMON IN SORREL SAUCE

❖   ❖   ❖

The rich flavor of salmon is enhanced by the slight acidity of sorrel in this dish created by Murdo MacSween, head chef at Oakley Court near Windsor. Murdo, who is a nephew of the famed novelist Sir Compton MacKenzie, is a Scot who speaks fluent Gaelic. He naturally specifies Scotch salmon for the dish, but I have made it successfully with salmon from other than Scottish waters, and with sea (salmon) trout. Serve with a Chardonnay.

4 slices of salmon fillet, each 6 ounces
Salt, freshly ground pepper
2 tablespoons minced shallots
½ cup dry white wine

¼ cup heavy cream
4 cups loosely packed sorrel, about 8 ounces
4 tablespoons butter
Garnish: parsley sprigs

Lightly flatten the salmon fillets and season with salt and pepper. Combine the shallots and wine in a small saucepan and simmer, uncovered, until the liquid is reduced to ¼ cup. Pour in the cream, bring almost to a boil, cover, and set aside.

Cut the stems and coarse ribs from the sorrel leaves, stack and roll them, and shred them very fine. Set aside. Heat 2 tablespoons of the butter in a skillet and sauté the salmon over moderate heat until it is done, 5 to 6 minutes. Arrange the salmon on 4 warmed plates. Add the sorrel to the reserved sauce and bring to a boil over fairly high heat. The sorrel will melt into a purée. Add the remaining butter, cut into bits, all at once, and taste the sauce for seasoning. Stir sauce and pour over the salmon. Garnish with parsley sprigs.

S E R V E S 4.

SALMON WITH WATERCRESS SAUCE

❖   ❖   ❖

Edouard Hari, executive chef of the Inn on the Park in London, cares a great deal about the people who come to eat at the Inn's restaurants. He wants the food to taste and look superb. A little bit of himself goes into every meal that is served, he says. His aim is to keep natural flavors unspoiled and never to mix flavors that will conflict with each other. Like Shaun Hill of Gidleigh Park in Devon, he dislikes bizarre garnishes that no one can eat. An optimistic and ebullient man, he delights in creating new dishes, this one very tempting. Serve with a Pouilly-Fuissé.

½ recipe Puff Pastry (see Index)
2 bunches of watercress, about 8
   ounces
2 tablespoons butter
2 tablespoons minced shallots
2 fillets of fresh salmon, each
   about 6 ounces

Salt, freshly ground white pepper
½ cup Fish Stock (see Index)
½ cup dry white wine
¼ cup heavy cream

Make puff pastry. Roll the pastry out into 2 pieces, each 4 by 6 inches, and bake them in a preheated moderate oven (350°F.) until well risen and lightly browned, about 25 minutes. Allow to cool, then split each into halves. Set aside in the turned-off oven to keep warm.

Wash and pick over the watercress. Discard the stems. Drop the cress into a saucepan of briskly boiling water and blanch for 1 minute. Drain thoroughly, rinse under cold running water, and drain again. Purée the cress in a blender or food processor until very smooth. Divide the purée into 2 parts and set it aside.

In a skillet large enough to hold the fish comfortably, heat the butter. Add the shallots and cook over moderate heat until they are softened, about 1 minute. Season the salmon with salt and pepper and cook in the skillet over low heat, turning once, until the salmon is done, 5 to 6 minutes. Lift out to a plate and keep warm, covered. Pour the fish stock into the skillet and reduce the liquid to half over fairly high heat. Add the wine and reduce the liquid in the pan to ½ cup. Add the cream, bring to a simmer, then stir in half of the watercress purée. Taste for seasoning, adding salt and pepper if necessary. If any juices have collected on the plate with the salmon, add them to the sauce.

To assemble the dish, spread both pieces of each of the pastry cases with the remaining watercress purée. Place the bottom halves on each of 2 warmed plates and top with the salmon. Spoon the watercress sauce on the salmon and top with the lid.

S E R V E S 2.

SALMON WITH WALNUTS, GRAPES AND SCALLOPS

❖   ❖   ❖

Chris Oakes, head chef at the Castle Hotel in Taunton, Somerset, has created a medley of flavors that harmonize beautifully in this dish. Serve with a Chardonnay.

1½ pounds center-cut salmon
  fillet, skinned and cut into 4
  slices
1 tablespoon minced fresh
  tarragon
Salt, freshly ground pepper
4 tablespoons (½ stick) butter

¼ cup chopped walnuts
½ cup seedless green grapes,
  peeled
4 large scallops, sliced
1 tablespoon lemon juice, or to
  taste

Make a slit in each piece of salmon and stuff each with ¼ teaspoon chopped tarragon. Season the fish with salt and pepper. Heat 2 tablespoons of the butter in a skillet large enough to hold the salmon in a single layer. Sauté the salmon over moderate heat for 2 to 3 minutes on each side. It should be firm to the touch. Be careful not to overcook as the fish dries out easily. Transfer the salmon to a warmed plate, cover, and keep warm.

Add the rest of the butter to the skillet. Add the walnuts, grapes, scallops and lemon juice, and toss over moderate heat for about 1 minute, or until the scallops are opaque. Season with salt and pepper and spoon the mixture over the salmon. Sprinkle with remaining tarragon. Serve immediately.

S E R V E S 4.

STUFFED ROLLED SALMON

❖   ❖   ❖

This is a grand dish, but worth the trouble for a special occasion. John King of the Ritz Club in London created the dish, which accurately reflects his culinary philosophy. He is a firm believer in chefs having a classical cuisine training which they should use as a springboard to launch themselves into an inventive future, always shunning gimmickry. Serve with a Chardonnay.

Mousse Stuffing

½ pound boned and skinned
   salmon
2 egg yolks

2 whole eggs
Salt, freshly ground pepper
1 cup heavy cream

Salmon

1½ pounds center-cut salmon
   fillet, skinned and cut into 4
   slices
¼ pound (1 stick) butter, plus
   butter for pan
2 tablespoons minced shallots
1 cup dry white wine

1 cup strong Fish Stock (see
   Index)
1 pound mixed wild mushrooms
   such as chanterelles, morels,
   oyster mushrooms
½ cup heavy cream
Garnish: parsley sprigs

To make the mousse combine the salmon, chopped coarse, in a blender or food processor with the egg yolks and process to a purée. Add the 2 whole eggs, and salt and pepper to taste, and process until smooth. Scrape into a bowl and refrigerate for at least an hour. When the mixture is cold beat in the cream with a wooden spoon. Taste for seasoning, add salt and pepper if necessary, and refrigerate until needed.

Very lightly flatten the 4 slices of salmon, which should measure about 5 by 4 inches. Season them with salt and pepper. Either pipe or spoon the chilled mousse along the short side of the salmon, then gently roll the fish up into a fat sausage. Secure the sausages with toothpicks to stop them unrolling. Butter an ovenproof dish large enough to hold the salmon in a single layer. Sprinkle the dish with the shallots, add the salmon, and pour in the wine and stock. Cover and cook in a preheated hot oven (425°F.) for about 10 minutes, or until the fish is done. Lift out the salmon to a warmed plate, cover, and keep warm.

Heat 4 tablespoons of the butter in a skillet and sauté the mushrooms for about 3 minutes. Transfer to a bowl and keep warm. Pour the liquid in which the salmon was cooked into a saucepan and reduce it to half over fairly high heat. Add the cream and reduce to 1 cup. Cut remaining butter into bits and beat it into the sauce. Taste for seasoning.

Arrange the salmon fillets on 4 heated plates and spoon the sauce over them. Sprinkle the salmon with the mushrooms and garnish with a few sprigs of parsley. Serve immediately.

S E R V E S 4.

N O T E: If there is any leftover mousse, make it into quenelles and poach in fish stock. Use to garnish other fish dishes. The uncooked mousse will keep, refrigerated, for 2 or 3 days.

BRAISED SALMON WITH PIKE MOUSSE

❖   ❖   ❖

The pike mousse in this recipe created by Bernard Rendler, the *sous-chef* at Gravetye Manor in East Grinstead, West Sussex, could not be easier to make. The dish is interestingly different from Martin Bredda's Haddock and Salmon Trout Surprise although the ingredients are very much the same. It demonstrates the creative originality of the chefs. When I find pike hard to get I substitute a nonoily white fish; I have also substituted sea (salmon) trout for the salmon with great success. Serve with a Muscadet.

Pike Mousse

8 ounces skinned and boned pike 1 large egg
  or other nonoily white fish 1 cup heavy cream
Salt, freshly ground pepper

(recipe continues)

Fish and Sauce

Butter
4 slices of salmon fillet, each
    about 5 ounces
2½ cups Fish Stock (see Index)
½ cup dry white wine
2 tablespoons minced shallots

4 medium-size mushrooms, sliced
4 medium-size tomatoes, peeled
    and chopped
½ cup heavy cream
2 tablespoons snipped chives

In a food processor or blender purée the pike or other fish until it is very light and smooth. Season with salt and pepper. Add the egg and process until thoroughly mixed. For a very fine, light texture rub the mixture through a sieve into a bowl, or simply scrape the mixture from the food processor into a bowl. Set the bowl in a larger bowl filled with ice and very slowly beat in the cream with a wooden spoon.

Butter a shallow flameproof dish large enough to hold the salmon fillets in a single layer. Pour in 2 cups fish stock and wine and bring to a simmer. Remove from the heat. Carefully spread the mousse over the fish. Arrange the fish in the baking dish and cook in a preheated hot oven (425°F.) for 15 minutes. Run under a broiler to glaze.

While the fish is cooking make the sauce. Pour remaining ½ cup fish stock into a saucepan. Add the shallots, mushrooms and tomatoes and simmer, uncovered, until the liquid is reduced to ½ cup. Add the cream and continue to simmer until the sauce reaches coating consistency. Season to taste with salt and pepper.

Pour the sauce onto 4 heated plates. Top with a salmon fillet and sprinkle with chives. Serve immediately.

S E R V E S   4.

HADDOCK AND SALMON TROUT SURPRISE

❖   ❖   ❖

Martin Bredda, chef to the Earl and Countess of Normanton who entertain visiting parties at the family seat, Somerley, at Ringwood in Hampshire, has a simple aim in cooking. He wants to cook well, present the food beautifully, and use the best of the good things available to him, the fish and game from the estate especially. He uses pike in this recipe. If it is not available, substitute a nonoily white fish such as sole or flounder. Serve with a Pouilly-Fuissé.

1 pound pike, or sole or flounder or similar white fish, skinned and boned
Salt, freshly ground pepper
4 egg whites
¾ cup heavy cream
Butter
5 haddock fillets, each 3 to 4 ounces
5 sea (salmon) trout fillets, each 3 to 4 ounces

1 cup light cream, or Fresh White Cheese or Junket Cheese (see Index)
12 ounces shelled medium shrimps
2 tablespoons tomato purée
2 tablespoons melted butter (optional)

Chop the pike or substitute fish coarse. Season with salt and pepper and put into a blender or food processor. Process to a purée. With the machine running, add the egg whites one by one until the whites are thoroughly incorporated and the mixture is light and fluffy. Scrape the purée into a bowl. Set the bowl into a larger bowl filled with ice and refrigerate for 1 hour.

Remove purée from the refrigerator and beat in half of the heavy cream, using a wooden spoon. Return the mousse to the refrigerator for 15 minutes, then beat in the rest of the cream. Refrigerate the mousse until ready to use.

Butter a ring mold. Season the haddock and sea trout fillets with salt and pepper. Using each type of fish alternately, line the mold, letting the ends of the fillets hang over the sides. Spoon the mousse into the mold, fold the ends of the fillets over the mousse, and press them lightly in place. Cover the mold with foil or parchment paper and set in a baking pan with hot water to come about halfway up the sides. Bake in a preheated moderate oven (350°F.) for 35 minutes, or until the fillets are firm to the touch. Remove the mold from the pan and allow it to rest.

While the mold is resting, make the sauce. In a medium-size saucepan combine the cream, or fresh white or junket cheese, the shrimps and tomato purée. Cook just long enough to warm through and cook the shrimps.

Unmold the salmon and haddock mousse on a warmed circular dish. Brush it with melted butter if liked. Serve the sauce separately.

SERVES 8.

COLD POACHED SALMON WITH SORREL MAYONNAISE

❖   ❖   ❖

Peter Jackson, whom I met first when he was head chef at Bodys-gallen Hall in Wales and later when he was head chef for a time at Eastwell Manor in Kent, is a passionate believer in fresh, natural food, but he does not believe in undercooking or combining ingredients that will quarrel with each other in the mouth; foods and flavors should complement each other. I enjoyed his salmon one brilliant summer day and feel his cooking lives up to his philosophy. He now has his own restaurant in Glasgow, Scotland—The Colonial. Serve with a Chardonnay.

1½ recipes Fish Stock (see Index)
1 tablespoon green peppercorns
1 whole salmon, 5 pounds, unskinned with head and tail left on
1 recipe Mayonnaise made with lemon juice (see Index)

2 teaspoons dry vermouth, preferably Noilly Prat
½ cup sorrel, stems and ribs removed, leaves shredded

In a fish kettle large enough to hold the salmon comfortably, bring the fish stock to a boil with the green peppercorns. Wrap the salmon in cheesecloth and lower it gently into the briskly boiling liquid. Bring the liquid back to a boil over high heat, cover, turn off the heat and allow to cool. The fish will be perfectly cooked, moist and tender. Lift it out to a large serving platter and carefully skin it. Leave head and tail intact.

Mix the mayonnaise with the vermouth and stir in the sorrel. Serve with the salmon. If liked, the salmon may be garnished with lemon slices or cucumber slices and cherry tomatoes. It may be accompanied by cucumber salad, green salad or potato salad.

S E R V E S 8.

FILLET OF TURBOT IN SORREL

❖ ❖ ❖

Martin Rowbotham of Huntstrete House, an eighteenth-century country manor house, now a country house hotel near Bath, did not start off as a cook, but fell in love with cooking and switched careers. He brings freshness and originality to cooking. Turbot is not a fish that swims in U.S. waters but fortunately halibut makes an excellent substitute. Serve with a Muscadet.

1 pound mushrooms, chopped fine
2 medium-size onions, chopped fine
½ garlic clove, crushed
Salt, freshly ground pepper
4 fillets of turbot or halibut or similar fish, skinned and boned, each 6 to 8 ounces

Large sorrel leaves, about 12
¼ pound (1 stick) butter
1 cup dry vermouth
½ cup heavy cream, or Fresh White Cheese or Junket Cheese (see Index)
1 tablespoon lemon juice

Combine the mushrooms, onions and garlic in a heavy skillet and cook over moderate heat until mushrooms have given up all their liquid. Shake or stir the contents of the pan so that they do not burn. Season with salt and pepper and set aside.

Season the fish with salt and pepper and cover with the reserved mushroom mixture. Wrap each fillet in sorrel leaves. Butter the skillet and arrange the fish in it. Pour in the vermouth and bring to a simmer. Cover and poach for about 10 minutes, or until the fish is done. Remove the fish and keep warm.

Reduce the liquid in the pan to half over moderately high heat. Add the cream and reduce until the sauce coats a spoon. Add the lemon juice, then whisk in remaining butter, bit by bit, over low heat until the sauce is light and creamy. If using fresh white or junket cheese simply stir it in, add the lemon juice, and warm gently through. Omit the butter. Taste for seasoning and add salt and pepper if necessary.

Pour the sauce onto 4 warmed plates and arrange a package of fish on each. Serve the rest of the sauce separately.

SERVES 4.

TURBOT AND SALMON WITH CHAMPAGNE SAUCE

❖   ❖   ❖

Simon Collins, head chef at Bishopstrow House in Warminster, Wiltshire, is brilliantly inventive. He has a talent for putting together quite ordinary ingredients in a way that transforms them into something very special. Instead of turbot, which is not available in the United States, use halibut; instead of dry Champagne, use a dry white wine from the Champagne region, or any dry white wine. Serve with a still Champagne.

¼ cup julienne strips of carrot
¼ cup julienne strips of celery
¼ cup julienne strips of white of leek
¼ cup julienne strips of mixed red and green bell peppers
Butter

Salt, freshly ground pepper
4 slices of turbot or halibut, or similar fish, 3 ounces each, cut on a slant
4 slices of salmon fillet, 3 ounces each, cut on a slant
1 bay leaf

Sauce

2 cups dry white wine
2 cups strong Fish Stock (see Index)
½ teaspoon chopped fresh tarragon, or ¼ teaspoon dried

Pinch of ground saffron
½ cup heavy cream

Combine the julienne strips of carrot, celery, leek and bell peppers in a saucepan of briskly boiling water and blanch for 2 minutes. Drain and refresh under cold water. Drain thoroughly.

Cut four 10-inch circles of aluminum foil, or wax or parchment paper, and butter generously. Season the fish with salt and pepper and place a slice of halibut on each circle. Top each with some of the vegetable julienne, a little bit of bay leaf and a teaspoon or so of fish stock. Top with the salmon slices and seal the paper or foil by folding it securely. Arrange the fish in an ovenproof baking dish and bake in a preheated hot oven (425°F.) for 6 minutes.

Meanwhile make the sauce. Pour the wine into a saucepan and reduce it to 1 cup over high heat. Add the fish stock, tarragon, saffron and a few grinds of black pepper and reduce the liquid again to 1 cup over high heat. Add the cream and continue to reduce, still over high heat, until the sauce reaches coating consistency. Season to taste with salt and pepper, strain, and warm through.

Pour the sauce onto 4 warmed plates. Take the fish out of the foil or paper and serve on top of the sauce. Garnish, if liked, with a sprig of fresh tarragon.

S E R V E S 4.

FILLETS OF TURBOT WITH LEEKS AND WILD MUSHROOMS

❖   ❖   ❖

This delectable dish is not difficult, but it requires attention to detail. Don't be put off by the long list of ingredients. Many of them are ordinary kitchen items. Use halibut instead of turbot, which is seldom available in the United States; halibut is an excellent substitute. Created by Raymond Blanc, the brilliant young chef-patron of Le Manoir aux Quat' Saisons at Great Milton near Oxford, I find I can do no better than describe it in his own words: "The color effect is magnificent, the textures so different, and the taste will fulfill the enchantment of this still life." Raymond is in love with cooking and this dish shows it. Serve with a Chardonnay.

6 ounces (1½ sticks) butter
2 tablespoons minced shallots
1⅓ cups Gewürztraminer or
    other dry white wine
½ cup mushrooms, chopped fine
6 turbot or halibut fillets, each
    about 5 ounces
Salt, freshly ground pepper
2 tablespoons lemon juice
2 tablespoons heavy cream
1 tablespoon snipped chives
12 baby leeks, trimmed, washed,
    tied up, blanched for 3 to 4
    minutes, then cut into ½-inch
    pieces

½ pound mixed wild mushrooms
    such as chanterelles (girolles),
    morels, etc.
2 tablespoons dry Madeira wine
2 tablespoons truffle juice
    (optional)
1 pound freshly cooked small new
    potatoes, kept warm

(recipe continues)

Set a flameproof dish, large enough to hold the fish in a single layer, over low heat. Melt ½ tablespoon of the butter in the dish, add the shallots, and cook until shallots are soft but not brown. Add the wine and simmer for 1 minute. Add the chopped mushrooms. Season the fish with salt and pepper. In a small saucepan melt 2 tablespoons of the butter and mix it with 1 tablespoon of the lemon juice. Arrange the fish on top of the shallot-mushroom mixture and brush with the lemon-flavored butter. Cover the dish and cook in a preheated moderately hot oven (400°F.) for 3 to 5 minutes. Strain the juices from the pan through a sieve into a saucepan. Cover the fish and keep warm in a turned-off oven.

Reduce the juices over fairly brisk heat by about one third. Add the cream, then whisk in all but 4 tablespoons of the butter, cut into bits. Add the chives, season to taste with salt and pepper, and add a little lemon juice if liked. Set aside and keep warm.

Meanwhile warm the leeks in a skillet with hot water and a little butter, about 1 tablespoon. Drain and keep warm.

Melt 1 tablespoon of remaining butter in a small skillet and sauté the wild mushrooms with a little of the remaining lemon juice for about 4 minutes. Lift out the mushrooms with a slotted spoon to a warm plate, cover, and keep them warm. Add the Madeira to the skillet and reduce it to half. Add the truffle juice, if using. Whisk in remaining 2 tablespoons of butter, cut into bits. Cover and keep warm.

To assemble the dish, have ready 6 warmed plates. Put a fish fillet in the middle of each plate and garnish the plate with alternate mounds of leeks and wild mushrooms. If necessary return the plates, covered with buttered paper, to the oven for 2 minutes to heat through. Pour the butter sauce over the fish, and the Madeira sauce over the mushrooms. Add the new potatoes and serve.

S E R V E S 6.

TURBOT FILLET "LAMBERT"

❖   ❖   ❖

This is another of Denis Woodtli's interestingly different fish dishes. He is head chef at Lochalsh Hotel, Kyle of Lochalsh, in Highland, Scotland. For turbot, use halibut; for langoustines use either crayfish or jumbo shrimps. The recipe can easily be doubled but it does make a lovely self-indulgent meal when one is dining alone and is not content to dine less than well. Serve with a dry Moselle.

1 turbot or halibut fillet, 5 to 6 ounces	½ cup medium-dry white wine
2 langoustines, crayfish or jumbo shrimps, whole, unpeeled	½ cup strong Fish Stock (see Index)
2 large scallops	2 tablespoons tomato purée
2 tablespoons butter	¼ cup brandy
½ medium-size onion, chopped fine	½ cup heavy cream, or Fresh White Cheese (see Index)
	Salt, freshly ground pepper

Lightly flatten the turbot or halibut fillet. Shell one of the langoustines, crayfish or jumbo shrimp and place it, with one of the scallops, on the fish. Roll it up and secure it with a toothpick. Generously butter a small skillet. Add the onion, white wine, fish stock and stuffed fish. Bring to a simmer, cover, and cook for 5 to 6 minutes, or until done.

In another skillet heat a little butter and toss the other crayfish or jumbo shrimp, unshelled, in the pan over moderately high heat for 1 or 2 minutes. Add the tomato purée, stir, then pour in the brandy. When brandy is warm, ignite it. Add half of the cream and cook until the sauce reaches coating consistency. Add salt and pepper to taste.

Lift the fish out of the first skillet and put it on a heated plate. Cover and keep warm. Reduce the liquid in the skillet to half its volume, add remaining cream and the scallop and reduce the sauce to coating consistency. Season with salt and pepper.

Pour the white-wine sauce onto half of the fish and plate, and the tomato purée sauce onto the other half. Put the scallop on the tomato sauce, and the whole crayfish or jumbo shrimp on the white-wine sauce. The finished dish looks very attractive and tastes wonderful. It is worth the trouble. Serve with a green salad.

SERVES 1.

If I want to avoid cream, I stir in fresh white cheese and warm it through. The dish will be quite heavy enough and as the scallop only needs minimal cooking it will cook while the cheese is heating through.

FILLET OF TURBOT WITH QUAIL EGGS AND WILD MUSHROOMS

❖   ❖   ❖

Every now and then an elegant dish is needed for a special occasion. Michael Croft, head chef at the Royal Crescent Hotel in Bath, Avon, has a special genius for creating such culinary elegance. Instead of turbot, use halibut. I have also cooked the dish with sea (salmon) trout very successfully. Serve with a Sancerre.

Sauce

2 tablespoons minced shallots
½ cup minced mushrooms
1 sprig of thyme
½ garlic clove, crushed
2 cups dry red wine

½ cup strong Fish Stock (see Index)
1 tablespoon glace de viande
Salt, freshly ground pepper
2 tablespoons butter

Fish

2 thick fillets of turbot or halibut, each about 5 ounces
2 tablespoons clarified butter
2 tablespoons raw butter
1 cup chanterelle (girolle) mushrooms, rinsed and dried
4 quail eggs, soft-cooked and shelled

½ teaspoon minced mixed herbs (parsley, chervil, chives and basil)
1 teaspoon lemon juice
½ cup Garlic Croutons (see Index)

To make the sauce, put the minced shallots, minced mushrooms, thyme and garlic in a saucepan. Pour in the wine and reduce over moderately high heat to ½ cup. Strain the sauce, return it to the saucepan, and add the fish stock and *glace de viande*. Bring back to a simmer, taste for seasoning, and add salt and pepper if necessary. Whisk in the butter, set aside and keep warm.

Season the fish with salt and pepper. Heat the clarified butter in a small heavy skillet large enough to hold the fish comfortably and sauté the fish over moderately high heat for about 2 minutes each side. Remove from the pan and keep warm, covered. Add the raw butter to the pan and let it brown slightly. Add the chanterelle mushrooms and sauté for 1 minute. Add the eggs, herbs, lemon juice and croutons.

Pour the sauce onto 2 heated plates. Put a fish fillet in the center of each plate and garnish with the mushroom mixture.

S E R V E S 2.

N O T E : *Glace de viande* is available from specialty food shops and many supermarkets; otherwise simply reduce some rich brown stock to a syrupy consistency.

MONKFISH AND TURBOT IN CHIVE SAUCE

❖   ❖   ❖

Alan Vikops, head chef at the County Hotel in Canterbury, Kent, likes his sauces to have a distinct flavor but not so overwhelming as to mask the taste of the food they accompany. He also likes his dishes to look attractive, pleasing both eye and palate. I think he succeeds very well in this simple recipe. Use halibut instead of turbot. Serve with a Pouilly-Fuissé.

8 pieces of skinned and boned
  monkfish, each about 2 ounces
4 pieces of skinned and boned
  turbot or halibut fillet, each
  about 3 ounces
Salt, freshly ground pepper
4 tablespoons sweet paprika

¾ cup dry vermouth, preferably
  Noilly Prat
¾ cup strong Fish Stock (see
  Index)
¼ pound (1 stick) butter, cut
  into bits
½ cup snipped chives

Season the fish with salt and pepper then roll it in the paprika. Put it into a skillet large enough to hold it in a single layer. Pour in half of the dry vermouth. Bring to a simmer, cover, and cook over very low heat until the fish is done, 3 to 4 minutes. Transfer the fish to a warmed plate, cover, and keep warm.

Pour the rest of the vermouth and the fish stock into the skillet and reduce it over high heat to half. Whisk in the butter and the chives.

Arrange the fish on 4 heated plates and pour the sauce round them. The reddish-brown of the fish, colored by the paprika, will make an attractive contrast to the white sauce, flecked with green.

S E R V E S 4.

TURBOT WITH CRAYFISH

❖   ❖   ❖

Aidan McCormack, the young Welsh head chef at Middlethorpe Hall, a lovingly restored Queen Anne house in York, now a small hotel, has a forthright philosophy of cooking; what is on the plate is to eat, and overdecoration with fussy garnishes give good cooking a bad name. He believes in the virtues of simplicity and true flavor, and the use of the nose, as a sauce is right when it smells right. I enjoyed two of his fish dishes, the recipes for which bear out his philosophy. The crayfish tails in the recipe can be replaced with shrimps. Use halibut in place of turbot. Serve with a Riesling.

1 cup medium shrimps or
  crayfish, shelled, and shells
  reserved
2 tablespoons minced shallots
½ cup dry vermouth
2 cups Fish Stock (see Index), or
  clam juice
4 pieces of skinned and boned
  turbot or halibut fillets, each 6
  ounces

Salt, freshly ground pepper
2 tablespoons butter
¼ cup heavy cream
¼ cup chopped, peeled and
  seeded tomatoes
2 tablespoons chopped parsley or
  chervil

If whole crayfish are available, reserve four of the heads as a garnish, if liked. Otherwise chop the shrimp or crayfish shells and put into a medium-size saucepan with the shallots, vermouth and fish stock. Bring to a simmer and cook, uncovered, for 10 minutes. Strain and set aside. For a simpler stock, omit the shallots and simply add the vermouth to the fish stock or clam juice.

Season the fish with salt and pepper. In a skillet large enough to hold the fish in a single layer, heat 1 tablespoon of the butter. Add the fish and pour in enough of the stock to cover. Reserve any remaining stock. Bring to a simmer, cover, and cook over low heat for 5 to 8 minutes, or until the fish is done. Lift the fish onto a warmed plate, cover, and keep warm.

Add the reserved stock to the skillet and reduce over high heat until thick and syrupy. Add the cream, bring to a simmer, and cook until sauce is of coating consistency. Add the tomatoes and the crayfish tails or shrimps, season to taste with salt and pepper, and cook for

1 minute, until the shellfish is done. Off the heat stir in remaining tablespoon of butter, cut into bits.

Put the fish onto 4 heated plates, spoon the sauce over, and sprinkle with the herbs. Garnish each plate, if liked, with a crayfish head.

SERVES 4.

MONKFISH WITH LIME AND GARLIC

❖   ❖   ❖

This is another of Aidan McCormack's simple and imaginative fish dishes that I have enjoyed. If lime juice is not available, use lemon juice. Serve with a Muscadet.

4 slices of boned and skinned
  monkfish, each about 6 ounces
1 cup chopped, peeled and seeded
  tomatoes
3 tablespoons minced shallots

2 garlic cloves, chopped
3 tablespoons chopped parsley
1 cup dry white wine
½ cup Mayonnaise made with
  lime juice (see Index)

In a skillet large enough to hold the fish in a single layer combine the fish, tomatoes, shallots, garlic, parsley and wine. Bring to a simmer and cook, covered, for about 3 minutes, or until the fish is done. Lift the fish out onto a warmed dish, cover, and keep warm.

Reduce the liquid in the skillet over moderately high heat to about one quarter. Pour in any liquid that has collected on the plate with the fish. Bring to a simmer, remove from the heat, and whisk in the mayonnaise.

Arrange the fish on 4 heated plates and mask with the sauce. Serve immediately.

SERVES 4.

MONKFISH WITH GINGER SAUCE

❖   ❖   ❖

Robert Gardiner, the young head chef of Ardsheal House Hotel at Kentallen, Highland, in Scotland, uses ginger very imaginatively in this simple, well-flavored, unusual fish dish. Serve with a white Hermitage.

Sauce

¼ pound (1 stick) unsalted butter, sliced

2 tablespoons fine-grated fresh gingerroot

4 garlic cloves, minced

¼ jalapeño pepper, seeded and chopped fine, or use any fresh, hot green chili pepper

½ cup light soy sauce such as Japanese usukuchi shoyu

2 tablespoons dry white wine

½ cup mixed minced red and green bell peppers

Fish

2 pounds monkfish, skinned and boned and cut into 6 slices

1 cup minced parsley

Melt the butter in a heavy saucepan over very low heat. Add the gingerroot, garlic and jalapeño pepper, cover, and simmer over very low heat for 10 minutes. Add the soy sauce and wine and simmer for 5 minutes longer. Stir in the mixed red and green bell peppers and simmer for 2 minutes longer. Taste the sauce; if it is too salty, add a little more white wine.

Put the fish on a bed of parsley into a steamer and steam for about 3 minutes, or until it is no longer opaque. Do not overcook. Put the fish onto 6 warmed plates and spoon the sauce over it. Serve with rice.

S E R V E S 6.

MONKFISH WITH GINGER AND SPRING VEGETABLES

❖   ❖   ❖

Kenneth Bell's Monkfish with Ginger could not be more different from Robert Gardiner's creation although both are original and delicious, one from an old master in the kitchen, the other from a relative newcomer. Kenneth owns and runs sixteenth-century Thornbury Castle, near Bristol, which he has converted into a restaurant and hotel. Serve with a white Hermitage.

2 medium-size carrots, scraped
   and cut into cork shapes
2 small turnips, peeled and cut
   into cork shapes
2 tablespoons butter
2 pounds monkfish, skinned,
   boned, and cut into ¾-inch
   pieces

1 tablespoon drained, thin-sliced
   stem ginger in syrup
¾ cup diced celery, about 2 ribs
2 cups dry white wine
Salt, freshly ground pepper
½ cup heavy cream
½ cup chopped parsley, dill or
   chervil

Blanch the carrots and turnips in briskly boiling salted water for 5 minutes. Drain and set aside.

In a large skillet heat the butter and add the fish, ginger, celery, carrots, turnips and the wine. Season with salt and pepper, and simmer for 10 minutes. Lift out the fish and arrange it on a warmed serving dish. Cover and keep warm. Add the cream to the sauce and simmer for 5 minutes longer, uncovered. Taste for seasoning. Reduce sauce over moderately high heat if it is too thin. It should be almost of coating consistency. Taste the sauce and add salt and pepper if necessary.

Pour the sauce over the fish and sprinkle with the herbs. Serve immediately, with new potatoes and a green salad.

SERVES 4.

I have made this successfully with Fresh White Cheese (see Index) for friends avoiding cream. Do not reduce the cheese, just stir it in and warm it through.

STUFFED FILLET OF PINK TROUT

❖   ❖   ❖

When pink trout is not available I use sea (salmon) trout for this. The recipe created by David Nicholls, head chef of Waltons in London, makes a superb lunch or dinner for two. Serve with a Chardonnay.

1 cup light cream
¼ garlic clove, crushed
1 teaspoon butter, plus butter for pan
¼ cup julienne strips of carrot, celery and leek
Salt, freshly ground pepper
Skinned and boned fillets from 1-pound pink trout

½ cup dry vermouth, preferably Noilly Prat
½ cup dry white wine
¼ cup strong Fish Stock (see Index)
½ medium-size tomato, peeled, seeded and chopped
Garnish: dill sprigs

In a small saucepan combine ½ cup of the cream, the crushed garlic clove, the teaspoon of butter and the julienne of vegetables and simmer until the cream is thick and the vegetables tender, about 5 minutes. Season with salt and pepper. Cool.

Place the fillets on a board and season with salt and pepper. Put half of the cream and vegetable mixture on each fillet about one third of the way up from the tail end. Fold the tail end over the vegetables, then fold the other end over. Fasten with toothpicks. Lightly butter a skillet big enough to hold the 2 fillets comfortably. Arrange the fish in the pan and pour in the vermouth, dry white wine and fish stock. Cover and poach until the fish is cooked, about 8 minutes. Lift out onto a warmed plate, cover, and keep warm.

Add remaining ½ cup cream to the pan and simmer until the sauce reaches coating consistency. Season to taste with salt and pepper. Add the tomato and cook for 1 minute longer.

Spoon the sauce onto 2 heated plates and arrange a stuffed fillet on each plate. Garnish with sprigs of dill. Serve with new potatoes or noodles, and a green salad.

S E R V E S 2.

FILLET OF TROUT WITH VEGETABLES

❖   ❖   ❖

Sam Chalmers, formerly chef-patron of Le Talbooth Restaurant in Dedham, and now chef at his own restaurant, Chimneys at Long Melford, Suffolk, constantly comes up with attractively simple variations on classic dishes, transforming the well-known into something fresh and new. This is a good example of his special talent. Serve with a Chardonnay.

1 medium-size carrot, scraped and cut into julienne strips
1 celery rib, cut into julienne strips
1 small white turnip, peeled and cut into julienne strips
1 small leek, white part only, thoroughly washed and cut into julienne strips

2 tablespoons butter
Salt, freshly ground pepper
16 trout fillets, skinned and boned, lightly flattened
½ cup dry white wine
1 cup Fish Stock (see Index)

Sauce

¼ cup minced shallots
2 tablespoons lemon juice
1 cup dry white wine

1 large egg yolk, lightly beaten
½ cup whipped cream

Sauté the carrot, celery, turnip and leek in the butter in a skillet until vegetables are soft. Season with salt and pepper. Cool slightly and spread the mixture over half of the trout fillets. Top with the other half. Arrange the fillets in a skillet large enough to hold them in a single layer. Pour in the wine and stock, bring to a simmer over moderate heat, cover, and reduce the heat to as low as possible. Poach the fish for 8 minutes. Carefully pour off the poaching liquid.

While the fish is cooking make the sauce. In a saucepan combine the shallots, lemon juice and wine and reduce to half over brisk heat. Off the heat, beat in the egg yolk, then fold in the whipped cream. Season to taste with salt and pepper. Pour the sauce over the trout and run the skillet under a preheated broiler to glaze the top.

Lift the trout onto 8 heated plates and spoon any sauce from the skillet over them. Serve with new potatoes, baby carrots and a green vegetable.

S E R V E S 8.

BAKED RED GURNARD

❖   ❖   ❖

Roy Richards has an imaginative way with fish as the recipe on page 140 shows. He says of the red gurnard that it is an unlovely fish to look at, and much underappreciated, as despite its looks its texture and flavor are sensational. Gurnard is sold in U.S. markets as searobin. If gurnard are not available, the best substitutes are halibut or John Dory, but any firm white fish can be used. This is a delightfully simple recipe needing very little time. Serve with a Sauvignon Blanc.

Butter
6 fillets of gurnard or other white
  fish, each about 6 ounces
Salt, freshly ground pepper
1 recipe Velouté Sauce (see
  Index), made with ⅔ cup dry
  white wine, ⅔ cup fish stock
  and ⅔ cup light cream

2 tablespoons grated Gruyère
  cheese

Generously butter an ovenproof dish large enough to hold the fish in a single layer. Season the fillets with salt and pepper and arrange them in the baking dish. Make a velouté sauce with wine, fish stock and cream. Stir in the grated cheese, then pour the sauce over the fish. Bake in a preheated hot oven (425°F.) for about 10 minutes, or until the fish is done.

S E R V E S 6.

PANACHE OF FISH

❖   ❖   ❖

Shaun Hill, head chef at Gidleigh Park, a secluded Edwardian manor, now a charming country house hotel on the edge of Dartmoor, Devon, started cooking as an enthusiastic amateur, a classics scholar with no notion of cooking as more than a hobby. Cooking won, and he acquired some training and found himself quite quickly promoted to head chef at prestigious restaurants. His enthusiasm survives and his recipes reflect his philosophy that cooking should celebrate the qualities and flavors of the ingredients the cook is using. This is a delicious dish, pretty to look at and worthy of its name as it is a kind of flourish. It is not half as complicated as it looks, and the results are more than worth it. Serve with a Chardonnay.

Butter Sauce with Tomato

½ cup strong Fish Stock (see Index)
1 tablespoon tomato purée

¼ pound (1 stick) butter, cut into bits
Salt, freshly ground pepper

Butter Sauce with Broccoli

½ cup dry white wine
1 tablespoon puréed cooked broccoli

¼ pound (1 stick) butter, cut into bits

¾ pound fresh salmon fillet, cut into 4 slices
¾ pound turbot or halibut fillet, cut into 4 slices

4 large scallops, with coral (roe) if possible
8 jumbo shrimps, peeled

To make the Butter Sauce with Tomato, pour the fish stock into a small heavy saucepan, add the tomato purée and reduce over moderately high heat until only about 1 tablespoon of liquid remains. Reduce the heat to low, then whisk in the butter, bit by bit, to make a smooth sauce. Taste for seasoning, add salt and pepper to taste, and set aside in a warm place until needed.

In another small saucepan combine the wine and broccoli purée and reduce over moderately high heat until only about 1 tablespoon of liquid remains. Reduce the heat to low, then whisk in the butter, bit by bit, to make a smooth sauce. Season to taste with salt and pepper, remove from the heat and set aside in a warm place until needed.

Arrange the fish and shellfish in a steamer over boiling water and steam until done, about 4 minutes. Be careful not to overcook. Have ready 4 warmed plates. Arrange the fish and shellfish in the center of the plates and pour the sauces over them so that each sauce covers half of the fish and shellfish in the center of the plate, or pour the sauces separately onto each side of the plates. The effect is very pretty with the brilliant red and green sauces, pink and white fish, pink shrimp and white scallop with its coral. Any combination of fish and shellfish can be used according to what is best at the market.

SERVES 4.

HALIBUT FILLETS
WITH GREEN GRAPES

❖   ❖   ❖

Roy Richards, chef-patron of the Manor House restaurant, at Pickworth in Rutland, Lincolnshire uses Pineau de Charentes, a sweet fortified wine of the Cognac region, in this recipe. It is a very pleasant apéritif but not easy to buy outside France or even outside the Cognac region. I have used a demi-sec white wine successfully in place of the Pineau. A teaspoon of brandy added to the wine is an advantage. Serve with a Muscadet from the Loire.

Butter	½ pound seedless green grapes
6 halibut fillets, each about 8	½ cup semisweet white wine
ounces	1 teaspoon brandy
Salt, freshly ground pepper	½ cup heavy cream

Generously butter an ovenproof baking dish large enough to hold the fish in a single layer. Season the fillets with salt and pepper and arrange them in the dish. Scatter the grapes over the fish. Pour in the white wine mixed with the brandy and the heavy cream. There should be enough liquid barely to cover the fish, but it should not be swimming in it. Add more wine if necessary. Bake in a preheated hot oven (425°F.), basting frequently until the fish is done, 10 to 15 minutes. The sauce should be golden and glistening, with a creamy sweetness in contrast with the slight acidity of the grapes.

S E R V E S 6.

BAKED FILLETS OF STRIPED BASS WITH CHIVE AND LEMON SAUCE

❖   ❖   ❖

Nothing could be simpler than Chris Oakes' recipe. Chris, who is head chef at the Castle Hotel in Taunton, Somerset, has a strong feeling for cooking methods that preserve the fresh taste of foods. Striped bass is such a delicate fish that this recipe is perfect for it. The chive and lemon sauce is an attractive and equally simple accompaniment. Serve with a Sauvignon Blanc.

2 tablespoons butter
2 striped bass fillets, each 6 to 7 ounces

Salt, freshly ground pepper
1 cup dry white wine

Sauce

1 large lemon
¼ cup mild white-wine vinegar
1 cup olive oil

Salt, freshly ground pepper
⅛ teaspoon sugar
½ cup snipped chives

Butter a flameproof baking dish large enough to hold the fillets comfortably. Season the fish with salt and pepper and arrange in the dish. Pour the wine over it, dot with the rest of the butter, cover with aluminum foil, and bring the liquid to a simmer on top of the stove. Bake in a preheated moderate oven (350°F.) for 5 minutes, or until the fish is springy to the touch. Lift out onto 2 heated plates.

Remove the rind from the lemon and cut it into very fine julienne strips. Squeeze the juice from the lemon. In a bowl combine the julienne strips and lemon juice. Stir in the vinegar, then whisk in the oil, a little at a time, until the mixture is thick. Season to taste with salt, pepper and sugar. Add the chives. Spoon the sauce over the fish.

S E R V E S 2.

BRILL À LA BREVEL

❖   ❖   ❖

Brill, like turbot, does not swim in the waters on the American side of the Atlantic, so use halibut in this recipe. This comes from Tim Cumming, chef-patron of the Hole in the Wall restaurant in Bath, Avon. Tim had his first job there when trailblazer George Perry-Smith, now of the Riverside in Helford, Cornwall, was running it and helping to start the British culinary revolution. That was in 1965. Now twenty years later Tim is back where he began, still young and very creative. The restaurant has been expanded into a Restaurant with Rooms. Tim's wife Sue, herself a fine cook, had also worked at the Hole in the Wall earlier. A pleasant homecoming for them. Serve with a Muscadet.

Butter for dish, plus 1 tablespoon
1 tablespoon minced shallots
2 halibut fillets, each 6 to 8 ounces
2 medium-size tomatoes, peeled, seeded and chopped

4 medium-size mushrooms, sliced thin
Salt, freshly ground pepper
¼ teaspoon dried thyme
½ cup dry white wine
2 tablespoons heavy cream

Generously butter an ovenproof dish large enough to hold the fish in a single layer. Scatter the shallots over the bottom of the dish, add the fillets, top with the tomatoes and mushrooms, and season with salt, pepper and thyme. Cut the tablespoon of butter into bits and dot the fish with it. Pour in the wine. Cover and bake in a preheated moderate oven (350°F.) for 12 to 15 minutes, or until done. Carefully remove the fish and keep warm.

Pour the juices from the ovenproof dish into a small saucepan and reduce them over fairly high heat to ½ cup. Lower the heat, stir in the cream, and heat through. Taste for seasoning.

Pour half of the sauce over each fish fillet. Serve with new potatoes, or rice and a green salad.

SERVES 2.

The sauce can be finished if liked, with Fresh White Cheese, Junket Cheese or Yogurt Cheese (see Index) instead of cream.

SKATE WINGS BRAISED IN CIDER

❖   ❖   ❖

Paul Gayler, head chef at Inigo Jones restaurant in London, likes cooking with fish, especially as he has a supplier who brings it to him fresh daily and lets him choose just what he wants. He also likes to put together ingredients that do not usually find themselves in the same dish and does this with impeccable good taste. He is a very creative chef. Serve with a Sauvignon Blanc or a white Bordeaux.

4 tablespoons butter, plus butter
   for dish
1 tablespoon minced shallot
2 medium-size tomatoes, peeled,
   seeded and diced
1 large tart cooking apple, peeled,
   cored and diced
4 medium-size skate wings
Salt, freshly ground pepper

½ cup dry cider
¼ cup dry white wine
1 cup Fish Stock (see Index)
½ cup light cream
1 teaspoon Dijon mustard
¼ cup Calvados
2 tablespoons chopped fresh
   tarragon leaves

Butter a flameproof dish large enough to hold the skate wings. Add the shallot, tomatoes and apple. Season the fish with salt and pepper and arrange on top of the shallot mixture. Pour in half of the cider, the wine and the fish stock. On top of the stove bring the cooking liquid to a simmer. Cover the dish with buttered wax paper and bake in a preheated moderate oven (350°F.) for 10 to 15 minutes, or until the skate is cooked. Remove the fish to 4 warmed plates and keep warm.

Pour the liquid into a saucepan, add the cream, and reduce over moderately high heat until the sauce coats a spoon. Beat in remaining butter, cut into bits, the mustard, the rest of the cider and the Calvados. Taste for seasoning and add salt and pepper if necessary.

Spoon the sauce over the fish and sprinkle with chopped tarragon. Serve immediately with new potatoes.

S E R V E S 4.

STEAMED FISH
IN BUTTER SAUCE

❖   ❖   ❖

Raymond Duthie, whom I first met when he was head chef at the
Royal Crescent Hotel in Bath, has decided ideas about food. He
believes in following traditional methods of preparation, but at the
same time wants the dishes he prepares to be clean-tasting, crisp,
uncomplicated and eye-catching. He is a Scot and a perfectionist
without being overfussy. His food is subtle and delicious. Serve with
a Pouilly-Fuissé.

2 pounds assorted fish fillets,
*   from 4 varieties if possible,*
*   including striped bass, John*
*   Dory, striped mullet, red porgy*
*   or similar fish, cut into 1-inch*
*   pieces*
Salt, freshly ground pepper
1 medium-size onion, chopped

1 medium-size carrot, scraped
*   and chopped*
1 sprig of thyme
1 teaspoon black peppercorns,
*   lightly crushed*
Seaweed, if available
1 recipe Beurre Blanc (White
*   Butter Sauce) (see Index)*

Season the fish with salt and pepper and set aside. In the bottom part
of a steamer combine the onion, carrot, thyme, peppercorns and a
generous amount of salt, with water to cover. Line the basket of the
steamer with seaweed and arrange the pieces of fish on top. Cover,
and steam until the fish is cooked, about 6 minutes.

Have ready the butter sauce and pour it onto 4 warm, not hot,
plates. Arrange the pieces of fish on top of the sauce. Serve any extra
sauce separately.

S E R V E S   4.

RISOTTO OF MUSSELS WITH SAFFRON

❖ ❖ ❖

This is an extremely simple, entirely delicious dish created by Simon Hopkinson of Hilaire restaurant in London. It is perfect for entertaining friends at an informal weekend supper, accompanied by a green salad and plenty of wine, such as a Sancerre.

1 *quart mussels, cleaned*
½ *cup dry white wine*
6 *tablespoons butter*
6 *tablespoons shallots, chopped fine*
2 *cups Arborio (Italian risotto) rice*

2 *cups Chicken Stock (see Index)*
Salt, freshly ground pepper
1 *teaspoon saffron, ground*
½ *cup minced parsley*

Put the mussels into a large shallow pan with a lid. Pour in the wine, cover, and simmer for 5 minutes. Lift out and reserve the mussels. Discard the shells. Discard any unopened mussels. Strain the liquid in the pan through a sieve lined with a double layer of dampened cheesecloth and measure it. There should be about 2 cups. Make up the quantity, if necessary, with equal amounts of chicken stock and dry white wine.

In a large heavy saucepan melt the butter. Add the shallots and sauté until shallots are soft, about 5 minutes. Add the rice to the pan and stir over low heat until all the rice is coated with the butter but not browned. Pour in the chicken stock and mussel liquor. Season with salt and pepper and stir in the ground saffron. Bring to a simmer over moderate heat, stir and cook, covered, over very low heat until the rice is almost tender, about 20 minutes.

Add the reserved mussels and the parsley, stir to mix and cook just long enough to heat the mussels through and finish cooking the rice. Serve with a green salad.

S E R V E S 6.

SCALLOPS AND MUSSELS WITH SCALLOP MOUSSELINE

❖　　　❖　　　❖

Sonia Blech, chef-patronne of Mijanou restaurant in London, experiments with dishes. She seeks the ideal combination of flavor, texture and taste. This simple and beautiful-to-look-at dish achieves that aim. It is not difficult to make, but is very impressive both to see and eat, though not for everyday cooking. Serve with a Sauvignon Blanc or a white Bordeaux.

Scallop Mousseline

12 large scallops with coral (roe)
1 whole egg
1⅓ cups heavy cream
1 teaspoon lemon juice

1 teaspoon Cognac or other
　brandy
Salt, freshly ground pepper
Butter

Scallops and Mussels

12 mussels, thoroughly scrubbed,
　cleaned and soaked
½ cup dry white wine
1 tablespoon minced shallots
¾ cup Veal or Chicken Stock
　(see Index)

¼ cup heavy cream
1 teaspoon Cognac or other
　brandy
12 medium shrimps, shelled

Carefully remove the coral (roe) from the scallops and put the coral into a blender or food processor. Reserve the scallops. Add the egg and process to a purée. Scrape out of the blender or food processor into a bowl and chill thoroughly. Return the mixture to the blender or food processor and, with the machine running, gradually pour in the cream. Flavor with the lemon juice and Cognac and add salt and pepper to taste. Butter 2 ramekins or small soufflé molds and fill with the mixture. Set in a baking pan with water to come about halfway up the ramekins. Bake in a preheated moderate oven (350°F.) for 15 to 20 minutes, or until done. Unmold, cover, and keep warm.

While the mousseline is cooking, put the mussels into a shallow pan with a tight-fitting lid. Add the wine and shallots, cover, and cook over moderately high heat for 5 minutes, or until the mussels have opened. Lift out the mussels and discard the top shells. Strain the liquid in the pan and pour it into a saucepan. Add the veal or chicken stock and simmer until the liquid is reduced to half. Season with salt and pepper if necessary, pour in the cream, and Cognac, and simmer for 1 or 2 minutes. Add the mussels in their half shells, the scallops and the shrimps. Cover and simmer for about 1 minute, until the scallops and shrimps are cooked and the mussels warmed.

To serve, pour the sauce onto 2 heated plates. Place the mousseline in the center of each plate and surround it with the mussels and scallops alternately. Place a shrimp above each scallop.

S E R V E S 2.

SCALLOPS WITH AVOCADO SAUCE

❖   ❖   ❖

The delicate flavor of avocado complements the equally delicate flavor of the scallops in this elegantly simple and lovely-to-look-at dish created by Allan Garth, head chef at Gravetye Manor, East Grinstead in West Sussex. It takes only a brief time to prepare and requires only a very few ingredients, ideal for the cook in a hurry who wants to make something special. Serve with a Chardonnay.

1 cup Fish Stock (see Index)
2 cups light cream
1 large ripe avocado
Salt, freshly ground pepper

20 large scallops, with roe if possible
1 cup wild rice, or long-grain rice, freshly cooked

Pour the stock and cream into a saucepan and simmer over moderate heat, uncovered, until reduced to 1½ cups. Peel and pit the avocado and mash with a fork until smooth. Stir it into the reduced fish stock and cream mixture. Season with salt and pepper and warm through. Keep warm, not hot.

Steam the scallops for 2 to 4 minutes or until they have lost their opaque look. Be careful not to overcook.

Spoon the cooked hot wild rice or long-grain rice onto 4 heated plates. Divide the scallops among the plates and spoon the sauce over them.

S E R V E S 4.

VEGETABLES
AND
SALADS

⬧　　⬧　　⬧

TODAY'S BRITISH chefs have a keen appreciation of vegetables. They dislike the old-fashioned concept of a plate with heaped vegetable servings jostling for space with meat, poultry or fish. They want vegetables to be esteemed in their own right and presented gracefully to the diner. A favorite presentation is a selection of vegetables arranged on a small round or crescent-shaped plate served with the main course. These are often selections of *primeurs*, tiny little carrots still with their tufted green tops, little new potatoes unpeeled but for a strip round the middle, baby white turnips, tender snow peas, skinny little green beans, baby peas, delicate green asparagus tips, broccoli sprigs and cauliflowerets all at their freshest, youngest best, three or four served neatly arranged.

Many chefs wanting to please vegetarian diners have devised attractive dishes that can be served to both vegetarians and nonvegetarians alike as main courses, and there are more elaborate vegetable dishes that enhance the main course they are served with.

Vegetable purées and purées combining root vegetables are favorites with them. They like to present a selection of purées such as beets, carrots or broccoli in flavorful heaps separately or sometimes on main-course plates. Potatoes with parsnips, or potatoes with Jerusalem artichokes, liven up routine tastes.

There is also a whole new attitude to salads. They can be served as first courses or as main courses; can contain meat, poultry, fish or shellfish; can be served warm as well as chilled with a variety of greens and a variety of dressings using different oils and vinegars. There is a whole new dimension of food, taking advantage of today's magnificent abundance.

PARSNIP AND POTATO PURÉE

❖   ❖   ❖

Enliven winter dishes with this purée while waiting for the delicious tiny *primeurs* of spring. The mixture gives bland vegetables a lift.

1 pound boiling potatoes, peeled
  and halved
1 pound parsnips, peeled and
  quartered

4 tablespoons butter
Salt, freshly ground pepper

In a large saucepan combine the potatoes and parsnips. Pour in enough cold water to cover, add 1 teaspoon salt, bring to a boil, and simmer until the vegetables are tender, about 20 minutes. Drain, cover, and shake over low heat for about a minute, then purée in a food processor with the butter. Season with salt and pepper and serve with any meat or poultry.

S E R V E S 6.

V A R I A T I O N : Instead of parsnips, scrape and slice 1 pound Jerusalem artichokes and cook with the potatoes. Purée as above.

PURÉED BEETS

❖   ❖   ❖

Simon Hopkinson, of Hilaire restaurant on the Old Brompton Road in London, serves beet purée with roast teal, a most unusual and exciting combination. Teal is a small wild duck not usually available, however the beet purée is good with any wild duck. I have found it agreeable with domestic duckling and other poultry. Beets also look attractive in combination with other vegetables. Serve the beet purée with mashed potatoes and carrot purée in three neat heaps on the plate with plainly cooked poultry. If liked a gravy or sauce can be served separately.

2 pounds fresh beets
Salt, freshly ground pepper

2 tablespoons butter, cut into bits

Scrub but do not peel the beets. Trim the stems. Put into a saucepan of boiling salted water to cover and simmer, covered, until tender, about 30 minutes. Drain, cool, and rub off the skins. Chop beets coarse and purée in a blender or food processor. Return to the rinsed out and dried saucepan and season to taste with salt and pepper. Add the butter and heat through, stirring to mix.

S E R V E S 6.

Puréed Carrots:

Carrots can be puréed in the same way. They should be trimmed, scraped and sliced, then cooked until tender in boiling salted water. Very young carrots will take about 10 minutes, older ones up to 30 minutes.

BROCCOLI, BRUSSELS SPROUTS AND OTHER PURÉES

❖   ❖   ❖

Both broccoli and Brussels sprouts are delicious as purées. They seem to have a new and different flavor in this form, and they add a special touch to meat and poultry dishes as their flavor is robust. Many other vegetables are also good puréed. They are all cooked in the same way and puréed in a blender or food processor.

Green peas, green beans and cauliflowerets all take between 5 and 8 minutes in boiling salted water. Broccoli and Brussels sprouts take about 8 minutes. Check the vegetables when cooking so as not to overcook.

If any of the vegetables seem watery, drain them in a sieve for about 10 minutes, then reheat with a little butter to bind them. Vegetables with skins or fibers can be rubbed through a large sieve for a smooth purée, then reheated with a little butter. Green peas need this extra step.

John Hornsby, whose cooking I enjoyed when he was head chef at the Castle Hotel in Taunton, Somerset, served two purées, spinach and beet, with pheasant and other feathered game and with duckling. Robert Jones of Ston Easton Park, Somerset, serves onion purée with spring lamb, a delicious combination. Young turnips, cooked until

(recipe continues)

tender, puréed and drained in a sieve, then mixed with about a quarter of their volume of potato to give them body, are also good with lamb. Finish them with a little butter if liked.

Julian Waterer serves a leek purée and fresh peaches, lightly poached, with lamb. The combination is equally good with veal or chicken breasts. Robert Gardiner serves puréed cucumber and new potatoes with poached salmon, and Denis Woodtli likes mint with his green beans. I find their ideas stimulatingly imaginative.

BEETS WITH CELERIAC SAUCE

❖   ❖   ❖

Michael Coaker, head chef at the Britannia Hotel's restaurant in London, says vegetables should never be dull. He takes delight in creating new vegetable dishes. This is good to eat and anything but dull.

Beets

1½ cups coarse-chopped cooked
   beets
3 tablespoons butter
¼ cup heavy cream, or Fresh
   White Cheese (see Index)
   (optional)

Salt, freshly ground pepper

Celeriac Sauce

1 cup cooked celeriac, puréed
2 tablespoons heavy cream, or
   Fresh White Cheese (see
   Index) (optional)

1 tablespoon butter
1 cup Chicken Stock (see Index),
   approximately
1 teaspoon lemon juice

In a food processor or blender combine the beets, butter and heavy cream or fresh white cheese and process to a purée. Season to taste with salt and pepper and transfer to a small saucepan. Set aside. The cream or fresh white cheese may be left out.

In a saucepan combine all the ingredients for the sauce. Stir to mix and heat gently. The sauce should be as thick as heavy cream. Thin with chicken stock if necessary. The cream or fresh white cheese may be left out. Keep the sauce warm.

Heat the beet purée. It should be thick enough to hold its shape in a spoon. Pour the sauce onto 4 warm plates. Mold the beets with tablespoons into quenelles and put on top of the sauce.

SERVES 4.

MUSHROOMS WITH FENNEL

❖ ❖ ❖

This unusual and simple dish comes from chef-patron John Evans of Meadowsweet restaurant in Llanrwst, Gwynedd, Wales. It can be served as a vegetable accompaniment to any plainly cooked meat or poultry, or as a vegetarian main course. John Evans created the dish after gathering mushrooms the morning after a rainy night. It gave him the special appreciation of the fresh grown vegetables and herbs in which he delights.

7 tablespoons butter
3 tablespoons all-purpose flour
1 cup milk
1 cup minced onions
1 cup minced peeled fennel bulb
2 tablespoons minced parsley

1 pound mushrooms, chopped
1 tablespoon minced fennel fronds
Salt, freshly ground pepper
⅛ teaspoon freshly grated nutmeg
Garnish: fennel fronds

Heat 3 tablespoons of the butter in a small heavy saucepan. Stir in the flour and cook over very low heat, without letting the mixture color, for 2 minutes. Off the heat gradually stir in the milk. When the mixture is smooth return it to the heat and simmer, stirring from time to time, over low heat for 5 minutes. The sauce will be very thick. Set aside.

In a medium-size heavy skillet heat the rest of the butter. Add the onions, fennel, parsley, mushrooms and fennel fronds. Season to taste with salt and pepper, add the nutmeg, cover, and simmer over moderate heat for 8 minutes, or until the vegetables are tender. Stir in the reserved sauce and simmer over low heat for 1 to 2 minutes to heat through.

For a vegetarian main course serve on a bed of rice and garnish with fennel fronds.

SERVES 2 or 3 as a main course, 4 to 6 as a vegetable course with plainly cooked meat or poultry.

MUSHROOM AND QUAIL EGG TARTLETS

❖   ❖   ❖

Nicholas Knight, the young head chef at Master's Restaurant in Kensington, London, puts his imagination combined with his cooking expertise to work to produce dishes that are simple to cook but complex in flavor and texture. He uses his considerable artistry in the presentation of his dishes. This one, for example, is pretty to look at, with poached quail eggs nestling together in tartlet shells. Quail eggs are now readily available but handling the tiny things requires what I call good hands, which not all of us are blessed with, especially when we are in a hurry. I've made the tartlets using ordinary hen's eggs and it works perfectly well. It is a good dish for non-meat eaters, and makes a satisfying main course for lunch or dinner.

4 tart shells, 4-inch size, made
    with Short-Crust Pastry (see
    Index) and baked blind
2 tablespoons butter
6 tablespoons minced shallots

2 pounds mushrooms, chopped
    fine
32 quail's eggs, or 8 hen's eggs
Vinegar
Salt

Sauce

1 cup Chicken Stock (see Index)
1 cup heavy cream, or Fresh
    White Cheese (see Index)

2 tablespoons snipped chives, or
    more to taste

Make the tart shells and set them aside. In a large skillet heat the butter and add the shallots. Cook over very low heat until they are softened. Add the mushrooms and cook over moderate heat, stirring from time to time, until they have given up all their liquid, about 5 minutes. Let the mixture cool, then spread it over the bottom of the tart shells.

If using quail eggs, have ready a shallow dish of vinegar large enough to hold all of them at the same time. Break the eggs into the vinegar, then carefully pour the contents into a large skillet of briskly boiling salted water, over high heat. As soon as the water returns to a boil, remove from the heat. Lift out the eggs with a slotted spoon and slide them into a bowl of cold water. Set aside until ready to use. If using hen's eggs break them, then slide them into a saucepan of boiling water mixed with 1 tablespoon vinegar to each quart of water. Simmer for 3 to 4 minutes, spooning the white over the yolk as the eggs cook. Lift out into cold water and set aside.

To make the sauce put the stock, cream and chives into a saucepan and simmer until the mixture is reduced to a light coating consistency. If using fresh white cheese, simply whisk it in to mix and heat through.

To serve, put 8 quail or 2 hen's eggs into each of the tart shells and heat through in a preheated moderate oven (350°F.) for 3 to 4 minutes. Coat lightly with the warm sauce. Serve with a green salad or an assortment of vegetables arranged on a small separate plate.

SERVES 4.

VARIATION : The tarts make a good cocktail, buffet or appetizer dish when made with eight 3-inch tart shells and 4 quail eggs or 1 hen's egg per tart.

SERVES 8.

CRISPY BAKED POTATOES

❖   ❖   ❖

Everyone, or almost everyone, likes potatoes. Vaughan Archer, head chef at the very beautiful 90 Park Lane Restaurant in London, has created a recipe that I find irresistible. Chef Archer has his potatoes trimmed to perfect 1-inch cylinders before slicing them, but I don't as the recipe works perfectly well for the home cook prepared to tolerate less than artistic perfection.

2 large potatoes, peeled and sliced   4 tablespoons butter
    thin
Salt, freshly ground pepper,
    nutmeg

Season the potatoes with salt, pepper and a few grinds of nutmeg. In a skillet heat the butter and toss the potatoes until they begin to soften. Do not let them brown.

Have ready 4 nonstick flan rings, 3 inches around and ½ inch deep, on a baking sheet, and fill them with the potato slices, arranging them round the edge, then filling in the center. Bake in a preheated hot oven (400°F.) until crispy and golden, about 30 minutes. Lift off the flan rings. Using a spatula, slide the potatoes onto heated plates. Serve at once.

SERVES 4.

STUFFED POTATOES

❖   ❖   ❖

These potatoes are an interesting variation on the usual stuffed baked potato. Chef Vaughan Archer created them when he needed a lighter version of stuffed potatoes to accompany steak or other meat or poultry dishes. Use your favorite vegetables for the stuffing.

2 medium-size potatoes, each
   about 5 ounces
1 cup cooked mixed vegetables
   (carrots, celery, green beans,
   white turnips, zucchini, etc.)

2 teaspoons minced truffle
   (optional)
2 teaspoons beaten egg
Salt, freshly ground pepper
2 tablespoons butter

Peel the potatoes and trim if necessary to a neater shape. A roughly cylindrical potato is the best choice. Using an apple corer, make a hole through the center of each potato. Simmer potatoes in boiling salted water for 5 minutes. Drain. Mix the vegetables with the truffle, if using it, the beaten egg, and salt and pepper to taste and stuff firmly into the potatoes. Melt the butter in a small baking pan. Roll the potatoes in the butter, then bake in a preheated hot oven (425°F.) for about 20 minutes, or until tender. Cut each potato into 6 slices.

S E R V E S 2 to 4.

BUTTERED LEEKS

❖   ❖   ❖

This is a very simple and quick way to cook leeks, keeping all their delicate flavor and texture. Serve as a green vegetable.

4 tablespoons butter
6 medium-size leeks, trimmed,
   thoroughly washed and chopped
   coarse

Salt, freshly ground pepper

Melt the butter in a large skillet with a lid. Add the leeks, season with salt and pepper, and stir to mix. Cover and cook over moderate heat for about 5 minutes, or until leeks are tender and still crisp. Do not let them brown.

SERVES 6.

VEGETABLE-STUFFED ONION CUPS

❖   ❖   ❖

This is another of the delectable vegetable dishes created by head chef Vaughan Archer.

4 medium-size Bermuda-type onions, about 3 inches in diameter
Chicken Stock (see Index)
4 small carrots, trimmed, scraped, and cut into 1-inch pieces
4 small turnips, peeled and quartered

4 small zucchini, trimmed and cut into 1-inch pieces
½ cup thin green beans, trimmed and cut into 1½-inch pieces
8 snow peas, sliced into 3 diagonally
4 baby sweetcorn tips, about 1 inch
Butter

Peel the onions and trim the root end. Slice off the top of each onion. Using a small serrated spoon scoop out the flesh, leaving a solid shell of 2 or 3 layers. Use the scooped-out onion in a soup or stew. Put the onions into a shallow saucepan or skillet with a lid. They should fit snugly. Pour in enough stock to come about halfway up the onions. Cover and poach until the onions are tender, about 45 minutes. Test with a toothpick or skewer for tenderness.

While the onions are cooking, cook the vegetables in boiling salted water until they are tender but crisp. It is better to cook them separately, then divide them into 4 portions. As soon as the onions are done, lift them out of the poaching liquid and keep them warm. Toss each portion of vegetables in a little butter and fill the onion cups. Serve immediately.

SERVES 4.

CARROT PUDDINGS WITH FRESH HERB SAUCE

❖   ❖   ❖

Young Pierre Chevillard, head chef at Chewton Glen Hotel, New Milton, Hampshire, an elegant country house hotel on the edge of the New Forest, has been cooking since his apprenticeship at the age of 15. His carrot puddings can be served either as a vegetable or as a first course. The herb sauce complements the flavor of the carrots.

1½ pounds young carrots,
   scraped and sliced thin
6 cups Chicken Stock (see Index)
½ teaspoon sugar
Salt
1 tablespoon olive oil
1 cup chopped mushrooms

Freshly ground pepper
4 large eggs, lightly beaten
2 cups grated Gruyère cheese
3 tablespoons chopped fresh
   chervil, or 1 tablespoon dried,
   or use chopped parsley

Sauce

1 cup Chicken Stock (see Index)
1 tablespoon minced shallot or
   scallion
1 cup heavy cream, or Fresh
   White Cheese (see Index)
1 tablespoon butter, softened at
   room temperature

1 tablespoon each of chopped
   fresh chervil, chives, tarragon
   and parsley, or other fresh
   herbs

Combine the carrots, stock, sugar, and salt to taste in a large saucepan and simmer, covered, until carrots are very tender, about 25 minutes. Let the mixture cool to lukewarm, then remove the carrots and purée them in a blender or food processor. Return the purée to the liquid and stir to mix. Pour into a large bowl.

Heat the oil in a skillet and sauté the mushrooms with salt and pepper to taste over moderately high heat for about 5 minutes, or until all the liquid has evaporated. Cool the mushrooms, then stir them into the purée. Add the eggs, cheese and chervil; mix well. Taste for seasoning and add salt and pepper if necessary. Pour the mixture into 6 buttered ¾-cup ramekins. Bake in a preheated moderate oven (350°F.) for 30 minutes, or until a knife inserted in the center comes out clean. Let the puddings cool for a few minutes, then run a knife around the inside of each ramekin and unmold onto 6 warmed plates.

While the puddings are baking, make the sauce. Combine the chicken stock and shallot in a saucepan and reduce over moderately high heat to ¼ cup. Stir in the cream and simmer until the mixture has thickened lightly; or stir in the fresh cheese and warm through. Pour through a sieve into a bowl. Stir in the butter and herbs, season to taste with salt and pepper, and pour over the puddings.

S E R V E S 6.

CARROT AND GREEN PEPPERCORN SAUCE

❖ ❖ ❖

This unusual sauce is another of Nicholas Knight's versatile recipes. He uses it as a coating sauce for steak or lamb chops. It is also good with plainly cooked rabbit or poultry, and I have enjoyed it with a bland fish like cod and a vegetable like broccoli. It is not time-consuming to make, and when I use fresh white cheese instead of cream, it is also pleasantly low in fat.

2 cups thin slices of peeled carrots
1½ cups milk, approximately
2 egg yolks
1 cup heavy cream, or Fresh
   White Cheese (see Index)

Salt
1 tablespoon green peppercorns

Put the carrots in a medium-size saucepan and pour in enough milk to cover. Bring to a simmer and cook, partially covered, over low heat until the carrots are tender, about 20 minutes. Drain and discard any remaining milk. Purée the carrots in a blender or food processor. Rinse out and dry the saucepan and return the carrot purée to it.

In a bowl combine the egg yolks and cream or fresh white cheese. Whisk into the carrot purée over low heat and cook, whisking, for a few minutes until the sauce is light and fluffy. Season to taste with salt and stir in the green peppercorns. Coat the steak with the sauce, or use to coat lamb chops, poultry, fish or green vegetables.

S E R V E S 4 generously.

SAVORY RICE

❖   ❖   ❖

Michael Collom, head chef at the Priory Hotel in Bath, likes to serve this rice with Garnished Pork Scallops (see Index). I enjoy it with the pork dish, and also with any dish served with rice.

2 tablespoons butter
2 tablespoons minced shallots or
  scallions
1/4 cup chopped red bell pepper
2 cups long-grain rice
4 cups Chicken Stock (see Index)

1/8 teaspoon ground saffron
Salt, freshly ground pepper
1 sprig of fresh thyme
1 bay leaf
1/2 cup raisins

In an 8-cup flameproof casserole heat the butter and sauté the shallots and bell pepper until they are tender but not browned. Add the rice and cook, stirring, over very low heat for 2 to 3 minutes. Pour in the chicken stock, saffron, salt and pepper to taste, thyme and a bay leaf. Bring to a simmer, cover, and cook in a preheated moderate oven (350°F.) until the rice is tender and all the liquid absorbed, about 20 minutes. If preferred, cook on top of the stove over very low heat. While the rice is cooking soak the raisins in warm water. Drain and add to the cooked rice.

S E R V E S 6.

CASSEROLE OF GREEN VEGETABLES

❖   ❖   ❖

Peter Jackson, chef-patron of the Colonial Restaurant in Glasgow, Scotland, loves vegetables, especially fresh green ones. This is one of his favorite ways of serving a medley of green vegetables to accompany meat or poultry dishes.

1/2 cup broccoli flowerets
1/2 cup baby peas
1/2 cup green beans (haricots
  verts), cut into 1/2-inch pieces
1 cup sliced zucchini

1/2 cup sugar peas, sliced
  diagonally
2 tablespoons butter
Salt, freshly ground pepper

Cook the vegetables separately in boiling salted water until crisply tender. Drain and rinse quickly in cold water to set the color. In a saucepan melt the butter and toss the zucchini, then add the other vegetables. Season with salt and pepper and serve hot on small side plates.

SERVES 4.

STUFFED GARNISHED ARTICHOKE HEARTS

❖   ❖   ❖

Michael Collom, head chef at the Priory Hotel in Bath, has found an increasing number of guests who are vegetarian, and he has created dishes to please them. This is pleasant for non-meat eaters but also makes an ideal dinner party first course as it can be made ahead of time except for the last-minute egg white and cheese topping.

2 tablespoons butter
2 tablespoons minced shallots or
  scallions
1 sprig of fresh thyme, chopped,
  or ⅛ teaspoon dried thyme
8 ounces mushrooms, chopped
  fine

Salt, freshly ground pepper
6 large artichoke hearts, cooked
6 egg whites
1½ cups grated Cheddar cheese

In a skillet heat the butter and sauté the shallots, thyme and mushrooms over moderately high heat for about 5 minutes, or until mushrooms have given up most of their moisture. Season with salt and pepper. Fill the artichoke hearts with the mixture, and arrange them on a baking sheet.

When ready to cook, beat the egg whites with a pinch of salt until they stand in firm peaks. Fold in half of the cheese and spoon the mixture on top of the artichoke hearts. Sprinkle with the rest of the cheese. Bake in a preheated hot oven (400°F.) for 10 to 15 minutes, or until the tops are golden brown. Serve with a green salad as a vegetarian main course, or as a first course.

SERVES 6.

ASPARAGUS TIPS IN CHIVE SAUCE

❖　　　❖　　　❖

This is another of Michael Collom's attractive vegetarian dishes that can be enjoyed both as a vegetarian main course and a first course to lunch or dinner. For heartier appetites serve double portions as a main course.

8 ounces Puff Pastry (see Index)	½ cup plain yogurt
Egg wash made with 1 egg yolk	½ cup heavy cream
mixed with 1 teaspoon water	1 tablespoon snipped chives
24 green or white asparagus tips,	Salt, freshly ground pepper
cooked	

Roll out the puff pastry and cut it into 6 rectangles, 6 by 4 inches. Place on a baking sheet and brush with egg wash. If there are any scraps of pastry left over, cut them into small decorative shapes and decorate the tops of the pastry pieces. Refrigerate for 1 hour, then bake in a preheated hot oven (425°F.) for about 15 minutes, or until the pastry is risen and golden brown. Place on a wire rack to cool. Split into halves and put 1 bottom half on each of 6 warmed plates.

Warm the asparagus tips and put four onto each of the pastry pieces. Put the other half of the pastry on top.

While the pastry is baking, make the sauce. In a small saucepan combine the yogurt, cream, chives, and salt and pepper to taste, and heat gently. Pour the sauce round the pastry and serve immediately.

S E R V E S　6.

SAVORY AVOCADO CHEESECAKE

❖　　　❖　　　❖

Margaret Brown, who taught herself to cook from the *Time-Life Foods of the World* series of cookbooks before she became chef-patronne of Simonsbath House Hotel in Exmoor, Somerset, has become an expert on early English cooking, particularly Elizabethan and Georgian cooking. This modern recipe, her own creation, is a delicious departure from her principal area of interest. It makes a good first course and a fine vegetarian lunch dish.

6 tablespoons butter
2 cups saltine cracker crumbs
4 teaspoons grated lemon rind
Salt, freshly ground pepper
2 envelopes unflavored gelatin,
    7 grams each
3 large ripe avocados
3 tablespoons lemon juice
3 large eggs, separated
½ pound cream cheese
1 tablespoon snipped fresh chives

1 teaspoon chopped mixed
    parsley, tarragon and chervil,
    or ½ teaspoon dried fines
    herbes
1 cup heavy cream, or Yogurt
    Cheese or Fresh White Cheese
    (see Index)
Pinch of cream of tartar
Garnish: avocado slices and
    watercress sprigs

Melt the butter in a heavy skillet and stir in the cracker crumbs and 2 teaspoons of the grated lemon rind. Season with salt and pepper and cook over low heat until the butter and seasonings are thoroughly mixed with the cracker crumbs. Have ready a lightly oiled 9-inch springform pan. Pack the cracker crumb mixture into the bottom of the pan and chill in the refrigerator for 30 minutes.

Pour ½ cup cold water into a small saucepan and sprinkle the gelatin over it. Set it aside to soften. Peel and pit the avocados and mash them in a bowl. Add the remaining 2 teaspoons of grated lemon rind and the lemon juice to avocados. In another bowl beat the egg yolks until they are light and lemon-colored. Mash the cream cheese, chives and mixed herbs into the egg yolks. Add the avocado mixture and stir until it is smooth. Set the saucepan with the softened gelatin over low heat and stir to dissolve. Stir gelatin into the avocado mixture. Add the cream, or yogurt cheese or fresh white cheese, mix well, and season with salt and pepper to taste. Beat the egg whites with a pinch of salt and the cream of tartar until they stand in firm peaks. Stir a tablespoon or two of the whites into the avocado mixture, then fold in remaining egg whites gently but thoroughly. Turn the mixture into the springform pan. Smooth the top, cover with foil, and chill in the refrigerator for 4 hours, or until firm.

Remove the sides of the pan and slide cheesecake onto a flat dish. Garnish with avocado slices and watercress sprigs.

S E R V E S 12 as an appetizer, 6 as a luncheon main course.

EGGPLANT CASSEROLE WITH TOMATO SAUCE

❖   ❖   ❖

Michael Coaker, head chef at the Britannia Hotel in London, likes to take traditional recipes and present them in a new form. This one is simplicity itself yet subtly changes Provençal ratatouille into a different dish.

2 tablespoons olive oil
1 medium-size onion, chopped
   fine
1 tablespoon minced shallot
1 small garlic clove, minced
2½ cups diced unpeeled eggplant
¾ cup diced zucchini
½ cup diced red bell pepper
½ cup diced green bell pepper

¼ cup chopped, peeled and
   seeded tomato
Salt, freshly ground pepper
⅛ teaspoon dried thyme
1 teaspoon tomato purée
Butter for soufflé dish
1 cup Tomato Sauce (see Index)
Garnish: chervil sprigs or parsley

Heat the oil in a skillet and sauté the onion and shallot over low heat until onion is soft. Add the garlic and cook for a minute or two longer. Add all the other vegetables, season to taste, and add the thyme and tomato purée. Cook, stirring from time to time, until all the vegetables are tender and the mixture is well blended.

Butter a 4-cup soufflé or similar dish and pack in the vegetable mixture. Set the dish in a baking pan with water to come about halfway up, and cook in a preheated moderately hot oven (375°F.) for about 10 minutes, or until heated through.

Heat the tomato sauce, which should be fairly thick, and pour it onto a warmed serving dish. Turn the vegetables out of the mold onto the sauce and garnish with chervil or parsley sprigs.

SERVES 4.

VARIATION: Vaughan Archer, head chef at 90 Park Lane Restaurant in London, also likes to serve eggplant dishes to accompany main courses. He serves fresh asparagus tips with his Eggplant Casserole, a delightful combination. His recipe, like Michael Coaker's, is inspired by a traditional dish, this one from Turkey—Imam Bayildi (the Imam fainted), so called because the Imam is said to have swooned with delight. Chef Archer does not aim to produce fainting fits with this version. His aim is simply to please.

2 long eggplants, each about
  ½ pound, peeled
¼ pound (1 stick) butter
1 tablespoon olive oil
Salt, freshly ground pepper

1 cup button mushrooms
2 medium-size tomatoes, about
  ½ pound, peeled, seeded and
  chopped

Cut the eggplants into 20 thin lengthwise slices. In a large skillet heat
4 tablespoons of the butter and the oil and sauté the eggplant slices
until lightly browned on both sides. Fit a slice into the bottom of four
3-inch ramekins or small soufflé dishes, then line the molds leaving
the long pieces to hang over the sides. Chop remaining eggplant fine
and sauté it in a little of the remaining butter. Season with salt and
pepper and set aside. Sauté the mushrooms in a little more of the
butter in the skillet; season and set aside. Toss the tomatoes in remaining butter, season, and set aside.

Fill the ramekins with layers of eggplant, mushrooms and tomato.
Fold over the overhanging eggplant. Set the ramekins in a baking pan
with water to come about halfway up. Bake in a preheated hot oven
(425°F.) for 20 minutes.

Remove from the oven, let stand for a few minutes, then invert
onto 4 warmed plates and serve with fresh asparagus tips.

S E R V E S 4.

FRESH PEAR VINAIGRETTE

❖   ❖   ❖

This imaginative, fresh-tasting salad is one of the felicitous creations of Michael Quinn. It demonstrates his special ability for balancing flavors and textures to contrast and blend sweet and savory, firm and soft. It could make the main course of a light luncheon, preceded by soup and followed by dessert or cheese.

6 *large pears*	16 *large fresh mint leaves*
½ *cup white-wine vinegar*	10 *fresh tarragon leaves*

Dressing

4 *tablespoons white-wine vinegar*	*Salt, freshly ground pepper*
½ *cup fresh mint and tarragon,*	*Superfine sugar*
chopped fine	¼ *pound smoked ham, chopped*
6 *tablespoons lemon juice*	*fine*

Using a vegetable peeler, peel the pears, leaving the stems attached. Put pears into a saucepan large enough to hold them in a single layer; add the vinegar, 10 mint leaves and the tarragon leaves. Pour in enough water barely to cover and poach the pears, covered, over low heat until they are tender, about 10 minutes. Pour off the cooking liquid and allow the pears to cool.

To make the dressing, mix the vinegar, chopped mint and tarragon leaves and lemon juice in a bowl. Season to taste with salt, pepper and superfine sugar. Stir to mix and dissolve the sugar. Add the chopped ham and mix thoroughly.

Slice the tops off the pears and very carefully scoop out the cores. Using a small spoon, fill the pears with the ham dressing. Pull away the stems from the pears and replace with remaining fresh mint leaves. Serve with any remaining dressing or with a mint- and tarragon-flavored mayonnaise.

S E R V E S 6.

N O T E : The dressing may be too sharp for some tastes. When making it, halve the vinegar and lemon juice, and add the rest a little at a time until the right balance of flavors is achieved.

FANTAIL OF DUCK SALAD WITH LEEK AND SPINACH SAUCE

❖ ❖ ❖

This brilliantly original dish created by Michael Quinn is robust enough to make the main course for lunch or dinner.

4 leeks, using white part only,
trimmed and washed
1 cup loosely packed leaf spinach
6 tablespoons butter
Salt, freshly ground pepper
1 cup Chicken Stock (see Index)

1 whole duck breast, skinned and
boned
9 snow peas
½ cup heavy cream
2 tablespoons snipped chives
Slices of truffle (optional)

Chop the leeks to coarse pieces. Wash and chop the spinach and set aside. In a saucepan heat 2 tablespoons of the butter, add the leeks and cook, covered, over very low heat until leeks are softened but not browned, about 4 minutes. Season to taste with salt and pepper. Pour in the chicken stock, cover, and simmer for a few minutes longer. Add the spinach and simmer for about 3 minutes. Cool. Pour the mixture into a blender or food processor and process to a very smooth purée. For a finer texture, push through a sieve.

In a skillet heat remaining butter. Season the duck with salt and pepper and cook in the butter, turning once, until done, 6 to 8 minutes. The duck should be pink inside. Slice each breast half lengthwise into 5 or 6 slices. Keep warm.

Drop the snow peas into a saucepan of boiling water and blanch for 1 minute. Lift out and dry. Cut 6 snow peas diagonally into halves, then slice into a fan shape. Cut remaining 3 snow peas into julienne strips.

Return the sauce to the heat, stir in the cream, and warm through. Pour the sauce onto each of 2 plates. Top the sauce with the duck breast and sprinkle chives round the edge of the plate. Garnish the duck with the snow pea fans and sprinkle with the julienne peas and truffle slices, if using them.

SERVES 2.

ROCK LOBSTER TAIL SALAD WITH STRAWBERRY VINAIGRETTE

❖ ❖ ❖

Denis Woodtli, head chef at Lochalsh Hotel, Kyle of Lochalsh on Scotland's west coast, likes to use strawberries in an unorthodox way. He feels their tart sweetness makes them ideal with shellfish, and he has created this salad as proof.

4 small rock lobster tails, each about 4 ounces	4 tablespoons olive or vegetable oil
1 cup hulled strawberries	1 large ripe avocado, pitted,
Salt, freshly ground pepper	peeled and quartered lengthwise
1 tablespoon red-wine vinegar	4 teaspoons caviar (optional)

Cook the lobster tails in salted water for 5 or 6 minutes. Lift them out of the water and let them cool, then shell them and cut each into quarters lengthwise. In a blender or food processor purée the strawberries, then sieve to remove the seeds. Season with salt and pepper and return to the blender or food processor. With the machine running, add the vinegar then pour in the oil in a slow, steady stream.

Pour the sauce onto 4 lightly chilled plates. Arrange a slice of avocado on each plate with the sliced lobster tails in a fan round it. Garnish the tails with a teaspoon of caviar, if using it.

S E R V E S 4.

QUAIL BREASTS WITH BACON AND GRAPES ON A MIXED SALAD

❖ ❖ ❖

Anthony Blake, chef de cuisine of Eastwell Manor at Ashford in Kent, believes that dishes should be presented with color and imagination but not served in excessively large portions. They should also be simple and light in accordance with modern ideas. This versatile salad could be served as a salad course or make a good beginning to a meal, followed by fish or shellfish as the main course of a warm-weather lunch or dinner.

8 quail breasts, skinned, boned
  and halved
Salt, freshly ground pepper
Butter
4 slices of bacon, cut into
  crosswise strips

24 seedless green grapes, peeled
  and halved
Assorted salad greens: oakleaf
  lettuce, endive, escarole,
  chicory, radicchio, Boston
  lettuce

Walnut Oil Dressing

1 tablespoon butter
4 tablespoons minced shallots
¼ cup dry red wine

2 tablespoons red-wine vinegar
¼ cup walnut oil

Season the quail breasts with salt and pepper. Reserve the rest of the carcasses for making stock. Heat 2 or 3 tablespoons butter in a heavy skillet and cook the quail breasts over moderate heat, turning once, for about 4 minutes. They should still be pink inside. Lift out of the skillet and keep warm. Add the bacon strips to the pan and sauté over moderate heat until they are crisp. Lift out onto paper towels to drain, then add to the quail breasts to keep warm. Add the grapes to the pan and sauté for 1 or 2 minutes. Lift out and add to the quail breasts.

Choose enough salad greens to serve 4, balancing color and texture. Wash and dry the greens and pile into a salad bowl. Make the dressing: In a skillet heat the butter and sauté the shallots until soft but not brown. Season with salt and pepper. Add the wine and vinegar and simmer, uncovered, over moderate heat until the mixture is reduced by half and thickened. Remove from the heat and pour into a bowl. Whisk in the walnut oil, and cool.

Toss the assorted salad greens with the walnut oil dressing and arrange them on 4 plates. Arrange 2 quail breasts on each plate on top of the greens and garnish with the bacon and grapes. Serve warm.

SERVES 4.

AVOCADO AND MELON FILLED WITH CRAB MEAT AND SHRIMPS

❖   ❖   ❖

Allan Holland of Mallory Court, a superb beginning-of-the-century home now a country house hotel in Warwickshire, near Leamington Spa and Stratford-upon-Avon, came to cooking from a deep interest in food. Elizabeth David's cookbooks started him off, and he has gone on learning ever since. His eclectic attitude increases his creativity. This dish, classic in its simplicity, is ideal for lunch as a main course but could be served as an appetizer for a grand meal.

¾ cup Mayonnaise (see Index)
1½ cups cooked crab meat,
    picked over to remove any
    cartilage
1 cup cooked shelled medium
    shrimps
Salt, freshly ground pepper
Lemon juice

1 large ripe avocado, peeled,
    pitted and quartered lengthwise
1 medium-size Ogen melon,
    quartered
1 or 2 teaspoons tomato purée
½ cup sour cream
Parsley sprigs

In a bowl combine 4 tablespoons of the mayonnaise with the crab meat and shrimps. Taste for seasoning and add salt, pepper and a little lemon juice if necessary.

Have ready 4 chilled plates. Place a quarter slice of avocado on each plate and fill with a quarter of the crab-meat and shrimp mixture. Arrange a slice of melon next to the avocado, fitting the two together to enclose the filling. Continue with the rest of the ingredients.

Stir the tomato purée into the rest of the mayonnaise to color it pale pink. Coat the avocado with the mayonnaise. Stir the sour cream until it is smooth and coat the melon with it. Garnish with a sprig of parsley.

SERVES 4.

AVOCADO, CUCUMBER AND PROSCIUTTO SALAD

❖   ❖   ❖

Julian Waterer, a young chef whose passion is cooking, is chef at The Salisbury restaurant at Old Hatfield, Hertfordshire. He is immensely creative and original. I first met him at Greywalls, a country house hotel at Gullane, Lothian, Scotland.

6 ounces sliced prosciutto, cut
  into julienne strips
¼ large seedless cucumber, cut
  into julienne strips
3 large avocados, peeled, halved
  and pitted

1 cup Oil and Vinegar Dressing
  made with lemon juice or wine
  vinegar and olive oil (see
  Index)
Garnish: watercress sprigs

Arrange the prosciutto and cucumber in the center of 6 salad plates. Put each avocado half, cut side down, on a chopping board; keeping the narrow ends intact, cut the avocados into thin lengthwise slices. Put a half avocado on top of the prosciutto and cucumber and press it gently to spread the slices like a fan. Spoon the vinaigrette over and around the avocado and garnish the plates with watercress. Serve as a salad, a light main course, or as a first course.

S E R V E S 6.

DUCK BREAST SALAD

❖   ❖   ❖

John King, chef de cuisine of the Ritz Club in London, was born in Kent, the son of a gamekeeper. He grew up in rural surroundings and always wanted to be a chef. He set out at an early age to get the best training possible. He has a fine feeling for green things, and fresh fruits, and combinations of them with other ingredients, as this salad shows.

1 whole breast of fresh duckling, skinned and boned	4 sprigs of lamb's lettuce
Salt, freshly ground pepper	2 ruby grapefruits, peeled and segmented
1 tablespoon vegetable oil	2 seedless oranges, peeled and segmented
2 tablespoons butter	3 tablespoons walnut oil
1 bunch of watercress	1 tablespoon red-wine vinegar
1 small head of chicory	
1 small head of radicchio	

Season both halves of the duck breast with salt and pepper. Heat the oil and butter in a skillet and sauté the breast halves until they are lightly browned on both sides but still pink in the middle, about 8 minutes. Lift out, cool, slice thin, and set aside, but do not refrigerate.

Wash the watercress, chicory, radicchio and lamb's lettuce and drain thoroughly. Remove the stems from the watercress and discard any wilted leaves from the cress and lettuces. Dry the salad greens, and tear into bite-size bits. Set aside in a bowl.

Peel the skin from the grapefruit and orange segments and remove any seeds. Set aside.

In a small bowl beat the walnut oil and vinegar together with salt and pepper to taste. Toss the salad greens in the dressing and arrange the salad in the center of 4 dessert plates. Lay alternate slices of duck breast, grapefruit and orange segments on top of the salad greens. Pour any remaining fruit or vinaigrette over the salad and serve.

S E R V E S 4.

WARM CHICKEN AND PEPPER SALAD

❖　　　❖　　　❖

Having enjoyed chef Melvin Jordan's Watercress Soup, I looked forward to trying his salads. His cooking has a simplicity and directness I find appealing, and his presentation is attractive. Green and red peppers with cubes of chicken breast contrast with the salad greens in appearance, taste and texture.

1 large garlic clove, crushed
4 tablespoons butter
1 whole chicken breast, halved, skinned, boned and cubed
1 small red bell pepper, seeded and cut into strips
1 small green bell pepper, seeded and cut into strips
Salt, freshly ground pepper
1 recipe Garlic Croutons (see Index)

1 tablespoon lemon juice
Assorted salad greens (Boston lettuce, romaine, radicchio, leaf lettuce, lamb's lettuce, etc.), washed, dried and torn into bite-size bits
Oil and Vinegar Dressing (see Index)

Combine the garlic and butter in a small heavy skillet and sauté the chicken cubes and pepper strips until vegetables are tender and the chicken cooked, 4 to 6 minutes. Sprinkle the croutons with the lemon juice. Add them to the pan and heat through.

Toss the salad greens in the dressing and arrange on 4 salad plates. Top with the warm chicken, pepper and crouton mixture. Serve immediately.

S E R V E S 4.

V A R I A T I O N : Omit the peppers and substitute sliced roast squab (pigeon) breasts for the chicken. Sprinkle the finished salad with minced parsley.

RADICCHIO AND WARM SCALLOP SALAD

❖   ❖   ❖

This is one of the elegant salads Michael Quinn created while he was Maître Chef des Cuisines at the Ritz in London, the first British chef ever to hold the position. He was one of the founding members of Country Chefs Seven when he was head chef at Gravetye Manor in West Sussex. He is now head chef at Ettington Park Hotel near Stratford-upon-Avon. The salad is eye-catching even when arranged quite haphazardly. Either way it tastes good.

1 recipe Oil and Vinegar
  Dressing, using lemon juice
  (see Index)
8 large endive leaves
½ small head of radicchio

8 large scallops, with roes, if
  possible
Salt, freshly ground pepper
4 tablespoons butter
Chervil sprigs

Make the dressing with lemon juice instead of vinegar. Toss the endive and radicchio separately in a little of the dressing. Arrange the endive leaves round the edges of 2 salad plates. Put the radicchio in a pile in the middle.

Season the scallops with salt and pepper. In a small heavy skillet heat the butter and sauté the scallops over moderate heat until they are lightly colored. Lift out and arrange on top of the radicchio. Garnish with chervil sprigs. Serve the rest of the dressing separately.

S E R V E S 2 to 4.

HUNTER'S SALAD

❖   ❖   ❖

This is a very grand salad for a special occasion. A whole boned partridge breast is used, but only the suprêmes, the whole breast, halved and boned, of the pheasant and chicken. The other parts of the two birds can be used for a simpler family meal. The salad is the creation of Pierre Chevillard, the young head chef at Chewton Glen Hotel in Hampshire, taking advantage of the readily available game in the area.

Oil and Vinegar Dressing (see Index)
2 teaspoons Meaux mustard
1 whole partridge breast, boned
½ boned pheasant breast, 1 suprême
½ boned chicken breast, 1 suprême

4 tablespoons (½ stick) butter
1 potato, peeled and sliced very thin
1 small head of radicchio
¼ small head of chicory
1 cup corn salad, approximately
1 small bunch of black grapes, pitted and peeled

Make the oil and vinegar dressing using olive oil and adding the Meaux mustard. Set aside. Cut each of the breasts into 4 lengthwise slices. In a skillet heat the butter and sauté the slices lightly, turning once. The partridge and pheasant should remain pink inside.

Arrange the slices of potato in a broiling pan and drizzle them with melted butter. Broil under moderate heat to make potato chips. Store-bought chips can, of course, be used instead.

Wash and dry the salad greens and toss them in the dressing. Arrange the greens on 4 plates and top with the sliced breasts, making sure each plate has a slice of each meat. Arrange a few grapes on each plate and scatter the potato chips over the salad.

SERVES 4.

FROGS' LEGS AND JUNIPER BERRY SALAD

❖   ❖   ❖

Andrew Stacey, the young *chef garde-manger* at The Bell Inn at
Aston Clinton in Buckinghamshire, has developed dishes that he feels
keep their natural flavor and delicately balanced composition. This
unusual salad is refreshing and makes a good lunch or summer dinner
main course.

2 tablespoons juniper berries
1 tablespoon medium dry or dry
  sherry wine
2 pairs frogs' legs
3 tablespoons light cream
2 teaspoons lime or lemon juice
Salt, freshly ground pepper
1 small head of Boston lettuce
½ small head of chicory

4 leaves of radicchio
4 leaves of corn salad
2 medium-size tomatoes, peeled,
  seeded and halved
Flour for dredging the frogs' legs
4 tablespoons butter
1 tablespoon each of snipped
  chives, chopped parsley and
  chervil

Salad Dressing

2 tablespoons medium dry or dry
  sherry wine
2 teaspoons Dijon mustard

2 teaspoons celery seeds
2 teaspoons red-wine vinegar
5 tablespoons olive oil

Put the juniper berries into a small bowl with 1 tablespoon sherry and
set aside. Bone the frogs' legs, if liked, or leave them whole. Put them
into a bowl with the cream, lime or lemon juice, and salt and pepper
to taste, and turn to coat well. Set aside.

Wash and drain the salad greens and dry thoroughly. Discard any
discolored leaves. Make the dressing by mixing together the sherry,
mustard, celery seeds, vinegar and salt and pepper to taste, then
gradually beating in the oil. Toss the greens in the dressing. Arrange
the salad on 4 plates. Slice the tomato halves and arrange around the
salad.

Drain the frogs' legs and pat them dry with paper towels. Dredge
them with flour, shaking to remove excess flour. Heat the butter in
a large skillet and fry the frogs' legs until they are golden brown,
turning frequently, for about 5 minutes. Drain on kitchen towels.

Arrange the frogs' legs on top of the salad and sprinkle with the herbs. Drain the juniper berries and sprinkle them over the salad.

S E R V E S 4 as a salad, 2 as a main course.

BROCCOLI AND RED BELL PEPPER SALAD

❖   ❖   ❖

This healthy and delicious salad was given me by Alan Casey when he was head chef at Culloden House, Inverness, in Scotland. He likes the new trends in cooking because they emphasize the use of fresh ingredients.

1-pound head of calabrese
 (purple-headed broccoli),
 trimmed
Salt
6 tablespoons walnut oil
1 tablespoon red-wine vinegar
1 tablespoon lemon juice
½ teaspoon English dry mustard
⅛ teaspoon minced garlic

¼ teaspoon salt
¼ teaspoon sugar
1 teaspoon minced seeded fresh
 hot green chili pepper
1 red bell pepper, seeded and cut
 into thin strips
2 tablespoons flaked almonds
 (optional)

Slide the calabrese gently into a large saucepan of briskly boiling salted water and cook, uncovered, at a simmer until it is just tender, 10 to 15 minutes. Drain, and refresh quickly in cold water. Drain, place in a bowl, and chill in the refrigerator.

In a bowl make a vinaigrette dressing with the oil, vinegar, lemon juice, and mustard mixed with a little water, garlic, salt, sugar and hot chili. Beat with a whisk to mix. Pour over the calabrese.

Drop the red bell pepper strips into a saucepan of briskly boiling salted water for 3 minutes. Drain and refresh in cold water. Drain and pat dry. Arrange the pepper strips around the calabrese. Sprinkle the vegetables with the flaked almonds, if liked.

S E R V E S 4.

SQUAB SALAD WITH PINE NUTS

❖   ❖   ❖

This richly flavored, hearty salad could easily be the main course of a light meal. It is the creation of Nicholas Gill, the head chef at Hambleton Hall in Oakham. Nick is an imaginative cook and a perfectionist.

2 squabs
1 medium-size onion, chopped
1 medium-size carrot, scraped
    and sliced
1 celery rib, chopped
4 parsley sprigs
1 garlic clove, chopped
6 peppercorns
Salt
Enough mixed salad greens to
    serve 4, such as lamb's lettuce,
    spinach, endive, radicchio and
    chicory, washed and dried

¼ cup Oil and Vinegar Dressing
    (see Index), made with Dijon
    mustard
1 tablespoon chopped fresh herbs
    (parsley, chives, chervil,
    tarragon)
½ cup pine nuts
Freshly ground pepper
1 teaspoon chopped fresh thyme,
    or ½ teaspoon dried
2 tablespoons vegetable oil

Carefully cut the breasts from the squabs and set them aside. Chop the carcasses of the birds and put them into a large saucepan with the onion, carrot, celery, parsley sprigs, garlic and peppercorns. Add cold water to cover, bring to a boil and simmer, skimming from time to time, for 2 to 3 hours. Strain the stock through a fine sieve, pushing down hard on the solids with the back of a spoon or ladle to extract all the juices. Pour the strained stock into a small saucepan and season very lightly with salt. Boil down vigorously to reduce to caramel consistency. Set aside.

Make the dressing with mustard and stir in the tablespoon of chopped fresh herbs. In a bowl toss the salad greens with the dressing and the pine nuts. Arrange the salad on each of 4 plates and set aside.

Season the squab breasts with salt, pepper and thyme. In a skillet heat the oil and sauté the breasts over fairly high heat for 2 minutes on each side. The meat should remain pink. Slice the breasts very thin lengthwise. Arrange in a fan on top of the salad greens and glaze with the caramelized stock. Serve warm.

S E R V E S 4.

CRAB, GRAPEFRUIT AND CUCUMBER SALAD

❖   ❖   ❖

This simple, fresh-tasting summer salad is typical of the cooking of John Evans, chef-patron of Meadowsweet restaurant at Llanrwst in Wales.

1 hothouse (long) cucumber
1 tablespoon white-wine vinegar
2 or 3 grapefruits, preferably pink, peeled, separated into segments and chilled

Heart of 1 romaine or other crisp lettuce, shredded
½ pound cooked fresh crab meat, picked over for cartilage

Dressing

5 tablespoons heavy cream
2 teaspoons tomato purée
1 tablespoon brandy
4 tablespoons grapefruit juice
Salt, freshly ground pepper

⅛ teaspoon cayenne, or less to taste
Paprika
Parsley sprigs

Score the cucumber with a fork and cut it into thin slices. Put it into a bowl with the vinegar and 2 cups cold water for 2 hours. Drain and pat dry. Arrange the cucumber slices round the edges of 4 chilled salad plates. Arrange a circle of grapefruit segments inside the cucumber. Fill the center of the plate with shredded lettuce. Arrange the crab meat on top of the lettuce.

In a bowl whisk together the cream, tomato purée, brandy, grapefruit juice, salt and pepper to taste, and cayenne. Pour over the crab meat, sprinkle with paprika, and garnish with parsley sprigs.

S E R V E S 4.

AVOCADO SALAD

❖   ❖   ❖

This very pretty salad belies all the criticism of the *nouvelle cuisine* idea of the picture-on-the-plate. It isn't gimmicky or skimpy. It demonstrates the sort of originality that makes the cooking of Murdo MacSween, head chef at Oakley Court, near Windsor, so attractive.

Salad Dressing

3 tablespoons olive oil
1 tablespoon Dijon mustard
1 tablespoon red-wine vinegar

2 tablespoons tomato juice
Salt, freshly ground pepper

Salad

8 radicchio leaves
½ small head of chicory, chopped
10 cooked green beans, cut into
   1-inch lengths

2 tablespoons minced shallots
1 avocado, peeled, pitted and
   sliced lengthwise
2 tablespoons lemon juice

In a bowl combine all the dressing ingredients, whisking thoroughly to blend. Set aside until ready to use.

Arrange the radicchio leaves in a flower shape on 2 salad plates. Toss the chopped chicory and green beans in the dressing and pile them in the center of the radicchio flower. Sprinkle with the shallots. Brush the avocado with the lemon juice and arrange in a fan shape on top of the lettuce and beans. Drizzle with any leftover dressing.

SERVES 2.

SCALLOP SALAD

❖   ❖   ❖

Sam Chalmers, chef-patron of Chimneys restaurant, Long Melford, Suffolk has a lovely way with food. He uses the techniques of classical cooking, then puts things together in a new way. He has had wide experience, including time in foreign countries, which gives his cooking an imaginative touch.

1 recipe Beurre Blanc made with lemon juice (see Index)
2 teaspoons heavy cream

16 large scallops, cut into halves
Fish Stock (see Index)
Mixed salad greens for 4

Make the Beurre Blanc using lemon juice instead of vinegar. When it is done, gradually stir in the cream. Set the sauce in a larger saucepan of warm water to keep it warm without curdling.

Put the scallops into a small heavy saucepan and pour in enough fish stock to cover. Cook over moderate heat for about 1 minute, or until scallops have lost their translucent look. Be careful not to overcook. Drain. Toss with the salad greens and the Beurre Blanc. Serve immediately.

SERVES 4.

HOT SCALLOP SALAD

❖　　　❖　　　❖

I met Raymond Duthie when he was head chef at the Royal Crescent Hotel, before he left and Michael Croft went there. I was very impressed by his cooking and by his meticulous approach to his craft. He sticks to traditional methods of preparation, but does not hesitate to create new dishes when inspiration seizes him. This salad could not be simpler or more delicious.

Mixed salad greens: radicchio,
　escarole, watercress and endive
¼ cup olive oil
16 large scallops, sliced
2 tablespoons minced shallots
¼ pound button mushrooms

1 celery rib, chopped fine
1 tablespoon dry sherry wine
1 tablespoon sherry vinegar
Salt, freshly ground pepper
½ cup minced parsley
½ cup minced chervil

Wash and dry the salad greens and tear them into bite-size bits. Arrange the salad greens around the edge of a large platter.

Heat the olive oil in a large heavy skillet. Add the scallops, shallots, mushrooms and celery and sauté over high heat, stirring constantly, for 30 seconds. Add the sherry and stir, then add the vinegar, stir, and season to taste with salt and pepper. Heap the mixture into the middle of the platter and sprinkle with chopped parsley and chervil. Serve immediately.

SERVES 4.

POULTRY AND FEATHERED GAME

POULTRY IS deservedly popular. It is versatile, inexpensive and always available, as well as being nutritionally desirable in these health-conscious days. British chefs have met the challenge to create new dishes for poultry with enthusiasm. They have developed delectable recipes for both chicken and duckling, some elegant and suitable for parties, some very simple and quick to cook for put-together-in-a-hurry meals.

Game has always been a great favorite in Britain. Chefs have created new and attractive recipes for pigeon (squab), grouse, quail and pheasant.

In the meat business a chicken breast is the entire breast portion of the bird but for most of us a skinned and boned chicken breast is a half breast and I have used this term throughout. It is what the French call a *suprême*. Most butchers and super-markets sell the breasts ready prepared often with skin still on. This is easy to remove.

Most ducklings weigh 4½ to 5 pounds and are sold frozen. If fresh birds are available use them, otherwise simply defrost the frozen birds. I find them very satisfactory.

CHICKEN AND VEGETABLE TERRINE

❖　　　❖　　　❖

Kenneth Bell, chef-patron of Thornbury Castle, has created the perfect summer luncheon dish in this terrine. It is delicious and healthy too. Serve with a Bordeaux.

1 pound chicken breasts, skinned
　and boned
3¾ cups heavy cream, chilled
Salt, freshly ground white pepper
Butter
½ pound young zucchini,
　trimmed and cut into
　lengthwise strips

½ pound baby carrots, scraped
　and cut into lengthwise strips
½ pound calabrese, trimmed and
　separated into small sprigs
2 ounces snow peas, trimmed
¼ pound thin small green beans,
　trimmed

Chop the chicken breasts and purée in a blender or food processor. Gradually pour in the cream with the machine running and blend for 30 seconds, or long enough to mix thoroughly. Transfer to a bowl and season to taste with salt and pepper. Chill in the refrigerator for about 15 minutes.

Butter the bottom and sides of a terrine about 10 inches long by 4 inches wide and put a thin layer of the chicken mixture on the bottom. Cook the vegetables separately in briskly boiling salted water; the time will depend on the vegetables. They should be tender but still crunchy. Drain, refresh in cold water and drain again thoroughly, chilling them for a few minutes if necessary.

Make a layer of the zucchini on top of the chicken, cover with a layer of chicken mixture, top with the carrot strips, cover with chicken mixture, and top with the calabrese sprigs. Cover the calabrese with chicken and top with snow peas. Add more chicken and cover with the beans. Finish with a layer of chicken mixture. Set the terrine in a baking pan and pour in hot water to come about halfway up the terrine. Cover the terrine with aluminum foil and cook in a preheated moderate oven (350°F.) for 35 to 45 minutes. It will feel firm to the touch when cooked. Cool, then chill in the refrigerator for at least 4 hours.

Unmold and slice. Serve with a chilled light tomato sauce.

S E R V E S 6.

Tomato Sauce

4 medium-size tomatoes, about 1   Salt, freshly ground pepper
    pound, peeled, seeded and   1 tablespoon tomato paste
    chopped

Purée the tomatoes in a food processor or blender with salt and pepper
to taste. Add the tomato paste. Pour into a bowl and chill. Serve
with the sliced terrine.

M A K E S about 1½ cups.

MELON RAJ

❖   ❖   ❖

Michael Collom, head chef at the Priory Hotel in Bath, Avon,
likes to experience the cooking of other countries and is sometimes
inspired by what he finds. He calls this Melon Raj because of the
curry powder, but the real inspiration is his own. Serve with a Côte
du Rhône.

2 small ripe melons such as   ¼ pound black grapes, halved
    honeydew or Ogen   and pitted
2 cooked chicken breasts, skinned   ¼ pound seedless green grapes,
    and boned   halved
½ cup Mayonnaise (see Index)   Garnish: crushed ice, parsley
Pinch of curry powder, or to   sprigs
    taste

Halve the melons and scrape out the seeds. Trim the base so the melon
halves sit firmly. Cut the chicken into ½-inch cubes and fill the melon
halves with the chicken. Mix the mayonnaise with the curry powder
and coat the chicken with it. Alternate the black and white grapes
around the edge of each melon half and place a parsley sprig in the
middle. Serve on a bed of crushed ice, if liked.

S E R V E S 4.

CHICKEN WITH AVOCADO

❖   ❖   ❖

This simple and subtly flavored chicken dish takes little more than half an hour to cook. It is the creation of Sam Chalmers, who was chef-patron of Le Talbooth Restaurant at Dedham in Essex, and now runs Chimneys restaurant at Long Melford in Suffolk. Serve with a red Bordeaux.

4 chicken breasts, skinned and   *1 large ripe avocado*
  boned   *2 tablespoons dry sherry wine*
Salt, freshly ground pepper   *½ cup heavy cream, or Fresh*
4 tablespoons minced shallots   *White Cheese (see Index)*
4 tablespoons butter

Season the chicken breasts with salt and pepper. Sauté the shallots in a medium-size skillet in 2 tablespoons of the butter. Add the chicken breasts, cover and sauté over low heat, turning once, until chicken is tender but not browned, about 8 minutes.

While the chicken is cooking peel and halve the avocado. Remove and discard the pit. Cut 1 half into thin slices. In a bowl, mash the other half.

When the chicken breasts are cooked, remove from the skillet, cover, and keep warm. Pour the sherry into the skillet and bring to a simmer, stirring. Add the cream, simmer for 1 to 2 minutes, season with salt and pepper, and stir in the mashed avocado. Beat in remaining butter. Remove from the heat.

Arrange the chicken breasts on 4 heated plates, mask with the avocado sauce, and garnish with slices of avocado.

S E R V E S 4.

BREAST OF CHICKEN WITH MANGO, GINGER AND CORIANDER SAUCE

❖　　　❖　　　❖

Stanley Matthews, the young head chef at the Feathers Hotel in Woodstock, Oxfordshire, always wanted to be a chef. His earliest memories of learning to cook are of licking his mother's wooden spoons to find out what things tasted like. He has asked questions ever since. He loves his work and is dedicated to the idea of giving his guests (for that is how he thinks of them) well-balanced, nutritious and exciting food. This chicken breast dish meets his requirements, and is also extremely simple to cook. Serve with a Beaujolais.

2 chicken breasts, skinned and boned	1 cup thin-sliced or chopped fresh mango
Salt, freshly ground pepper	1 tablespoon minced fresh coriander
2 tablespoons butter	
1 teaspoon grated fresh gingerroot	4 tablespoons heavy cream

Season the chicken breasts with salt and pepper. Heat the butter in a flameproof casserole and add the chicken breasts, turning them in the butter. Bake in a preheated moderately hot oven (400°F.) for about 10 minutes, or until they are springy to the touch. Remove breasts from the casserole, cover, and keep warm.

Pour off any excess fat from the casserole. Add the gingerroot, mango and coriander, stir to mix, and simmer on top of the stove for 1 minute. Add the cream, stir, and cook for a minute or so longer to reduce the sauce slightly and blend the flavors. Serve with boiled new potatoes and broccoli or green beans.

S E R V E S 2.

CHICKEN BREASTS
STUFFED WITH CRAB

❖   ❖   ❖

This recipe developed by Christopher Grist at Great Fosters at Egham in Surrey could hardly be less like the recipes of Francis Coulson or Baba Hine, but it is just as easy to cook and just as delicious to eat. Serve with a Beaujolais.

6 chicken breasts, skinned and
   boned
¾ pound fresh or frozen crab
   meat, picked over to remove
   any cartilage
Salt, freshly ground pepper

3 tablespoons butter
1 recipe Béarnaise Sauce (see
   Index)
Garnish: watercress sprigs and 12
   asparagus tips (optional)

Trim the chicken breasts and reserve small pieces for another use. Flatten the breasts and top with the crab meat but without going to the edge of the breasts. Season with salt and pepper. Roll up chicken gently and secure with toothpicks. In a large heavy skillet that will hold all the chicken breasts comfortably, melt the butter. Add the stuffed chicken breasts, turning to coat them with the butter. Cook over low heat, turning once or twice, until the chicken is done, about 8 minutes, without letting it color. Lift out the chicken breasts onto the tray of a broiler, mask with the béarnaise sauce, and glaze quickly under a preheated broiler until they are golden brown.

Serve garnished with watercress sprigs and, if liked, the asparagus tips. Accompany with a green salad.

S E R V E S 6.

CHICKEN BREASTS WITH GINGER
STUFFING AND ORANGE SAUCE

❖   ❖   ❖

David Adlard, chef-patron of Adlard's at Wymondham in Norfolk, spent years in industry before cooking claimed him. Now, after getting his training in a number of kitchens, he has his own restaurant. He bases his cuisine in the restaurant on seasonal foods, as many as possible available locally, and on foods he gathers from the wild, assisted by his American fiancée who runs the restaurant while he cooks. The result is food out of the ordinary. Serve with a Beaujolais.

2 cups minced mushrooms	Salt, freshly ground pepper
1 tablespoon minced shallot	6 chicken breasts, skinned and
1 tablespoon grated fresh	boned
gingerroot	1 cup Chicken Stock (see Index)

Orange Sauce

Grated rind of 2 oranges	1 cup heavy cream, or Fresh
⅔ cup orange juice	White Cheese (see Index)
1 tablespoon sugar	Garnish: 1 orange, peeled and
3 tablespoons white-wine vinegar	separated into segments
2 cups Chicken Stock (see Index)	

Put the mushrooms into a nonstick skillet and cook over low heat until the moisture has evaporated. Take out and set aside in a bowl. Add the shallot and cook for 2 minutes. Add the gingerroot and cook for 2 minutes longer. Return the mushrooms to the skillet, stir to mix, and season with salt and pepper. Cool. When the mixture has cooled, cut a slit in each of the chicken breasts and stuff with the mixture. Fasten with a toothpick.

Put the grated orange rind into a heavy saucepan with the orange juice and the sugar and simmer until it has reduced to a light caramel syrup. Add the vinegar and simmer until the caramel has dissolved and the mixture is syrupy. Stir in 2 cups chicken stock and simmer, uncovered, until reduced to 1 cup. Add the cream, season to taste with salt and pepper, and simmer over very low heat for 10 minutes. If using fresh white cheese, just heat it through.

Pour the cup of chicken stock into a large baking pan that will hold the chicken breasts comfortably. Bring to a simmer. Arrange the breasts, seasoned with salt and pepper, in the pan and cover. Bake in a preheated moderate oven (350°F.) for 10 to 12 minutes, or until done. Drain.

Arrange 1 breast on each of 6 heated plates and cover with the sauce. Garnish with orange segments. Serve with rice.

S E R V E S 6.

CHICKEN BREASTS WITH LEEKS AND GINGER

❖   ❖   ❖

Fresh gingerroot and soy sauce transform the chicken breasts into something out of the ordinary in this easy-to-cook dish, the invention of Simon Collins, head chef of Bishopstrow House, at Warminster in Wiltshire. Serve with a Côte du Rhône.

6 leeks, thoroughly washed, white part cut into julienne strips, green part reserved for sauce
1 cup julienne strips of fresh gingerroot

4 chicken breasts, skinned and boned
Salt, freshly ground pepper
1 cup Chicken Stock (see Index)

Sauce

1 medium-size onion, chopped
¼ pound (1 stick) unsalted butter
½ cup dry sherry wine
6 cups unsalted Chicken Stock (see Index)

2 tablespoons light soy sauce
½ cup Sauce Demi-glace (see Index)

Blanch the julienne of leek and ¼ cup of the gingerroot julienne in briskly boiling water for 1 minute. (Reserve remaining gingerroot for the sauce.) Drain and refresh in cold water. Drain thoroughly. Season the chicken breasts with salt and pepper and cut a pocket in each one. Stuff with the julienne of leek and gingerroot and secure with a toothpick. Set aside.

In a saucepan cook the reserved green part of the leeks, chopped, reserved ¼ cup gingerroot and the onion in 2 tablespoons of the butter over low heat until vegetables are soft. Add the sherry and simmer until the liquid is reduced by half. Add the stock and simmer until it is reduced to 1 cup. Strain through a fine sieve. Return the sauce to the pan, add soy sauce and demi-glace, and set aside.

In a skillet poach the chicken breasts in the cup of chicken stock, covered, over very low heat for about 8 minutes, or until springy when pressed with a finger. Be careful not to overcook. To finish the sauce, bring it to a boil, lower the heat, and whisk in the rest of the butter, cut into bits.

Place a chicken breast on each of 4 heated plates and mask with the sauce. Serve with rice pilaf garnished with toasted slivered almonds.

SERVES 4.

CHICKEN BREASTS "FRANÇOIS" WITH JUNIPER BERRY SAUCE

❖   ❖   ❖

Francis Coulson, chef-patron of Sharrow Bay hotel, Lake Ullswater, Cumbria, one of the forerunners of the renaissance of British cooking, is continuingly inventive. This dish makes a splendid main course, which can be prepared ahead of time with little fuss and does not keep the cook in the kitchen after the guests arrive, making it very special for entertaining. Serve with a Côte de Nuits or Burgundy.

8 chicken breasts, skinned and boned
2 large egg whites
Salt, freshly ground pepper
1 cup heavy cream, or Fresh White Cheese (see Index)
2 tablespoons minced mixed fresh herbs such as chervil, mint, thyme, marjoram, tarragon, parsley

1½ pounds Puff Pastry (see Index)
1 egg yolk

Juniper Berry Sauce

⅓ cup juniper berries
3 tablespoons butter
3 tablespoons all-purpose flour
2 cups Chicken Stock (see Index)
½ cup dry cider

½ cup heavy cream, or Fresh White Cheese (see Index)
Garnish: 1 cup seedless white grapes, halved

Set aside six of the breasts. Chop remaining 2 breasts and purée them in a blender or food processor. Add the egg whites and process until thoroughly mixed and smooth. Season with salt and pepper. Add the

(recipe continues)

cream gradually with the machine running and process for 30 seconds longer. Add the herbs and process only long enough to mix. Transfer the mousseline to a bowl and chill in the refrigerator for 30 minutes.

Using a sharp pointed knife, cut a lengthwise pocket in each of the 6 breasts and stuff with the mousseline. Chill again in the refrigerator.

Roll out the pastry to about ⅛-inch thickness and cut into 6 rectangles large enough to enclose the chicken breasts. Place a breast on each piece of pastry. Beat the egg yolk with 1 teaspoon water; using a pastry brush, paint the edges of the pastry, then fold it over to cover the breast, sealing well. Use a knife or the fingers to decorate the edge and, if necessary, trim it neatly. Brush the tops with the egg wash. The pastry can be refrigerated until ready to bake. When ready to cook arrange the pastry on a lightly oiled baking sheet. Bake on the middle shelf of a preheated moderate oven (350°F.) for 35 minutes, or until golden.

While the pastry is baking make the sauce, or make it ahead of time. In a spice, nut or coffee grinder pulverize the juniper berries and put them into a small bowl. In a medium-size saucepan heat the butter. Stir in the flour and cook, stirring with a wooden spoon, over low heat for 1 minute without letting the mixture color. Off the heat stir in the chicken stock and cider until the mixture is smooth. Return to the heat and cook for 10 minutes, stirring from time to time. Stir in the juniper berries and simmer for 5 minutes longer. Strain through a fine sieve into a bowl. Rinse out and dry the saucepan. Return the sauce to the pan, add the cream, season to taste with salt and pepper, and heat the sauce through.

To serve pour the sauce on each of 6 warmed plates and put a chicken breast on top. Garnish with a few of the seedless white grape halves. Serve with a green salad.

S E R V E S 6.

STUFFED CHICKEN BREASTS WITH TARRAGON AND SAFFRON SAUCE

❖   ❖   ❖

Baba Hine, chef-patronne of Corse Lawn House in the little village of Corse Lawn in Hereford and Worcester, has her own version of chicken with tarragon. It is very different from Terry Boswell's but no less delicious though it is a little more elaborate. It would make a very elegant dish for a party. Serve with a Côte du Rhône.

5 chicken breasts, skinned and
   boned
3 large egg whites
Salt, freshly ground pepper
⅛ teaspoon freshly grated nutmeg

⅓ cup heavy cream
Vegetable oil
½ cup dry white wine
½ cup Chicken Stock (see Index)

Sauce

⅓ cup heavy cream
⅛ teaspoon crumbled saffron

1 tablespoon minced fresh
   tarragon leaves

Set aside four of the chicken breasts. Chop remaining breast and purée it in a blender or food processor. With the machine running, add the egg whites and process until smooth. Season with salt and pepper and nutmeg. Add the cream and process for 30 seconds longer. Chill the mousseline in the refrigerator for 15 minutes.

With a sharp knife cut a lengthwise pocket in each of the 4 chicken breasts and fill it with the mousseline. Cut 4 sheets of aluminum foil 8 inches square. Lightly brush the foil with vegetable oil and place a chicken breast in the center of each one. Pour 2 tablespoons each of wine and stock over the chicken. Wrap the breasts in the foil, twisting it to seal it thoroughly. Place the packages on a lightly oiled baking sheet and bake in a preheated moderately hot oven (400°F) for 20 minutes.

Unwrap the packages and lift the chicken breasts onto a dish. Cover and keep warm in the turned-off oven with the door slightly ajar. Carefully pour the liquid in the packages into a saucepan. Add the cream, saffron and tarragon and reduce over brisk heat until the sauce coats a spoon.

Pour the sauce onto each of 4 heated plates, put a chicken breast on each plate and serve immediately, with rice, noodles or new potatoes, and a green vegetable or a green salad.

S E R V E S 4.

CHICKEN BREASTS WITH TARRAGON

❖   ❖   ❖

Thérèse (Terry) Boswell, chef-patronne of Combe House Hotel, at Gittisham in Devon, has her own, very attractive version of the classic *poulet à l'estragon*. It is a very quick dish made with chicken breasts but sometimes, for her family when she is at home, she cooks a whole chicken which takes about 1½ hours over low heat on top of the stove. For a summer lunch she sometimes bones the chicken, chops it, mixes it with the sauce, piles it into *vol-au-vent* cases, and serves it with a fresh green salad. Serve with a Côte du Rhône.

2 tablespoons butter	Salt, freshly ground pepper
1 tablespoon vegetable oil	¼ cup chopped fresh tarragon
1 medium-size onion, chopped fine	Grated rind of 2 lemons
2 garlic cloves, minced	4 tablespoons lemon juice
2 cups mushrooms, chopped	½ cup light cream
4 chicken breasts, skinned and boned	½ cup Chicken Stock (see Index), if needed

Heat the butter and oil in a flameproof casserole. Add the onion, garlic and mushrooms and cook, covered, over moderate heat for 5 minutes. Season the chicken breasts with salt and pepper and add them to the casserole; turn them over to coat them with the butter and oil mixture. Add the tarragon, grated lemon rind and lemon juice. Cover the casserole with aluminum foil and the lid and simmer over low heat for 15 minutes; or cook in a preheated moderately hot oven (400°F.) for 12 minutes, or until the chicken is done. Lift out the chicken breasts, cover, and keep warm. Pour the cream into the casserole and simmer, uncovered, until the sauce is lightly thickened. There should be about 1 cup. If the liquid is too scanty, add a little chicken stock. Season to taste with salt and pepper.

Put a chicken breast on each of 4 heated plates. Pour any liquid that has accumulated on the plate into the casserole; stir to mix. Pour the sauce over the chicken breasts. Serve with noodles or new potatoes. If liked the sauce may be puréed in a blender or food processor.

S E R V E S 4.

CHICKEN BREASTS, JACQUELINE

❖   ❖   ❖

Allan Holland, chef-patron of Mallory Court, Leamington Spa, near Stratford-upon-Avon in Warwickshire, has created a lovely contrast of flavors in this dish. The delicate chicken breast contrasts with the richness of duckling mousse, which can be prepared ahead of time. The whole dish can be assembled quickly as the chicken breasts take only about 10 minutes. The sauce is also quickly made. It is worth the effort for a delectable meal. Serve with a Margaux.

½ pound raw, boneless and
  skinless duckling meat
1 large egg white, lightly beaten
1 cup chilled heavy cream, lightly
  whipped

Salt, freshly ground white pepper
6 chicken breasts, skinned and
  boned, each 6 to 7 ounces
Butter
2 cups Chicken Stock (see Index)

Sauce

½ cup Tawny Port wine
1 cup heavy cream, or Fresh
  White Cheese (see Index)
Lemon juice

2 tablespoons butter, cut into bits
½ cup toasted flaked almonds
6 thin slices of truffle (optional)
Sprigs of fresh chervil or parsley

To make the mousse, chop the duckling meat coarse and purée it in a blender or food processor. With the machine running, slowly pour in the egg white and process until the mixture is smooth and well blended. Scrape the mixture into a bowl and refrigerate for 1 hour. Set the bowl in a larger bowl filled with ice and, using a wooden spoon, gradually beat in the whipped cream. Season with salt and pepper and return the mousse to the refrigerator.

Using a very sharp knife, make a lengthwise slit in the chicken breasts to make a pocket. Fill with the duck mousse. Do not overfill as the mousse expands during cooking. Place the stuffed chicken breasts in a buttered skillet large enough to hold them all in a single layer. Pour in the chicken stock. Cover the pan and simmer over low heat for 8 to 10 minutes, or until the breasts are just cooked. Remove the breasts from the skillet to a dish, cover, and keep warm while making the sauce.

Pour the Port into the skillet and boil it over high heat until Port

(recipe continues)

and stock are very reduced and syrupy. Add the cream and continue to simmer over low heat until the sauce has a coating consistency. Remove from the heat and add lemon juice and salt and pepper to taste. Beat in the butter, and keep the sauce warm.

Arrange the chicken breasts on 6 heated plates and coat with the sauce. Sprinkle with almonds and garnish with truffle if using. Surround with sprigs of chervil or parsley.

S E R V E S 6.

CHICKEN BREASTS STUFFED WITH VEAL SWEETBREADS

❖   ❖   ❖

This elegant creation comes from Gunther Schlender, the head chef at Rue St. Jacques restaurant in London. His aim is to provide interesting dishes made from the best ingredients, beautifully presented. His cooking, he says, is modern cuisine, not *nouvelle*. Serve with a Côte de Beaune.

5 chicken breasts, skinned and
    boned
Salt, freshly ground pepper
1 egg white
½ cup heavy cream

½ pound veal sweetbreads,
    cooked
½ pound spinach
½ cup Chicken Stock (see Index)

Sauce

6 tablespoons butter
2 tablespoons minced shallots
1 teaspoon fine-diced fresh hot
    red chili pepper
1 teaspoon fine-diced sweet red
    bell pepper

½ cup dry white wine
1 teaspoon tomato purée
2 cups heavy cream
Garnish: diced red bell pepper

Set aside one of the chicken breasts. Remove the fillets from the 4 remaining breasts. Flatten both the breasts and the fillets. Season with salt and pepper and set aside. Chop the reserved breast and purée it in a blender or food processor. Put it into a bowl and season with salt and pepper. Beat in the egg white. Gradually beat in the cream until the mixture is firm. Separate the sweetbread into small pieces. Make sure all skin and gristle is removed. Rinse and dry the spinach and tear it into small pieces. Fold the sweetbread pieces and spinach into the chicken mixture. Make a layer of the mousse on top of the chicken breasts but not right to the edge. Cover the filling with the flattened fillet and fold so that all the filling is covered. Wrap the stuffed chicken breasts in buttered aluminum foil. Arrange in a baking pan with the chicken stock. Bake in a preheated moderate oven (375°F.) for 15 to 20 minutes, or until the breasts feel springy to the touch. Keep warm.

While the breasts are cooking make the sauce. In a saucepan heat 2 tablespoons of the butter and cook the shallots over very low heat until they are soft. Add the chili and bell pepper and cook for 2 minutes longer. Add the white wine and tomato purée and simmer, uncovered, until the mixture is reduced to ¼ cup. Pour in the cream and continue to simmer until the sauce reaches coating consistency. Season to taste with salt and pepper and beat in remaining butter, cut into bits.

To serve, cut the breasts into thick slices and arrange each breast in a fan shape on a heated plate. Pour the sauce around each of the breasts and garnish with diced red pepper. If preferred, the breasts can be left whole and simply placed on 4 heated plates with the sauce.

S E R V E S 4.

CHICKEN BREASTS "DUICH"

❖   ❖   ❖

Denis Woodtli, head chef at Lochalsh Hotel on the Kyle of Lochalsh in Scotland, gets magnificent crayfish as well as other shellfish and fish. Jumbo prawns make a good substitute for the crayfish he uses in this recipe. The combination of chicken breast and shellfish is delicious. Serve with a Côte Chalonnaise.

4 crayfish or jumbo shrimps
2 chicken breasts, skinned and
    boned
¼ pound (1 stick) butter
4 tablespoons tomato purée
¼ cup brandy

1 cup heavy cream, or Fresh
    White Cheese (see Index)
Salt, freshly ground pepper
½ cup sliced mushrooms
½ cup medium-dry sherry wine
Garnish: parsley sprigs

Shell the crayfish or jumbo shrimps and set the heads aside. Cut a pocket in the chicken breasts and stuff with the shellfish. In a skillet heat half of the butter, add the shellfish heads, and sauté over moderately high heat for 1 or 2 minutes. Add the tomato purée, stir, then add the brandy and ignite it. Add half of the cream immediately and simmer over low heat until it has thickened. Season to taste with salt and pepper. Strain the sauce into a bowl, pressing down on the shellfish heads to extract all the juices.

Heat the rest of the butter in a skillet and sauté the chicken breasts over moderate heat, turning 2 or 3 times, until they are cooked through but not browned, about 8 minutes. Remove the chicken breasts, cover, and keep warm. Add the mushrooms and sherry to the skillet and cook for 3 or 4 minutes. Add remaining cream, season with salt and pepper, and simmer until the sauce is thickened.

To serve, warm the prawn sauce and pour it onto each of 2 heated plates. Place a chicken breast on each plate and cover with the mushroom sauce. Garnish with a parsley sprig.

S E R V E S 2.

BREAST OF DUCK WITH ORANGES IN A HONEY SAUCE

❖   ❖   ❖

This is one of the dishes I enjoyed when Willie MacPherson was head chef at The Feathers in Woodstock, Oxfordshire. It makes a very attractive dinner for two and takes little time to cook as the duck breast can be removed from the carcass of the duck and boned ahead of time. I suggest you do not serve wine with this dish.

1 whole duck breast, boned and halved	1 tablespoon brandy
Salt, freshly ground pepper	1 tablespoon clear honey
Flour	½ cup orange juice
2 tablespoons butter	1 cup Sauce Demi-glace (see Index)
1 tablespoon vegetable oil	1 orange, peeled and sectioned
1 shallot, chopped fine	¼ cup sliced almonds, toasted

Season the 2 duck breast halves with salt and pepper and dredge lightly with flour, shaking to remove excess flour. Heat the butter and oil in a heavy skillet and sauté the breasts until they are tender but still pink inside, about 4 minutes a side, or longer if better cooked duck is preferred. Lift out of the skillet onto a warm plate, cover, and keep warm.

Add the shallot to the skillet and sauté until soft but not browned. Add the brandy and ignite it. Add the honey, orange juice and demi-glace and simmer until the sauce reduces to coating consistency. Season with salt and pepper. Add the orange sections in the last few minutes of cooking.

To serve, cut each duck breast diagonally into 4 slices and arrange on 2 heated plates. Lift out the orange sections and arrange round the duck breast, then pour the sauce over and around them. Sprinkle with the almonds and serve. Serve with rice and a green salad.

S E R V E S 2.

N O T E : To toast almonds, put them on a baking pan in a preheated moderate oven (350°F.) for 10 minutes.

DUCKLING BREAST WITH BRUSSELS SPROUT PURÉE

❖ ❖ ❖

Michael Croft has a natural elegance in the way he deals with food, which is appropriate for the head chef of the Royal Crescent Hotel in Bath, itself the very essence of modern Georgian elegance. All the same, I was surprised by the flavor of the Brussels sprout purée. The vegetable emerges transformed. Serve with a Côte de Beaune.

1 whole duckling breast, boned
  and halved with skin left on,
  each half about 6 ounces
5 tablespoons butter

Salt, freshly ground pepper
1 cup Game Stock (see Index),
  or duck or chicken stock

Marinade

1 medium-size carrot, chopped
  fine
1 medium-size onion, chopped
  fine
3 tablespoons chopped shallots
1 parsley sprig
1 thyme sprig

1 bay leaf
1 teaspoon black peppercorns
4 tablespoons white-wine vinegar
¾ cup dry white wine
4 tablespoons olive or vegetable
  oil
½ teaspoon salt

Brussels Sprout Purée

1 pound Brussels sprouts,
  trimmed
2 tablespoons heavy cream

1 tablespoon butter
2 tartlet shells, made from Short-
  Crust Pastry (see Index)

Put the duckling breast halves in a bowl large enough to hold them comfortably. Combine all the ingredients for the marinade and pour them over the duckling breasts. Refrigerate for 24 hours, turning once or twice.

When ready to cook, lift the breasts out of the marinade and pat them dry with paper towels. Reserve the marinade. In a heavy skillet heat 2 tablespoons of the butter and sauté the breasts over moderate heat, turning once, until they are springy to the touch but still pink inside, about 8 minutes in all. Pour off and discard excess fat from the skillet. Put the breasts on a plate, cover, and keep warm.

Pour 1 cup of the marinade, including vegetables, into the skillet and simmer, uncovered, until liquid is reduced to 2 tablespoons. Add the game stock and bring to a boil. Simmer to reduce by half. Skim and strain. Return the sauce to the skillet and beat in remaining butter, bit by bit. Taste for seasoning, add salt and pepper if necessary, and keep warm.

For the Brussels sprout purée have ready a large saucepan filled with briskly boiling salted water. Add the sprouts, bring back to a boil over fairly high heat, then reduce the heat and cook the sprouts, uncovered, at a gentle simmer for 10 to 12 minutes, or until tender. If the sprouts are very small they will take only about 8 minutes. Drain and put into a blender or food processor with the cream and butter and purée until smooth. Transfer to a small saucepan, season with salt and pepper, and heat through. Have ready the tartlet shells. Fill them with the purée and keep warm.

To serve, remove the fat from the duck breasts and cut it into very fine julienne strips. Crisp it under a preheated broiler and set it aside. If preferred, discard the skin, or leave it on the duckling and crisp it under the broiler. Cut the breasts into slices and arrange them in a fan shape on 2 heated plates, or leave whole. Surround with the sauce and garnish with a tartlet of the sprout purée. If using the julienne of duck fat, garnish the breast with it.

S E R V E S 2.

BREAST OF DUCK WITH BLACKBERRIES AND DUCK LIVER TARTLET

❖   ❖   ❖

There is just enough tartness in the blackberries to make a contrast with the rich duck flavor, while the garnish of duck liver tartlet provides another sort of contrast. Chris Oakes, head chef at the Castle Hotel in Taunton, Somerset, put it all together in a felicitous manner. Serve with a Chianti.

1 duckling, 4½ to 5 pounds, if frozen thoroughly defrosted	1 tablespoon heavy cream
Salt, freshly ground pepper	2 tartlet shells made of Short-Crust Pastry (see Index), baked blind
2 tablespoons butter	
1 cup fresh ripe blackberries	1 cup duck stock
Sugar, if necessary	2 sprigs of lemon thyme, or any fresh herb
Liver from duck	
1 egg yolk	

Remove the breast from the duckling and skin and bone it, or have the butcher do it. Cut the breast into halves. Reserve the rest of the carcass for another meal. Season the breasts with salt and pepper. Heat the butter in a skillet just large enough to hold the breasts and sauté them for 3 to 4 minutes on each side. They should remain pink. Remove the breasts from the skillet to a heated plate, cover, and keep warm.

Put the blackberries in a small saucepan with a little water. If they are very tart, add a little sugar. Warm them through over low heat for 3 to 4 minutes. Drain and keep warm.

Chop the duck liver and put into a blender or food processor with the egg yolk, cream and seasoning to taste; reduce to a purée. Pour the mixture into the 2 tartlet shells and bake in a preheated moderately hot oven (400°F.) for 3 to 4 minutes, or until lightly set. Pour the duck stock into a small saucepan and bring it to a boil over fairly brisk heat; simmer until the stock is reduced by half.

Pour the reduced duck stock onto 2 heated plates. Cut each breast half into 4 lengthwise slices and arrange them on the plate in the shape of a fan, or leave in one piece if preferred. Arrange the blackberries around the duck and put the tartlets at the bottom of each plate. Put a sprig of lemon thyme or other herb at the top.

S E R V E S 2.

TWO DUCKLINGS WITH TWO SAUCES

❖   ❖   ❖

This is another of the poultry recipes created by Francis Coulson, chef-patron of Sharrow Bay hotel at Pooley Bridge, Lake Ullswater, Cumbria. It is complicated and rather time-consuming, not suitable for the cook in a hurry but very worth cooking for a special occasion. Serve with a Côte de Beaune.

2 ducklings, each 4½ pounds, if frozen thoroughly defrosted
Salt, freshly ground pepper
1 cup mixed chopped celery, carrot and leek
Peel from 1 orange, chopped
Peel from 1 lemon, chopped
6 cups Chicken Stock (see Index)
1 tablespoon honey
2 large egg whites
½ cup heavy cream
Butter for molds

First Sauce

1 tablespoon flour
½ cup Tawny Port or dry red wine
½ cup chopped orange segments, or chopped pineapple, or red currants (optional)

Second Sauce

5 tablespoons butter
½ medium-size onion, chopped fine
¼ cup all-purpose flour
½ cup dry white wine
½ cup ground peeled hazelnuts (filberts)
2 bay leaves
1 cup heavy cream

(recipe continues)

Remove the legs from the ducklings and set them aside. Season the rest of the ducklings with salt and pepper and put into a baking pan with the mixed vegetables, orange and lemon peel and 1 cup of the chicken stock. Roast in a preheated moderate oven (350°F.) for 1 hour and 15 to 20 minutes. Remove from the oven and drizzle the honey over the duckling breasts. Return to the oven for 5 minutes, taking care the coating does not burn. Remove ducklings from the oven and let stand for a few minutes. Remove the breasts, halve, cover, and keep warm. Reserve the rest of the carcass for stock.

Pour off excess fat from the baking pan and stir in the flour to make the first sauce. Stir and cook on top of the stove for 1 or 2 minutes, then add the Port or dry red wine and 1 cup of the chicken stock. Simmer over low heat until the sauce has reduced to 1 cup. Season with salt and pepper and strain into a small saucepan. Stir in the chopped fruit, if liked, and set aside.

While the duckling breasts are roasting, bone the legs, chop the meat, then purée in a blender or food processor. With the machine running, add the egg whites and process until the mixture is very light and smooth. Scrape the mixture into a bowl and chill for 15 minutes. Set it over a bowl of ice and gradually beat in the ½ cup heavy cream. Butter four 1-cup soufflé or similar molds and fill with the mixture. Set in a baking pan filled with hot water and cover with foil. Bake in a preheated moderate oven (350°F.) for about 15 minutes, or until firm. Keep warm.

Make the second sauce. In a saucepan heat the butter and sauté the onion until soft but not browned. Stir in the flour and cook, stirring, over low heat for 2 to 3 minutes without letting the mixture color. Off the heat, stir in the wine and 4 cups chicken stock. Return the mixture to the heat and add the ground nuts and bay leaves. Simmer over low heat for 15 minutes. Strain the sauce and return it to the saucepan. Season to taste with salt and pepper and add the cream. If the sauce is too thin, simmer uncovered to reduce it a little.

To serve place 1 duckling breast half on each of 4 heated plates and mask with the first sauce. Unmold the mousses and coat with the second sauce. Serve with green vegetables and if liked a mixed fruit compote.

S E R V E S 4.

DUCKLING BREAST WITH MANGO AND LIME

❖   ❖   ❖

I first met John Hornsby when he was *sous-chef* to Anton Mosimann at the Dorchester in London, and later when he was head chef at the Castle Hotel in Taunton, Somerset. He is now in the United States. This recipe reflects his interest in using untraditional foods in the context of traditional British cooking. It works very well. I suggest that you skip wine with this dish.

1 duckling, 5 pounds, if frozen thoroughly defrosted	3 or 4 tablespoons lime juice
2 cups Chicken Stock (see Index)	2 tablespoons brown sugar
1 teaspoon tomato purée	½ cup dry white wine
1 large ripe mango	Salt, freshly ground pepper
Grated rind of 1 lime	2 tablespoons butter, melted

Remove the breasts from the duckling and skin and bone them. Set aside. Remove the legs and keep them for another meal. Chop the carcass roughly and put into a baking pan with the chicken stock and tomato purée. Brown in a preheated moderate oven (375°F.), basting from time to time until the carcass is browned. Strain, pressing down hard on the bones to extract all the juices. Set aside.

Peel the mango. Using a very sharp knife, cut down each side of the seed to get 2 thick slices. Dice half of the mango. Cut the other half into thin lengthwise slices. In a bowl mix the diced mango with the grated lime rind. In a small saucepan combine the lime juice, brown sugar and dry white wine and simmer, uncovered, to reduce by half. Add the stock from the duckling carcass and simmer to reduce to ½ cup. Add the diced mango and lime rind about halfway through the cooking. Set aside.

Season the duckling breasts with salt and pepper and brush generously with the melted butter. Broil under a preheated broiler for 2 minutes on each side, keeping them pink. Cut them into thin lengthwise slices. Put the mango slices in between the duckling slices. There will not be an equal number of slices so arrange accordingly. Warm the sauce, taste for seasoning and add salt and pepper if necessary.

Pour the sauce onto 2 heated plates and place the duckling and mango on top.

S E R V E S 2.

ROAST DUCKLING IN TWO SERVINGS

❖   ❖   ❖

Pierre Chevillard, head chef at Chewton Glen Hotel at New Milton in Hampshire, presents his ducklings in two separate servings with different garnishes, unusual and very appetizing. He uses two 2½ pound ducklings not available in the United States. One larger bird can be used instead. Serve with a Côte de Beaune.

1 duckling, about 5 pounds, if frozen thoroughly defrosted
Salt, freshly ground pepper
6 tablespoons butter
2 medium-size carrots, scraped and cut into julienne strips
1 leek, white part only, well washed, and cut into julienne strips
½ cup Grand Marnier or other orange-flavored liqueur
½ cup heavy cream

4 potatoes, peeled and cut into balls
1 onion, sliced thin
½ cup dry white wine
2 cups Veal or Beef Stock (see Index)
1 head of Boston lettuce, separated into leaves
4 ounces canned hearts of palm, rinsed and diced
½ cup Oil and Vinegar Dressing (see Index)

Pull away the excess fat from the cavities of the duckling. Season with salt and pepper and roast on a rack in a baking pan in a preheated hot oven (425°F.) for 45 minutes.

Heat 2 tablespoons of the butter in a saucepan and cook the carrots and leek until vegetables are soft. Add the liqueur and cream and simmer for 5 minutes, uncovered. Cover and set aside.

Heat 2 more tablespoons of the butter in a skillet and sauté the potato balls until they are tender and golden brown, about 10 minutes. Season with salt and pepper. Keep them warm.

When the duckling is cooked, remove it from the baking pan to a platter, and keep warm. Pour off the fat from the pan. Add the onion, wine and stock to the pan and simmer until onion is very soft and the liquid slightly thickened. Strain the sauce through a fine sieve into a saucepan, and stir in the remaining 2 tablespoons of butter, cut into bits. Season with salt and pepper, if necessary. Cover and keep warm.

For the first serving, cut the duckling breast into thin slices. Arrange the leek and carrot mixture on 4 heated plates and top with the sliced duckling. Spoon the sauce over and arrange the potatoes on the plates.

For the second serving toss the lettuce and hearts of palm with the dressing in a salad bowl. Slice the legs and arrange the meat on 4 plates. Garnish with the salad.

SERVES 4.

DUCKLING BREAST WITH WILD MUSHROOM SAUCE

❖   ❖   ❖

John Webber, whom I met when he was head chef at Gidleigh Park, in Chagford, Devon, dislikes the tendency in modern cooking to be dependent on fashion, nor does he like presentation so complex as to take hours or be overpowering to the eye of the diner. In his view flavor is the most important factor. Birmingham-born, he has an interesting background as he went straight into the Birmingham College of Food and Domestic Arts with no thought other than of becoming a chef. He was *sous-chef* to Anton Mosimann at the Dorchester before moving to Devon where he had a chance to develop his individual talent. He is now head chef at Cliveden, Taplow, in Buckinghamshire. Serve with a St. Emilion.

Sauce

½ pound dried cèpes
½ ounce dried morels
½ cup dry white wine
½ cup chicken consommé
2 cups Veal or Chicken Stock
  (see Index)

1 teaspoon tomato purée
½ teaspoon arrowroot
Salt, freshly ground pepper

Duckling

2 ducklings, about 5 pounds
  each, if frozen thoroughly
  defrosted
1 cup Veal or Chicken Stock (see
  Index)

1 tablespoon honey
1 teaspoon English dry mustard
½ cup fresh wild mushrooms

(recipe continues)

To make the sauce, start if possible the night before. Put the dried mushrooms, wine and consommé in a saucepan and bring to a boil. Remove from the heat and allow to stand for at least 2 hours; overnight is better.

When ready to cook, strain the sauce and remove and discard the soaked mushrooms, or add them to the stockpot to enrich the flavor. Return the liquid to the saucepan, add 2 cups of the veal stock, simmer and reduce by one third. Whisk in the tomato purée. Mix the arrow-root with a little water and stir it into the sauce to thicken it. Remove from the heat as soon as the sauce is thickened. Season with salt and pepper and keep warm.

Remove the breasts from the ducklings and cut off the wings but do not bone or skin them. Keep the rest of the ducklings for another meal. Make a glaze: Pour 1 cup veal stock into a small saucepan and reduce it over fairly high heat to ¼ cup. Whisk in the honey. Mix the mustard with a little water and stir it in.

Put the duckling breasts, skin side down, in a baking pan and roast in a preheated hot oven (425°F.) for 10 minutes. Turn the breasts over and brush the skin with the glaze. Cook for another 12 minutes, brushing every 4 minutes with the glaze. Add the fresh wild mushrooms to the sauce and simmer over very low heat for 5 minutes. Remove duckling breasts from the bone and slice with the skin on. Brush with the glaze.

Arrange the breasts on 4 heated plates and pour the mushroom sauce around them. Serve vegetables such as new potatoes and green peas separately.

S E R V E S 4.

CONFIT OF DUCK

❖   ❖   ❖

Simon Hopkinson, head chef of Hilaire restaurant in London, says of this dish that it is simple and completely effortless and is one of his favorites. It is also a favorite of mine and I like to serve it as supper for friends on a Sunday night. It is easier to prepare than the classical *confit*. Keep the breasts for another use. Serve with a St. Emilion.

6 *legs and thighs from 3*
  ducklings, each bird about 5
  pounds, if frozen, thoroughly
  defrosted
6 *tablespoons salt, preferably*
  coarse sea salt
Freshly ground black pepper
1 *bay leaf*

1 *teaspoon minced fresh thyme,*
  or ½ teaspoon dried
1 *pound duck or goose fat or lard*
2 *pounds potatoes, peeled and*
  sliced
2 *or 3 garlic cloves, chopped fine*
1 *cup minced parsley*

Put the duck pieces in a large bowl with the salt, freshly ground pepper, bay leaf and thyme. Mix all together, cover, and refrigerate overnight, turning once or twice. The next day wipe off the excess salt and herbs with kitchen towels and place the duck in a large baking pan. It is important to have a pan big enough so that the duck pieces do not overlap. Use 2 baking pans if necessary. Melt the duck or goose fat or lard and pour over the duck. There should be enough to cover the duck completely. Add more if necessary. Bake in a preheated moderate oven (350°F.) for 2 hours, or until the duck is very tender. Take duck pieces out of the baking pan and put into a container. Pour the fat over and store in the refrigerator, or in a cool place, for 1 week.

To serve, sauté the duckling in a nonstick skillet, or in a heavy skillet with a little of the fat, until the duck skin is crisp. In a separate pan sauté the potatoes with the garlic. Pile the duck and potatoes onto a heated large platter and sprinkle with the parsley.

S E R V E S 6.

STUFFED QUAIL
WITH JUNIPER SAUCE

❖　　　❖　　　❖

Baba Hine, chef-patronne of Corse Lawn House at Corse Lawn village near Tirley in Gloucestershire created this very attractive and appetizing dish. It does take a little time, and it is worth while getting the butcher to bone the quail as this makes it an easier and far less time-consuming dish. It is suitably festive for a dinner party. Serve with a Madeira.

¼ cup juniper berries　　　　　¼ cup dry Madeira wine

Stuffing

4 tablespoons (½ stick) butter　　⅔ cup fresh bread crumbs
6 chicken livers, chopped coarse　Salt, freshly ground pepper
2 tablespoons snipped fresh chives
1 tablespoon minced fresh
　tarragon, or 1 teaspoon dried

Quail

12 quail, boned, with wings and　¼ cup Sauce Demi-glace or Beef
　legs intact　　　　　　　　　　Stock (see Index)
12 slices of bacon, halved　　　　⅓ cup Chicken Stock (see Index)

In a small bowl soak the juniper berries in the Madeira overnight.

Make the stuffing: Heat the butter in a skillet and sauté the chicken livers with the chives and tarragon over moderate heat until livers are lightly browned outside but still pink inside. Remove from heat, add the bread crumbs, season with salt and pepper, and stir to mix.

Stuff the quail with the mixture and truss them. Arrange the birds in a baking pan just large enough to hold them in one layer. Top each one with 2 half-slices of bacon. Roast the birds in a preheated moderately hot oven (400°F.) for 20 minutes. Transfer with a slotted spoon to a platter and keep warm.

Pour any fat from the pan. To the juices in the pan add the juniper berries and the Madeira, the demi-glace or beef stock, and the chicken stock. Bring to a simmer and cook, stirring with a wooden spoon to scrape up any brown bits. Season with salt and pepper and cook for 2 minutes longer.

Pour the sauce over the quail. Serve immediately, with rice and a green salad, or with new potatoes and a green vegetable.

S E R V E S 6.

POT-ROASTED GROUSE WITH HONEY

❖   ❖   ❖

Anton Mosimann, Maître Chef des Cuisines at The Dorchester Hotel in London, is a chef of infinite creativity. His pot-roasted grouse is uncomplicated, needing little time in the kitchen. The end result is a subtly flavored, elegant main course. I suggest you do not serve wine with this dish.

¼ pound (1 stick) butter
1 cup minced mixed carrot, leek
* and celery*
½ teaspoon minced fresh thyme
4 young grouse
2 tablespoons honey, heather
* honey preferably*

1 cup dry cider
1½ cups Game Stock or rich
* Chicken Stock (see Index),*
* thickened with 2 teaspoons*
* arrowroot*
½ cup heavy cream
Salt, freshly ground pepper

In a heavy casserole heat half of the butter. Add the vegetables and thyme and cook over low heat until vegetables are soft. Add the grouse, spoon the honey over the breasts, cover, and cook in a preheated slow oven (325°F.) for 60 minutes. Remove birds from the casserole and keep them warm.

Pour the cider and stock into the casserole on top of the stove and deglaze over high heat, stirring to scrape up any brown bits. Simmer, uncovered, over moderate heat until the sauce is reduced to 1 cup. Strain the sauce through a fine sieve and return it to the casserole. Warm it through over low heat, stir in the cream, taste for seasoning, and simmer just until the sauce is slightly thickened. Beat in remaining butter, cut into bits. Taste, and if liked add a little more honey.

Arrange the grouse on 4 heated plates and serve the sauce separately.

S E R V E S 4.

PIGEON BREASTS WITH PRUNES IN ARMAGNAC

❖   ❖   ❖

This is a rich-tasting, luscious but not difficult dish, the creation of Stephen Ross, chef-patron of Homewood Park at Freshford, near Bath in Avon, whose cooking is a blend of traditional and new. In Britain squabs are called pigeons. Serve with Armagnac.

1 pound pitted prunes	*2 cups dry red wine*
½ cup Armagnac or other brandy	*½ cup dry Madeira wine*
8 squabs	*2 tablespoons red-currant jelly*
Salt, freshly ground pepper	

Put the prunes in a bowl, pour in the Armagnac, and leave to soak overnight, turning once or twice.

Season the squabs with salt and pepper and arrange in a baking pan. Roast in a preheated hot oven (425°F.) for 20 minutes. They should be kept pink. Remove from the oven and rest for 15 minutes. While the birds are resting, pour the red wine into the baking pan and bring to a simmer on top of the stove, scraping with a wooden spoon to take up any brown bits. Add the Madeira and the red-currant jelly and simmer until the sauce is reduced to a dark, rich consistency. Add the prunes and the Armagnac in which they have soaked.

Remove the breasts from the squabs and carve them into thin slices. Arrange on 8 heated plates and spoon the sauce over them. Serve with new potatoes or noodles and a green vegetable.

S E R V E S 8.

BREAST OF GROUSE WITH PORT JELLY

❖   ❖   ❖

This is another of Anton Mosimann's inspired recipes for grouse. It makes a lovely lunch or summer evening dinner. When I can't get

grouse I use chicken breasts or any game breasts for this. Serve with
Port wine.

1 envelope unflavored gelatin,
   7 grams
1 cup clear Game or Chicken
   Stock (see Index)
½ cup Tawny Port wine

4 breasts of grouse, or other
   game or chicken
Salt, freshly ground pepper
3 tablespoons butter

Salad

4 or more large lettuce leaves
2 cups diced fruits such as seeded
   orange or tangerine segments;
   sliced bananas; peeled, cored
   and chopped apples; black or
   white grapes, seeded and
   halved; sliced peeled kiwi
   fruits; strawberries; etc.

½ cup sour cream, or to taste
2 tablespoons snipped chives

Sprinkle the gelatin over ¼ cup cold water in a small bowl to soften.
In a small saucepan combine the stock and Port wine. Stir in the
softened gelatin and simmer over low heat, stirring, until the gelatin
has dissolved. Set aside until ready to use.

Season the grouse breasts with salt and pepper. Heat the butter in
a casserole, add the grouse, cover with buttered wax paper and the
lid, and cook in a preheated moderately hot oven (400°F.) for about
8 minutes, or until breasts are springy to the touch. Remove from the
oven, lift out and cool. If liked, the breasts may instead be poached
in game or chicken stock barely to cover on top of the stove for about
8 minutes. Lift out and cool.

Chill the gelatin mixture until it is syrupy. Put the breasts on a
wire rack and mask with the aspic. Any aspic that runs off may be
returned to the saucepan and warmed until liquid enough to use to
make a thicker coat of jelly. Refrigerate the breasts until the jelly is
set. Trim breasts neatly. Serve on slightly chilled plates with the salad
in a lettuce leaf alongside.

For the salad combine the fruits in a bowl with the sour cream and
spoon into the lettuce leaves. Sprinkle with the chives.

S E R V E S 4.

ROAST MALLARD DUCK WITH GINGER AND PORT SAUCE

❖   ❖   ❖

This is a gala way to prepare wild duck, and it merits a special occasion. It was created by Julian Waterer when he was head chef at Greywalls in Scotland. He has now returned to the south and is chef-patron at the Salisbury Restaurant at Old Hatfield, Hertfordshire. Serve with a Port wine.

1 tablespoon vegetable oil	1 tablespoon minced shallot
4 mallard ducks	4 pieces of stem ginger, chopped
Salt, freshly ground pepper	2 teaspoons grated fresh
1 tablespoon syrup from stem	gingerroot
ginger in syrup	2 teaspoons lemon juice
2 cups Game Stock or rich	¾ cup heavy cream
Chicken Stock (see Index)	2 pink grapefruits, peeled and
½ cup Tawny Port wine	separated into segments

Heat the oil in a baking pan. Season the ducks with salt and pepper and seal on all sides in the oil. Roast in a preheated hot oven (450°F.) for 20 to 25 minutes. Remove from the pan to a dish and allow to rest in a warm place while the sauce is made.

In a heavy pan combine the ginger syrup, game stock, Port and shallot and reduce to half. Add the chopped ginger, grated gingerroot and lemon juice. Continue to reduce over moderate heat until the sauce is almost syrupy. Add the cream and continue to simmer until the sauce reaches coating consistency. Season to taste with salt and pepper, strain, and keep warm.

Cut the legs from the ducks and remove the breasts. Reserve the carcasses for making stock. If liked, cut the breasts into 3 or 4 slices, or leave whole. Arrange the duck pieces on a large dish and put the grapefruit segments neatly over the duck. Put into the hot oven for 5 minutes.

Serve at once, with the sauce separate, with new potatoes, broccoli purée and carrot purée flavored with a little dry sherry.

S E R V E S   8.

ROAST PHEASANT WITH FRUIT GARNISH

❖   ❖   ❖

Christopher Pitman, head chef of the George of Stamford in Lincolnshire, enjoys game dishes and has turned this pheasant into something very special. The slight tartness of the fruit contrasts agreeably with the rich flavor of the pheasant. Serve with a Côte du Rhône.

1 young pheasant, about 2 pounds
6 tablespoons butter
4 slices of bacon, halved
6 small white onions, peeled
6 button mushrooms
2 slices of bacon, blanched, rind removed, and cut into ⅛-inch crosswise strips
½ cup Garlic Croutons (see Index)

10 seedless white grapes, halved
10 black grapes, peeled, halved and pitted
1 orange, peeled and sectioned
10 fresh cranberries
4 whole cooked chestnuts
2 tablespoons brandy
2 tablespoons chopped parsley

Spread the breast of the pheasant with 4 tablespoons of the butter softened at room temperature. Cover with the half bacon slices. Place on its side on a rack in a roasting pan and roast in a preheated hot oven (450°F.) for 25 to 30 minutes, turning the bird onto its other side halfway through the cooking. During the last 5 minutes of cooking remove the bacon and turn the bird breast side up to brown the breast. Remove the bird from the oven and turn it breast side down for 5 minutes to let the juices return to the breast. Turn it right side up, transfer to a platter, halve the bird, put on 2 heated plates, and keep warm.

In a medium-size heavy skillet heat remaining 2 tablespoons of butter and sauté the onions, mushrooms and bacon pieces over moderate heat until onions are tender. Add the croutons, white and black grapes, orange segments, cranberries and chestnuts and sauté for about 1 minute longer. Add the brandy, ignite it, and pour the mixture over the pheasant halves. Sprinkle with chopped parsley.

SERVES 2.

PHEASANT BREASTS IN GINGER AND WHISKY SAUCE

❖   ❖   ❖

Julian Waterer, who is one of the most brilliantly original chefs I have ever met, has a special way with game, often using ginger to point up its rich flavor. His recipes are seldom complicated and can be cooked in little time, coming to the table with their flavors fresh and vivid. This is a quite luxurious dish as pheasants are not everyday fare. Chicken breasts, though less robust in taste, can be used instead. Serve whisky with this dish instead of wine.

6 young pheasant breasts, boned
Salt, freshly ground pepper
6 tablespoons butter
¼ cup Scotch whisky
1 tablespoon syrup from stem
    ginger in syrup
½ teaspoon grated fresh
    gingerroot

1 tablespoon minced shallot
2 cups Game Stock (see Index)
½ teaspoon lemon juice
½ cup heavy cream
2 pieces of stem ginger in syrup,
    drained and chopped
½ pound zucchini, trimmed and
    cut into thin strips

Season the pheasant breasts with salt and pepper. Heat 3 tablespoons of the butter in a casserole large enough to hold the breasts comfortably. Add the breasts, skin side down, and sauté over moderate heat for 1 minute. Turn, cover with the lid, and cook in a preheated moderate oven (375°F.) for 8 to 10 minutes. The breasts should be pink inside. Remove from the casserole to a warmed platter and keep warm while making the sauce.

In a saucepan combine the whisky, ginger syrup, grated gingerroot and shallot and boil over moderate to high heat for 1 minute. Add the stock and lemon juice and simmer over moderate heat until the mixture is thickened. Add the cream and simmer for 3 minutes longer. Season to taste with salt and pepper and strain. Return to the saucepan, add the chopped stem ginger, and heat through.

Add remaining butter to a skillet and sauté the zucchini quickly over moderately high heat for a few minutes. Pieces should be slightly crisp. Pour the sauce onto 6 heated plates and arrange a pheasant breast on each one. Surround with the sautéed zucchini strips. If liked, slice the pheasant breasts into 6 slices and place on top of a bed of zucchini arranged over the sauce.

SERVES 6.

V A R I A T I O N : Graham Flanagan, head chef at the Cottage in the Wood, at Malvern Wells, Hereford and Worcester, has a simple and attractive variation on Julian Waterer's more sophisticated dish.

Four boned pheasant breasts are sautéed in a little butter and oil, removed from the pan, and kept warm. The fat is discarded and ½ cup Tawny Port is added to the pan and reduced over moderate heat to ¼ cup. Then 1½ cups of heavy cream, or Fresh White Cheese (see Index), are added to the pan and simmered until slightly thickened. If using fresh white cheese simply stir it in and warm it through. The sauce will be thick enough not to need reducing. The sauce is seasoned with salt and pepper and the pheasant breasts are returned to the sauce to heat through.

The breasts are served with the sauce poured over them and are garnished with sprigs of watercress. Straw potatoes are good with this.

S E R V E S 4.

BREAST OF PHEASANT WITH WILD MUSHROOMS

❖   ❖   ❖

Aidan McCormack, head chef of Middlethorpe Hall at York, has a talent for simplicity. He transforms the plainest of cooking with skillfully conceived garnishes into something special. Pheasant becomes a feast cooked this way. Serve with a Côte de Nuits.

4 breasts from 2 pheasants,
    boned
4 tablespoons butter
2 tablespoons minced shallots
½ pound assorted wild
    mushrooms (chanterelle,
    morel, etc.)

2 tablespoons brandy
½ cup Veal or Chicken Stock
    (see Index)
½ cup heavy cream
Salt, freshly ground pepper

In a large, heavy skillet sauté the pheasant breasts in 2 tablespoons of the butter until lightly browned on both sides. Add the shallots and mushrooms and continue to cook until the pheasant is done, turning from time to time, about 10 to 15 minutes. The pheasant should remain pink inside. Lift out the pheasant and the mushrooms, using a slotted spoon. Put on a plate, cover, and keep warm.

Add the brandy to the skillet and ignite it. Pour in the veal or chicken stock and simmer over moderate heat until the sauce has thickened. Stir in the cream and bring to a simmer. Season to taste with salt and pepper and beat in remaining 2 tablespoons butter, cut into bits. Add the mushrooms.

Arrange the pheasant breasts on 4 heated plates and coat them with the sauce. Serve with noodles and a green salad.

S E R V E S 4.

V A R I A T I O N : If wild mushrooms are not available, Aidan McCormack suggests using instead 4 medium-size celery ribs, cut into julienne strips.

MEATS AND
FURRED GAME

❖   ❖   ❖

THE INNOVATIVE chefs who are changing food in Britain hold British beef in high esteem, and they have created new dishes that do justice to the fine flavor of the meat. They use fillet steaks a great deal as these are very practical in restaurants, always tender, quickly cooked, and uniform in size. The home cook can use other steaks that are less expensive and just as suitable for the chefs' sauces and garnishes. These are not everyday dishes, with the exception of Braised Oxtail, but they can make a dinner party for special friends doubly special.

Lamb is exceptionally fine and chefs make fine use of it. They delight in this lean and succulent meat, which they consider both appetizing and healthful. But the Welsh chef does claim that Welsh lamb surpasses all other lamb; the Scots chef knows better, as Scots lamb is preeminent; while the English quite smugly know that nothing beats the best English lamb. It is fortunate the lamb is good enough to support all their claims.

Another favorite meat is venison, which is gaining in popularity with chefs, perhaps because it is another lean meat. Chefs have devised some really splendid venison recipes that would appeal to even the most jaded palates.

Good veal is not easy to get, but when it is, chefs have created some very imaginative recipes to take full advantage of the goodness. They have also developed tempting recipes for variety meats and for pork and rabbit dishes. Today's chefs very well understand the needs of the meat lover.

FILLET OF BEEF WITH FRESH FOIE GRAS

❖　　　❖　　　❖

Baba Hine, chef-patronne of Corse Lawn House, in a charming eighteenth-century house in Corse Lawn village, Gloucestershire has created this luxurious dish, irresistible to lovers of fresh foie gras. Since fresh foie gras is not an everyday sort of thing to have in the kitchen, I've tried the steaks without this special garnish and find Baba's subtly flavored and uncomplicated sauce entirely tempting. Sirloin or other steaks are equally suitable for this. Serve with a Chianti.

2 tablespoons clarified butter
4 fillet or other tender steaks,
　each 6 ounces
Salt, freshly ground pepper
½ cup thin-sliced chanterelle
　(girolle) mushrooms

¼ cup dry Madeira wine
½ cup Beef Stock (see Index)
2 tablespoons butter, cut into bits
4 thin slices of fresh foie gras,
　warmed
Garnish: parsley sprigs

Heat the clarified butter in a skillet large enough to hold the steaks comfortably. Season the steaks with salt and pepper and sauté for 3 to 4 minutes on each side for medium rare. Remove from the skillet and keep warm. Add the mushrooms to the pan and sauté for about 4 minutes. Add the Madeira and beef stock, and reduce slightly as the sauce should not be thin. Whisk in the butter.

Put the steaks onto 4 warmed plates, pour the sauce over them, and top each with a slice of foie gras. Garnish with parsley sprigs. Serve with an assortment of vegetables and potatoes separately.

SERVES 4.

FILLET OF BEEF WITH TWO PEPPERCORNS

❖   ❖   ❖

John Mann, head chef at The Old Lodge in Limpsfield, Surrey, is a chef of exceptional brilliance. His creations are always gratifying to the palate but are seldom sensible dishes for the home cook. This beef dish is part of a far more elaborate dish but since it is splendid by itself, is not complicated, and takes little time to cook, I have taken the liberty of abstracting it. Serve with a Côte de Nuits.

1½ tablespoons black peppercorns
1½ tablespoons white peppercorns
Salt
4 fillet steaks, about 1 inch thick, each 4 ounces

½ tablespoon vegetable oil
1 tablespoon butter
1 tablespoon brandy
1½ cups Veal Stock or rich Chicken Stock (see Index)

Mix the peppercorns together and crush coarsely with ½ teaspoon salt. Season the steaks with the peppercorn mixture, pressing it in firmly. Heat the oil and butter in a skillet and sauté the steaks for 3 to 4 minutes on each side for medium rare meat. Transfer the steaks to a platter and keep them warm.

Pour away any fat from the skillet, leaving only the pan juices. Flame with the brandy, then add the veal stock and reduce over moderately high heat until it is slightly thickened. Add any meat juices that may have collected on the platter and season the sauce to taste with salt.

Serve the steaks on 4 warmed plates with the sauce spooned over them. There will not be a great deal of sauce. Garnish the plate with boiled potatoes, young carrots and baby turnips cut into olive shapes, snow peas and some straw potatoes, if liked.

SERVES 4.

SIRLOIN STEAK WITH FOUR PEPPERS

❖   ❖   ❖

It isn't easy to come up with a new way of presenting sirloin steak, but this creation of famed chef Anton Mosimann of the Dorchester looks like it will become a classic. It is also uncomplicated and takes little time. It exemplifies the chef's philosophy: Make it simple, but make it perfect. Serve with a Côte de Nuits.

*4 sirloin steaks, 1 inch thick,
   each about 6 ounces
2 tablespoons each of crushed
   black and white peppercorns
Salt
4 tablespoons vegetable oil
¼ cup Cognac or other brandy*

*1 cup Veal or Beef Stock (see
   Index)
½ cup heavy cream
3 tablespoons butter, cut into bits
Freshly ground pepper
1 teaspoon each of pink and
   green peppercorns*

Season the steaks on both sides with the black and white peppercorns and salt to taste. Heat the oil in a heavy skillet and sauté the steaks for 3 to 4 minutes on each side for medium rare. Transfer the steaks to a platter and keep them warm. Pour off and discard any fat in the pan. Pour in the Cognac and ignite it. Add the stock. Reduce it to half over moderately high heat. Add the cream and reduce the sauce until it is lightly thickened. Whisk in the butter, bit by bit. Taste for seasoning and add as liked. Stir in the pink and green peppercorns, cover the steaks with the sauce, and serve immediately.

S E R V E S 4.

FILLET STEAKS WITH ASPARAGUS TIPS

❖   ❖   ❖

Chef Michael Collom of the Priory Hotel in Bath has come up with a way of lifting fillet steaks into a new dimension. If I have lots of time and some spare energy I make the béarnaise sauce, which adds a touch of luxury to the dish, otherwise I make this as one of my cook-in-a-hurry dishes, quickly cooked, quickly assembled and very appetizing. Serve with a Côte de Beaune.

½ cup Béarnaise Sauce (see Index) (optional)
6 fillet steaks, 1 inch thick, each about 4 ounces
Salt, freshly ground pepper
2 tablespoons butter
1 tablespoon vegetable oil

12 asparagus tips, white or green, cooked
1 cup Veal or Beef Stock (see Index)
1 cup dry Madeira wine
Garnish: watercress sprigs and straw potatoes

Make the béarnaise sauce, if using, and set it aside. Season the steaks with salt and pepper. In a skillet large enough to hold all the steaks comfortably, heat 1 tablespoon of the butter and the oil and sauté the steaks over moderately high heat for 3 to 4 minutes on each side. Remove from the pan and keep warm. Warm the asparagus tips.

Discard any fat from the skillet and pour any juices into a small saucepan. Pour in the stock and reduce the mixture to half over brisk heat. Add the Madeira, bring to a simmer, and continue to simmer the sauce over very low heat.

With a very sharp knife cut a diagonal pocket into each of the steaks and stuff with the asparagus tips. Garnish the asparagus with a spoonful of béarnaise sauce, if using it. Stir remaining tablespoon of butter into the sauce, which should have reduced to a slightly syrupy consistency. Put a steak onto each of 6 heated plates, pour the sauce round the steaks, and garnish with the watercress sprigs and straw potatoes.

S E R V E S 6.

V A R I A T I O N : Another attractive and inventive way of serving fillet or other steaks comes from Nicholas Knight, the youthful head chef at Master's Restaurant in Kensington, London. He masks steaks with a Carrot and Green Peppercorn Sauce which is light and delicious, the sweetness of carrot sharpened by the bite of green peppercorns. (See Index for recipe.)

FILLET OF BEEF WITH PICKLED WALNUT SAUCE

❖   ❖   ❖

Peter Jackson created this prizewinning dish when he was head chef at Bodysgallen Hall in North Wales. He is now chef-patron of his own establishment, The Colonial Restaurant on the High Street, in the heart of old Glasgow—a Scottish chef come home. Serve with a Médoc.

1 pound beef fillet, or more if liked
Salt, freshly ground white pepper
1 medium-size onion, chopped fine
1 celery rib, chopped fine
1 leek, white part only, chopped fine
1 medium-size carrot, scraped and chopped

½ cup juniper berries, crushed
2 cups Tawny Port wine
1 cup Sauce Demi-glace (see Index)
¼ cup pickled walnuts, chopped fine
Vegetable oil

Garnish

2 tablespoons butter
1 cup black grapes, halved and seeded
½ cup quartered mushrooms

¼ cup walnut meats
½ cup heavy cream (optional)
2 tablespoons minced parsley

Cut the beef into 4 slices. Season with salt and pepper and put into a fairly deep dish. Cover with the chopped onion, celery, leek and carrot and the juniper berries. Pour in the Port wine and leave to marinate in the refrigerator for 24 hours, turning occasionally.

When ready to cook, lift out the beef and pat dry with paper towels. Set aside and make the sauce: Pour all the marinade into a saucepan with the demi-glace and pickled walnuts. Simmer, uncovered, until the liquid is reduced to 1 cup. Strain, pressing down on the vegetables to extract all the juices. Rinse out and dry the saucepan and return the liquid to it. Set aside.

In a skillet heat a little vegetable oil and sauté the beef to the required degree of doneness, about 4 minutes a side for medium rare. Prepare the garnish: In another skillet heat the butter and sauté the grapes, mushrooms and walnut meats quickly over moderately high heat. Add the ½ cup heavy cream to the sauce, if using it, and simmer until sauce reaches coating consistency. Otherwise just warm the sauce through. Taste for seasoning and add salt and pepper, if necessary.

Place a fillet on each of 4 heated plates. Cover with the sauce and spoon the garnish over each one. Finish with a sprinkling of chopped parsley. Serve with new potatoes and a green vegetable.

S E R V E S 4.

BEEF FAN WITH ROQUEFORT CHEESE

❖   ❖   ❖

This unusual and richly flavored steak dish comes from Vaughan Archer of 90 Park Lane Restaurant, London. It is a luxurious dish that can be assembled in very little time, a great comfort to those who like to eat well but have minutes rather than hours available to spend in the kitchen. Serve with a Rioja.

2 cups dry red wine	*6 tablespoons butter*
1 cup Beef Stock (see Index)	*4 tablespoons Roquefort or other*
Salt, freshly ground pepper	*blue cheese*
4 fillet steaks, about 1 inch thick,	*2 tablespoons snipped chives*
each 6 ounces	*¼ cup fine-chopped mushrooms*

Combine 1 cup of the wine with the beef stock in a small saucepan and reduce to 1 cup over moderately high heat. Set aside.

Salt and pepper the steaks. Heat half of the butter in a heavy skillet and sauté the steaks for 3 to 4 minutes on each side for medium rare. Lift out the steaks and keep warm. Pour off any fat from the pan and add remaining cup of wine to the pan juices. Reduce over high heat until syrupy. Add the reserved wine and beef stock and the Roquefort cheese mashed with the rest of the butter. Season to taste with salt and pepper, if necessary. Stir in the chives and mushrooms, and keep warm.

Cut the steaks into lengthwise slices. Pour the sauce onto 4 warmed plates and arrange the steak in a fan on each plate. Serve with Stuffed Potatoes (see Index). If preferred the steak may, of course, be served unsliced.

S E R V E S 4.

FILLET OF BEEF, ST. CHRISTOPH

❖   ❖   ❖

Christopher Grist, head chef of Great Fosters, a Tudor mansion now a hotel and restaurant at Egham in Surrey, is a meticulous cook. He presents these steaks in puff pastry baskets that look very attractive. This is a step I am apt to omit as I find the steaks taste just as good with their luscious sauce poured in a small puddle on the plates, with the rest of it over the meat. It makes this luxurious dish both quick and simple to cook—unless there is some puff pastry in the freezer waiting to be used. Serve with a Médoc.

Puff Pastry (see Index)
2 fillet steaks, 1 inch thick, each
    about 4 ounces
Salt, freshly ground pepper
3 tablespoons butter
1 tablespoon chopped shallot
¼ cup Marsala wine
½ cup sliced chanterelle
    mushrooms

2 artichoke hearts, quartered
Pinch of dried tarragon, or ½
    teaspoon fresh tarragon leaves,
    chopped
½ cup heavy cream, or Fresh
    White Cheese (see Index)
Garnish: chopped parsley and
    watercress sprigs

Roll out some puff pastry to a thin sheet and cut two 3-inch circles. Prick lightly with a fork all over and place over two 1-cup ramekins or small soufflé molds. Bake in a preheated moderate oven (350°F.) until golden brown. Remove from the oven. When cool enough to handle lift cases gently from the molds. Keep the pastry baskets warm. These are the baskets in which the steaks will be placed. This step can be omitted for a simpler dish.

Season the steaks with salt and pepper. Heat 2 tablespoons of the butter in a heavy skillet and sauté the steaks over moderate heat, turning once, for 3 to 4 minutes on each side for medium rare. Set aside, covered, and keep warm. Add the shallot to the pan and cook until soft, 1 to 2 minutes. Pour in the Marsala and stir to scrape up any brown bits. Add the mushrooms, artichoke hearts, tarragon and cream and simmer until the sauce is reduced by half. If using fresh white cheese, just heat it through. Season to taste with salt and pepper. Add any juices that may have collected on the plate with the steaks. Stir in the remaining tablespoon of butter.

If using the pastry baskets, arrange the baskets on 2 heated plates and put a little sauce into each. Add the steak, then coat the steak with the rest of the sauce. Garnish with chopped parsley and a few sprigs of watercress.

SERVES 2.

SIRLOIN STEAK WITH STILTON CHEESE

❖   ❖   ❖

This recipe from Philip Burgess, head chef at the Arundell Arms in Lifton, Devon, a favorite hotel with salmon-loving anglers, takes even less kitchen time than Vaughan Archer's Beef Fan with Roquefort Cheese. It pleases both beef and cheese lovers as well as the economy minded, as leftovers from a whole Stilton cheese can be used. Serve with a Rioja.

1 cup dry red wine	1 tablespoon vegetable oil
1 cup Beef Stock (see Index)	4 sirloin steaks, each 8 ounces
½ pound Stilton cheese	Salt, freshly ground pepper
2 tablespoons butter	Garnish: watercress sprigs

Combine the red wine and beef stock in a saucepan and reduce over moderately high heat to 1 cup. Set aside. Mash the Stilton cheese with 1 tablespoon of the butter and set aside.

In a heavy skillet heat the oil and remaining tablespoon of butter. Season the steaks with salt and pepper and sauté over fairly high heat for 2 minutes on each side, longer if better done steak is preferred. Spread the steaks with the Stilton cheese mixture and broil until the cheese has melted. Pour the red wine sauce over the steaks.

Serve garnished with watercress and accompanied by green vegetables and potatoes.

SERVES 4.

BRAISED OXTAIL

❖   ❖   ❖

Philip Burgess is a Devonian, and now at the Arundell Arms he is back in his native county. Though young, he has had a wide experience of cooking, but he still relishes the good things of his childhood. He has developed his own version of this old favorite, which he describes as a warming winter dish. It is also satisfying. Serve with a Beaujolais.

½ cup all-purpose flour
Salt, freshly ground pepper
2 pounds meaty oxtails, cut into
    2-inch pieces
6 tablespoons beef dripping or
    vegetable oil
1 large onion, chopped coarse
1 large carrot, chopped coarse
1 celery rib, chopped
1 medium-size leek, trimmed,
    thoroughly washed, and
    chopped coarse, including a
    little of the green part

1 bay leaf
1 sprig of fresh thyme, or ⅛
    teaspoon dried
1 garlic clove, crushed
6 cups Beef Stock (see Index),
    approximately
1 tablespoon tomato purée
2 tablespoons dry sherry wine
Garnish: chopped parsley

Season the flour with salt and pepper and dredge the oxtails with the mixture, shaking to remove excess flour. In a large skillet heat 3 tablespoons of the beef dripping or vegetable oil and brown the pieces of oxtail, in batches if necessary. Lift them out into a large ovenproof casserole. Add the rest of the fat to the skillet and sauté the vegetables and herbs until the onion is softened. Sprinkle with a tablespoon of the flour and stir to mix. Continue cooking until the flour is lightly browned. Transfer the contents of the skillet to the casserole. Pour in enough stock to cover, adding a little more if necessary. Stir in the tomato purée and bring to a simmer on top of the stove. Cover, and put into a preheated moderate oven (350°F.). Cook until the meat is tender, about 3 hours.

Remove casserole from the oven and put the oxtail pieces into a serving dish. Keep them warm in the turned-off oven. Skim excess fat from the casserole and strain the liquid through a sieve into a clean saucepan. If the liquid seems very abundant or a little thin, reduce it over moderately high heat until it is lightly thickened. Season to taste with salt and pepper and stir in the sherry.

Pour the sauce over the oxtails and sprinkle with chopped parsley. Serve with plain boiled potatoes.

S E R V E S 4.

MUSTARD AND TARRAGON SAUCE FOR MEATS

❖   ❖   ❖

This easy-to-make, sturdily flavored sauce is the creation of Nicholas Knight, the young head chef at Master's Restaurant in Kensington, London. It is wonderfully useful for lifting an ordinary meat or poultry dish into a special category. I've also used it with a strong-flavored fish like halibut with great success. The chef feels it is best with white meats like veal, pork, chicken or turkey, and certainly it is good with these. I found that it is also surprisingly good with beef. Try it as a sauce topping on a hamburger. Serve with a Beaujolais.

1 tablespoon butter
2 teaspoons minced fresh tarragon
  leaves, or dried tarragon
  soaked in warm water,
  squeezed out and chopped
1 tablespoon coarse-grain
  mustard, such as Moutarde de
  Meaux

3 tablespoons Chicken Stock (see
  Index)
2 tablespoons dry white wine
Salt, freshly ground pepper
1½ cups heavy cream, or 1 cup
  Fresh White Cheese (see
  Index)

Heat the butter in a saucepan, stir in the tarragon, cover, and let it sweat over very low heat for about half a minute. Add the mustard, stock, wine, salt and pepper to taste and the cream and simmer, uncovered, until the sauce is slightly thickened. If using fresh white cheese, simply stir in and heat through.

S E R V E S 4.

VEAL AND LOBSTER WITH SHELLFISH AND SHERRY SAUCES

❖   ❖   ❖

This is one of the delectable recipes Michael Quinn created when he was head chef at the Ritz in London before going off to be in charge of the kitchen at Ettington Park, near Stratford-upon-Avon. When I find good veal hard to get, I make this with skinned and boned chicken breasts. Serve with sherry.

1 pound fillet of veal in one piece	Salt, freshly ground pepper
1 cooked lobster tail, 6 to 8 ounces	½ pound (2 sticks) butter

Shellfish Sauce

1 cup Shellfish Stock (see Index)	¼ cup heavy cream
1 teaspoon tomato purée	1 tablespoon brandy
1 tablespoon dry vermouth, preferably Noilly Prat	

Sherry Sauce

2 tablespoons minced shallots	¼ cup heavy cream
½ cup dry sherry wine	Garnish: sprigs of fresh chervil
½ cup Veal Stock (see Index)	(optional)

Cut a slit in the veal fillet, being careful not to cut right through the veal. Insert the cooked lobster tail, then tie the fillet into shape with kitchen string. Season with salt and pepper. In a skillet large enough to hold the veal comfortably, heat 2 tablespoons of the butter and quickly seal the meat on all sides over moderately high heat. Lower the heat to moderate and cook the fillet for 15 minutes, turning often. The meat should remain pink in the center. Transfer meat to a warmed platter and let it rest; keep it warm. When ready to serve, cut it into thin slices.

While the meat is cooking and resting, make the sauce. Pour the shellfish stock into a small saucepan with the tomato purée, dry vermouth and heavy cream and reduce to ½ cup. Stir in the brandy and taste for seasoning. Add salt and pepper, if necessary. Set aside and keep warm.

In another saucepan combine the shallots, sherry and veal stock and reduce over moderately high heat to 1 tablespoon. Add the cream, stir to mix, and strain through a fine sieve into the rinsed and dried saucepan. Over low heat beat in the rest of the butter, cut into bits, to make a creamy sauce. Taste for seasoning and add salt and pepper if necessary. Add a little more dry sherry. Keep warm.

To serve, spoon the shellfish stock onto 4 heated plates. Arrange the sliced veal on top of the sauce. Spoon the sherry sauce over the veal. Garnish, if liked, with sprigs of fresh chervil.

SERVES 4.

VEAL SCALLOPS WITH STRAWBERRY SAUCE

❖   ❖   ❖

Denis Woodtli, head chef at Lochalsh Hotel, Kyle of Lochalsh, in Scotland, uses the tart sweetness of strawberries to enhance the sauce for this simple, uncomplicated dish. Serve with a Beaujolais.

2 veal scallops, each 6 to 7 ounces
Salt, freshly ground pepper
1 cup, about 5 ounces, ripe strawberries

4 tablespoons clarified butter
½ cup heavy cream
Garnish: sliced strawberries and parsley sprigs

Flatten the veal scallops to ¼-inch thickness, or have the butcher do it. Season with salt and pepper. Purée the strawberries in a blender or food processor, then strain through a sieve set over a bowl. Set the strawberry juice aside. Spread the pulp on one half of each scallop and fold them over. Secure with a toothpick. Heat the butter in a skillet and cook the veal over low heat for 5 minutes on each side. Lift out onto a warm plate, cover, and keep warm.

Add the cream to the skillet and cook until it thickens to coating consistency. Add the strawberry juice and season to taste with salt and pepper.

Put the scallops on 2 heated plates and pour the sauce over them. Garnish with sliced strawberries and parsley sprigs.

SERVES 2.

MEDALLION OF VEAL
WITH LEMON

❖   ❖   ❖

This is another of the simple yet imaginative recipes of Christopher Grist, head chef of Great Fosters of Egham in Surrey. It takes very little time to cook and makes an ideal dish for two for an elegant dinner. Serve with a Beaujolais.

1 large lemon	Salt, freshly ground pepper
½ teaspoon sugar	¼ cup dry white wine
5 tablespoons butter	1 tablespoon chopped parsley
2 slices of veal fillet, each about 5 ounces	2 large leaves or 2 small sprigs of watercress

Cut the peel from half of the lemon in julienne strips. Put into a small saucepan with cold water to cover and bring to a boil over moderate heat. Drain, refresh in cold water, and drain again. Return the peel to the saucepan with the sugar and 1 tablespoon water and cook over very low heat until the water has evaporated. This intensifies the color of the peel. Set aside and keep warm.

Heat 2 tablespoons of the butter in a skillet. Season the veal with salt and pepper and sauté veal in the butter over moderate heat for about 5 minutes on each side. Remove veal slices to a plate, cover, and keep warm. Pour the wine into the skillet, scraping up any brown bits. Reduce the wine to 1 tablespoon, then beat in the rest of the butter bit by bit to make a creamy sauce. Add the chopped parsley and season with salt and pepper. Pour any juices that have accumulated on the plate with the veal into the sauce.

Put a slice of veal on 2 heated plates, and pour the sauce over them. Cut the unpeeled half of the lemon into 2 wedges and put on the side of the plates. Sprinkle the veal with the julienne of lemon peel and place a sprig or leaf of watercress on top. This is nice with rice and a mixture of young spring vegetables, tossed in butter. It is also very good made with boned chicken breast instead of veal.

SERVES 2.

FILLET OF VEAL STUFFED WITH HERB AND GARLIC CHEESE

❖   ❖   ❖

This is a delicate dish with a lively butter sauce sharpened with vinegar. Murdo MacSween, head chef at Oakley Court near Windsor, created it. The dish bears the stamp of his originality. Serve with a Côte de Nuits or a Margaux.

2 slices of veal fillet, each 4 to 5 ounces	¼ cup herb and garlic cheese Salt, freshly ground pepper

Butter Sauce

6 tablespoons butter	1 teaspoon chopped shallot
1 tablespoon white-wine vinegar	1 tablespoon heavy cream
5 tablespoons dry white wine	1 tablespoon snipped chives

Slit the veal slices to form pockets and stuff with the cheese. Season to taste with salt and pepper.

Cut 5 tablespoons of the butter into bits. Put the wine vinegar, dry white wine and shallot in a saucepan and reduce by half. Add the cream and bring to a simmer. Remove from the heat and whisk in the butter bit by bit to form a creamy sauce. Stir in the chives and keep warm.

Heat remaining tablespoon of butter in a small skillet and sauté the veal over moderate heat, turning once when lightly browned on the first side. The slices need only minutes to cook.

Arrange the sautéed veal on 2 heated plates and pour the sauce over them. Fresh noodles are a good accompaniment, with a green vegetable such as green peas.

S E R V E S 2.

VEAL KIDNEY WITH CABBAGE AND MUSTARD VINAIGRETTE

❖   ❖   ❖

Lovers of veal kidneys will welcome this unusual, simple, and most delicious dish, the creation of Simon Hopkinson, head chef of Hilaire restaurant on London's Old Brompton Road. This makes a perfect Sunday night supper. Serve with a Chianti.

2 veal kidneys, cleaned and cut into thick slices	¼ pound (1 stick) butter
	1 tablespoon olive oil
Salt, freshly ground pepper	1 large Savoy cabbage, sliced thin
Flour	1 garlic clove, chopped fine

Vinaigrette

2 tablespoons Dijon mustard	½ to ¾ cup olive oil, according
2 tablespoons sherry vinegar	to taste

Season the sliced kidneys with salt and pepper and dredge lightly with flour, shaking to remove excess flour. In a heavy skillet heat 2 tablespoons of the butter with the tablespoon of olive oil and sauté the kidney slices for 1 minute on each side. Transfer to a warm plate, cover, and keep warm.

Add remaining butter to the skillet. Season the cabbage with salt and pepper and sauté in the butter with the chopped garlic, quickly over moderate heat, stirring, for 4 to 5 minutes. The cabbage should remain green and fresh-tasting.

In a bowl beat the mustard and sherry vinegar together. Beat in the oil gradually, using ½ to ¾ cup to taste. Season with salt and pepper.

Divide the cabbage among 4 heated plates in neat mounds. Arrange the slices of kidney on top. If any juices have collected on the plate with the kidneys, add them to the vinaigrette. Pour the vinaigrette over the cabbage and kidney. Serve with mashed potatoes.

S E R V E S 4.

CALF'S LIVER WITH AVOCADO

❖   ❖   ❖

Melvin Jordan, head chef at Pool Court, Pool-in-Wharfedale, West Yorkshire, has an original way with calf's liver, this with avocado, and a variation with blackberries, both delicious. Serve with a Chardonnay.

8 slices of calf's liver
Salt, freshly ground pepper
¼ pound (1 stick) butter
16 fresh sage leaves
1 cup dry white wine

2 tablespoons lemon juice
1 large ripe avocado, peeled,
    pitted and cut into 8 lengthwise
    slices

Season the liver slices with salt and pepper. In a large heavy skillet heat 2 tablespoons of the butter and sauté the slices of liver over moderate heat for no longer than 1 minute a side. Lift out onto a heated plate, cover, and keep warm. Add the sage leaves and wine to the skillet, stir to scrape up any brown bits, and simmer until the liquid is reduced by half. Stir in the lemon juice, then whisk in the rest of the butter, cut into bits. The sauce will have a light coating consistency.

Arrange the liver slices on 2 warm plates and pour the sauce over them. Top with avocado slices.

S E R V E S 2.

V A R I A T I O N : Instead of the sage leaves, add 1 cup ripe fresh blackberries.

FILLET OF LAMB
WITH FRESH HERBS

❖   ❖   ❖

This is one of the simple and attractive dishes that John Hornsby worked out while he was head chef at the Castle Hotel in Taunton, Somerset. Serve with a Côte du Beaune or Côte de Nuits.

1 cup Veal or Chicken Stock (see
   Index)
½ cup dry white wine
2 tablespoons minced fresh herbs
   such as tarragon, rosemary,
   thyme, basil, mint and parsley

4 tablespoons butter
Salt, freshly ground pepper
2 slices of boneless loin of lamb,
   trimmed of fat, each 4 to 6
   ounces

In a small saucepan combine the stock and wine and simmer, uncovered, over moderate heat until reduced by half. Stir in the herbs. Cut 2 tablespoons of the butter into bits and beat into the sauce, a piece at a time, until they are all absorbed. Season the sauce with salt and pepper to taste and keep warm.

In a skillet just large enough to hold the lamb comfortably, heat remaining 2 tablespoons of butter. Season the lamb slices with salt and pepper and sauté in the butter over moderately high heat for 3 to 4 minutes, turning once. The lamb should be pink.

Pour the sauce onto 2 heated plates and arrange the slices of lamb on top. Serve with new potatoes and an assortment of vegetables such as green beans and cauliflower on a separate plate.

S E R V E S 2.

RACK OF LAMB WITH SAFFRON AND GARLIC SAUCE

❖ ❖ ❖

Martin Rowbotham, head chef at Huntstrete House, an eighteenth-century country manor house now a country house hotel near Bath, has created a pleasantly different dish with the saffron-flavored sauce in gentle contrast to the spinach. Serve with a Médoc or Margaux.

1 rack of lamb, about 6 chops	*1 small garlic clove, crushed*
Salt, freshly ground pepper	*½ cup dry white wine*
1 pound spinach	*1 cup Lamb Stock (see Index)*
2 tablespoons butter	*⅛ teaspoon crumbled saffron*

Ask the butcher to cut the lamb so that the chops can easily be carved. Pare away all excess fat. Season to taste with salt and pepper and roast on a rack in a preheated moderate oven (375°F.) for 25 minutes for rare, 30 minutes for medium rare. Remove the lamb from the oven and keep it warm.

While the lamb is cooking, blanch the spinach in a large saucepan of briskly boiling salted water for 4 minutes. Refresh under cold water and drain thoroughly. When ready to serve, reheat the spinach by tossing lightly in the butter.

Pour off excess fat from the roasting pan. Add the garlic and cook for about 30 seconds. Add the white wine and let it reduce over moderate heat to about one third. Add the lamb stock and the saffron and simmer until the sauce is reduced to ¾ cup.

Divide the spinach among 3 heated plates. Carve the lamb and put 2 chops on top of the spinach on each plate. Pour the sauce over it.

S E R V E S 3.

NOISETTES OF LAMB
WITH PLUM SAUCE

❖   ❖   ❖

David Harding, head chef at Bodysgallen Hall near Llandudno, North Wales, specifies Welsh lamb for this dish. Welsh lamb is exceptionally sweet and tender, but lamb from other parts of the world will also do well. Serve with a St. Emilion.

1 loin of lamb, 3 pounds, fat
   removed, boned and rolled
Salt, freshly ground pepper
1 pound plums
2 tablespoons sugar, or to taste

½ cup dry red wine
4 tablespoons Clarified Butter
   (see Index)
Garnish: watercress

Cut the lamb into 12 slices. Season with salt and pepper and set aside while making the sauce.

Put the plums into a saucepan with the sugar and wine and simmer until they are soft, 10 to 15 minutes. Put the plums through a fine sieve and return the purée to the saucepan. Taste and add more sugar if necessary. The sauce should be quite tart. If the plum purée is very thin, reduce it over moderate heat to the consistency of heavy cream. Cool.

In a large heavy skillet heat the butter and sauté the noisettes of lamb for about 2 minutes on each side. They should remain pink. Coat 4 heated plates with the plum sauce and arrange 3 noisettes on top of the sauce. Garnish with watercress.

SERVES 4.

For a lighter meal, serve 2 slices of lamb per person and serve 6.

LAMB WITH MINT

❖   ❖   ❖

Lamb has a natural affinity with herbs. In England it was tradi-
tionally served with mint sauce. John King, head chef at the Ritz
Club in London, has created a different kind of mint sauce, which
makes this simple lamb dish something very special. Serve with a St.
Emilion.

2 racks of lamb	*¼ cup vegetable oil*
Salt, freshly ground pepper	*4 tablespoons butter*
1 cup loosely packed fresh mint	*½ cup dry white wine*
sprigs	*2 teaspoons arrowroot*

Have the butcher remove the fillets from the racks of lamb and chop
the bones and meat trimmings. Make 1 recipe lamb stock with the
bones and trimmings (see Index). Cut the lamb fillets into 12 slices
and flatten them slightly. Season with salt and pepper.

Keep a few of the best mint leaves for a garnish. Chop the rest very
fine.

Heat the oil in a large heavy skillet and quickly sauté the lamb
scallops on both sides over fairly high heat for 1 or 2 minutes on each
side, keeping them pink inside. Lift out to a warmed dish and keep
warm. Pour off the oil from the skillet and add 2 tablespoons of the
butter. Add the chopped mint and cook over low heat for about 1
minute. Add the white wine and simmer for 2 or 3 minutes, then
pour in the lamb stock. There should be 2 cups. Simmer, uncovered,
to reduce this by about half. Whisk in remaining 2 tablespoons of
butter. Season to taste with salt and pepper if necessary. Mix the
arrowroot with a little water and stir into the sauce. Cook only until
the sauce is lightly thickened.

Arrange 3 slices of lamb on each of 4 heated plates, coat with the
sauce, and garnish with the reserved fresh mint leaves. Serve with
small new potatoes and a green vegetable.

S E R V E S 4.

COLLOPS OF LAMB WITH MORELS AND YOUNG TURNIPS

❖   ❖   ❖

Martin Lam, head chef at L'Escargot in London's Soho, has a very discriminating palate and a great love for traditional English food. He uses the old term "collop" for slice but puts together his ingredients in a refreshingly new and modern way. The rich morels are perfectly balanced by the clean taste of the young turnips. Serve with a Médoc or St. Emilion.

Fillets from 3 boned racks of lamb
½ cup olive oil
1 tablespoon chopped fresh thyme
Salt, freshly ground black pepper
¼ pound (1 stick) butter
3 tablespoons chopped shallots

½ pound fresh morels, or ¼ pound dried, soaked
1 cup dry Madeira wine
½ cup Veal Stock (see Index)
24 young white turnips, peeled and cooked

Marinate the lamb in the olive oil, thyme, salt and a generous amount of freshly ground black pepper overnight.

In a skillet heat 2 tablespoons of the butter and sauté the shallots until soft. Add the morels and sauté for 2 minutes longer. Add the Madeira and reduce by half. Add the veal stock and simmer for a few minutes longer to blend the flavors. Set aside and keep warm.

Lift the lamb fillets out of the marinade and wipe off the thyme with paper towels. Heat a little olive oil in a large heavy skillet that will hold the lamb comfortably and sauté it for 5 minutes, turning once or twice. It will be nicely pink. Cut the fillets into slices (collops).

Have ready 6 heated plates. Spoon the sauce onto the plates, making sure there are some morels on each plate. Divide the lamb among the plates. Arrange the turnips alternately with the lamb slices, or in any decorative way. Serve immediately.

S E R V E S   6.

LAMB SCALLOPS IN FRESH HERBS WITH POACHED PEARS

❖   ❖   ❖

I like the straightforward character of the dishes developed by Willie MacPherson, whose cooking I greatly enjoyed when he was head chef at The Feathers in Woodstock, near Oxford. The mixture of flavors here is delicious. Serve with a Médoc or St. Emilion.

4 firm pears, peeled
4 tablespoons lemon juice
½ cup sugar
1 pound boneless loin of lamb
Salt, freshly ground pepper
1 cup mixed chopped fresh herbs
   such as thyme, parsley, mint,
   tarragon, rosemary, chervil or
   basil

2 tablespoons butter
1 cup Sauce Demi-glace (see
   Index)
4 tablespoons dry red wine

Put the pears in a single layer into a large shallow saucepan. Add the lemon juice and sugar and cold water barely to cover. Bring to a simmer, cover, and poach until the pears are tender, about 15 minutes. Cool pears in the liquid. Lift out pears, halve and core them, then cut them into lengthwise slices. Set aside.

Season the lamb with salt and pepper, then roll in the chopped herbs, pressing lightly so that the herbs stick to the meat. In a skillet heat the butter and sauté the lamb over moderate heat, turning frequently so as not to burn the herbs. Cook for about 5 minutes, or longer if better done lamb is preferred. Lift lamb out of the skillet onto a board and cut it into 4 crosswise slices. Cut each slice lengthwise on a slant and arrange in an overlapping pattern on one side of each of 4 heated plates. Arrange the slices of pear on the other side of the plate.

Heat the demi-glace in a small saucepan with the wine and bring to a simmer. Pour the sauce onto the middle of the plates and serve immediately.

SERVES 4.

RACK OF LAMB WITH MUSTARD AND FRESH HERBS

❖   ❖   ❖

David Moir, whose cooking I enjoyed when he was head chef at Gleddoch House at Langbank near Glasgow in Scotland, uses much the same mixture of fresh herbs as Willie MacPherson, but the finished dish is very different. It is wonderfully well flavored, and delightful for a dinner party as it is not difficult or time-consuming. Serve with a Médoc or St. Emilion.

2 racks of lamb, cleaned of fat,
    rib bones trimmed
Salt, freshly ground pepper
3 tablespoons butter
2 tablespoons minced shallots
1 garlic clove, crushed
2 medium-size tomatoes, peeled,
    seeded and chopped

1 cup mixed chopped herbs such
    as mint, chives, rosemary,
    chervil and sage
3 tablespoons freshly made bread
    crumbs
4 tablespoons Dijon mustard
1½ cups reduced Lamb Stock
    (see Index) for gravy

Ask the butcher to cut the rack so that it is easy to carve through the chops. Season the lamb with salt and pepper and put it into a baking pan. Bake in a preheated moderate oven (350°F.) for about 20 minutes. The lamb will be pink.

While the lamb is cooking heat 1 tablespoon of the butter in a small skillet and cook 1 tablespoon of the shallots, the garlic and tomatoes for 3 to 4 minutes. Season to taste with salt and pepper and transfer to a bowl. Heat 2 tablespoons of the butter in the same skillet, add the rest of the shallots, and sauté until they are soft. Stir in the herbs and bread crumbs, season with salt and pepper, and stir to mix. Transfer to a bowl.

When the lamb is cooked, remove it from the oven and spread it liberally with the mustard, then coat with a layer of the tomato mixture topped with a layer of the herb and bread-crumb mixture. Return to the oven for a few minutes to reheat.

Serve on a heated large platter and carve into 2 chops per person. Serve with the lamb gravy and straw potatoes.

S E R V E S 6.

BONED RACK OF LAMB WITH FLAGEOLETS AND PORT SAUCE

❖ ❖ ❖

This makes a change of pace from the usual lamb dish, and is uncomplicated to cook. Robert Gardiner, head chef at Ardsheal House Hotel at Kentallen, of Appin in Scotland, developed the recipe, which has his own special touches in the way the beans are cooked and in the Port wine sauce. Serve with a white Port.

1½ cups dried flageolets, soaked in
   cold water overnight
1 onion, stuck with 2 or 3 cloves
8 tablespoons butter
1 tablespoon vegetable oil
1 medium-size onion, chopped
   fine
½ cup dry red wine
2 medium-size tomatoes, peeled,
   seeded and chopped
2 tablespoons tomato purée

2 garlic cloves, minced
Salt, freshly ground pepper
2 tablespoons minced parsley
1 rack of lamb, boned but with
   fillet still attached to the "flap"
   of meat, trimmed of fat
2 tablespoons chopped shallots
½ cup Tawny Port wine
1¼ cups Veal or Lamb Stock
   (see Index)
¼ cup light cream (optional)

Drain and rinse the soaked beans and put them into a large saucepan with cold water to cover by about 2 inches. Add the onion stuck with cloves. Bring to a boil, lower the heat and simmer, covered, until the beans are just tender, about 1 hour. The time will vary according to the freshness of the beans. Discard the onion. Drain the beans and put into a bowl. Reserve 1 cup of the cooking liquid.

Rinse out and dry the saucepan. Heat 2 tablespoons of the butter and the oil and sauté the onion until soft. Add the wine and reduce over moderately high heat by half. Add the tomatoes, tomato purée, garlic and the 1 cup cooking liquid from the beans. Simmer over low heat for about 20 minutes, or until the sauce is thick. Add the beans, mix thoroughly, and season to taste with salt and pepper. Just before serving reheat the beans and stir in the parsley.

Roll up the boned rack of lamb loosely and put into a baking pan with the folded end down. Cook in a preheated hot oven (425°F.) for about 25 minutes for rare, 30 minutes for medium rare. The exact time will depend on the thickness of the flap. Be careful not to

(recipe continues)

overcook as the lamb should be pink. Lift out of the baking pan and set on a warmed platter to rest for 10 minutes.

While the lamb is resting make the sauce. Pour off the fat from the baking pan and add 2 tablespoons of the butter. Add the shallots and sauté over moderate heat until they are soft. Pour in the Port wine and simmer until reduced almost to a glaze. Add the veal or lamb stock and simmer to reduce until it is thickened. Add the cream, if using it, heat through, and remove from the heat. Beat in remaining 4 tablespoons of butter, cut into bits. Taste for seasoning and add salt and pepper, if necessary.

Cut the lamb into 9 slices. Put a pile of beans in the center of each of 3 heated plates. Arrange the lamb slices around the beans and spoon the sauce over the lamb, or serve the sauce separately.

SERVES 3.

LOIN OF LAMB WITH FRESH HERB SAUCE

This is a rather grand dish, the creation of Nick Gill, head chef at Hambleton Hall, in Oakham, Leicestershire, an attractive country house hotel run by Tim and Stefa Hart with great flair. It is not a difficult dish to make. With a little organization and doing things ahead of time, it can be a splendid dish for a dinner party. Serve with a Médoc or St. Emilion.

2 to 2½ pounds boned loin of
   lamb
Salt, freshly ground pepper
¾ cup olive or vegetable oil
½ cup minced mixed herbs,
   preferably fresh
4 cups Lamb Stock or rich
   Chicken Stock (see Index)

½ cup each of chopped fresh
   tarragon, chervil, mint, thyme
   and parsley, or other fresh
   green herbs
3 tablespoons minced shallots
½ cup dry vermouth
1 cup heavy cream, or Fresh
   White Cheese (see Index)

Vegetable Garnish

3 pounds small new potatoes
2 pounds small white turnips,
  peeled
2 medium-size carrots, scraped
  and sliced

½ pound snow peas, trimmed
12 asparagus tips

A day ahead of time season the lamb with salt and pepper and put it into a shallow dish with ½ cup of the oil and the ½ cup chopped mixed herbs. Combine thoroughly, cover, and refrigerate overnight.

When ready to cook, pour the lamb stock into a saucepan and reduce over moderately high heat to 2 cups. Plunge the herbs into a large saucepan of briskly boiling salted water and blanch for 1 minute. Drain and refresh in cold water. Drain again thoroughly and put into a blender or food processor. Reduce to a purée. Add the shallots and vermouth to the lamb stock and simmer until the stock is reduced to 1 cup. Stir in the cream and simmer over low heat, uncovered, until the sauce is slightly thickened. If using fresh white cheese, stir it into the stock and heat through. Add the herb purée, taste for seasoning, and add salt and pepper to taste. Strain through a sieve into a saucepan, pushing down hard on the solids to extract all the juices. Reheat and keep warm.

Cook all the garnish vegetables separately in boiling salted water, and drain. Arrange on a heated platter, cover, and keep warm until ready to serve. Fry the cooked new potatoes in a little of the oil until golden.

Remove the lamb from the marinade and wipe off the herbs. In a large heavy skillet that will hold the lamb comfortably, heat remaining oil and sauté the lamb over fairly high heat, turning from time to time, until lamb is browned on the outside and pink inside, about 8 minutes. Remove from the pan and slice into medallions.

Have ready 8 heated plates and pour the herb sauce onto them. Arrange the lamb slices in a semicircle on each plate and arrange the vegetables in little heaps on the plates. Serve any extra sauce separately.

SERVES 8.

MELI-MELO OF LAMB WITH GARLIC AND ROSEMARY

❖   ❖   ❖

This is a most attractive way to serve a medley of lamb, using the innards as well as the loin. It is the inspiration of Paul Gayler, head chef at Inigo Jones restaurant in London. Serve with a St. Emilion.

Sauce

6 tablespoons butter
2 tablespoons minced shallots
4 garlic cloves, crushed
1 bunch of rosemary sprigs

½ cup dry white wine
1 cup Lamb Stock (see Index)
Salt, freshly ground pepper

Lamb

4 lamb tongues
1¼ pounds loin of lamb
½ pound lamb sweetbreads, blanched

4 lamb kidneys
1 tablespoon vegetable oil
8 large garlic cloves, unpeeled

Heat 2 tablespoons of the butter in a small saucepan and add the shallots, garlic and 1 sprig of the rosemary. Cover and cook over very low heat until shallots are tender. Add the white wine and simmer for 3 to 4 minutes. Add the lamb stock and simmer over moderately high heat until the sauce is thickened. Strain the sauce and stir in 1 tablespoon of the butter. Set aside.

Put the lamb tongues into a saucepan just large enough to hold them comfortably and add water to cover. Simmer until tongues are tender, for 1 to 1½ hours. Add salt halfway through the cooking. Lift tongues out and cut into lengthwise ¼-inch-thick slices. Return to the cooking liquid and keep warm.

Heat 1 tablespoon of the butter in a baking pan and sear the loin of lamb, turning to seal all over. Roast in a preheated moderate oven (375°F.), topped with a large sprig of rosemary, for 20 minutes. The lamb should be pink. Remove from the oven, cover, and keep warm.

Put the sweetbreads into a saucepan with salted water to cover and simmer, covered, for 15 minutes. Drain; cover with cold water. When cool remove any membranes. Sauté sweetbreads in remaining 2 tablespoons of butter. Cut into thin slices, cover, and keep warm.

Cut the kidneys into slices about ⅛ inch thick and sauté in the vegetable oil over moderately high heat for about 1 minute.

The garlic cloves can be cooked in the oven at the same time as the lamb. Wrap them in a piece of aluminum foil and put into the oven with the lamb. When the lamb is done, turn the oven up to 400°F. and cook the garlic cloves for about 30 minutes longer, or until they are soft. When cool enough to handle, peel off the skins.

To serve, have ready 4 heated plates. Cut the lamb into 4 slices, then cut the slices lengthwise and fan them out onto the plates. Arrange the tongues, sweetbreads and kidneys round the lamb, then pour the warmed sauce around the meats. Garnish with the garlic cloves and sprigs of rosemary. Serve immediately, with celeriac or spinach on a small plate.

S E R V E S 4.

V A R I A T I O N : Alan Vikops of the County hotel in Canterbury, Kent, has an interesting variation on Meli-Melo which he calls Potpourri of Lamb with Tarragon Sauce. Instead of loin, he uses the fillet of a boned rack of lamb, cut into 4 slices and sautéed quickly in butter for about 4 minutes in all. Instead of sweetbreads he uses 2 pairs of lamb brains, which are peeled, blanched, and cooked in lamb stock for about 8 minutes, then sliced and kept warm. He does not have the garlic cloves or rosemary as a garnish; instead, he uses two 2-inch-square puff-pastry cases, stuffed with 8 sautéed and sliced lamb kidneys.

The sauce is quite different. In a saucepan combine 1 cup dry white wine, 2 tablespoons tarragon vinegar, 1 tablespoon chopped shallot and a few tarragon stems. Bring to a simmer and cook, uncovered, until the liquid is reduced by half. Add 5 cups hot lamb stock and continue to simmer until the liquid is reduced to 1 cup. Strain. Return liquid to the saucepan. When ready to serve, warm it and beat in 3 tablespoons butter, cut into bits; keep the sauce warm. The tongues, simmered in lamb stock for 1 to 1½ hours, are sliced.

To serve, pour the sauce onto 4 heated plates. Put the stuffed pastry squares in the center of the plates and surround with the lamb, tongues and brains. Garnish with a sprig of tarragon.

S E R V E S 4.

LAMB SCALLOPS WITH HAZELNUTS AND ORANGE

❖   ❖   ❖

Roy Richards, chef patron of Manor House restaurant, Pickworth in Lincolnshire presents a leg of lamb in a new guise. This unusual, but not difficult recipe would make a fine party dish. Serve with a Beaujolais.

½ cup shelled hazelnuts
7-pound leg of lamb, boned
Freshly ground pepper
3 tablespoons vegetable oil

1 tablespoon grated orange rind
Salt
⅓ cup Cognac or other brandy
2 tablespoons minced parsley

Spread the hazelnuts on a baking sheet and toast them in a preheated moderate oven (375°F.) for 15 minutes. Wrap the nuts in a kitchen towel and let them steam for 15 minutes, then rub off the skins. Crush them coarse with a rolling pin.

Cut the lamb across the grain into ¼-inch scallops. Season them generously with freshly ground black pepper. Heat 1 tablespoon of the oil in a large heavy skillet and sauté about one third of the lamb scallops for 30 seconds. Turn them and sprinkle with one third of the orange rind, one third of the nuts, and salt to taste. Sauté for a further 30 seconds. Transfer to a platter, cover, and keep warm while cooking the rest of the scallops. Sauté remaining scallops in 2 batches in the same way. Transfer them to the platter and keep warm.

Pour the Cognac or other brandy into the skillet, set over moderate heat, and scrape up any brown bits. Sprinkle the lamb with the parsley and pour the Cognac mixture over it. Serve with potatoes and a green vegetable, or with a green salad.

S E R V E S   6.

PORK, KIDNEY AND CUCUMBER HOTPOT

❖   ❖   ❖

Graham Flanagan, head chef at the Cottage in the Wood, Malvern Wells, Hereford and Worcester, greatly values traditional regional cooking, which he feels is of real importance in a nation's cooking. It often needs updating, which he does while keeping the true spirit of the dish. Serve with a Rioja.

1 pound boneless pork, preferably loin, cut into 1-inch cubes
2 pork kidneys, cut into ½-inch slices
Flour for dredging
Salt, freshly ground pepper
2 tablespoons butter
1 tablespoon vegetable oil
2 medium-size onions, chopped fine
½ pound tart green cooking apples, peeled, cored, and cut into chunks

¾ pound hothouse cucumber, unpeeled, cut into pieces 1 by ½ inch
Pinch of dried sage, or 1 fresh sage leaf, chopped
1 bay leaf
1 tablespoon tomato purée
2 cups brown stock

Dredge the pork pieces and kidney slices with flour seasoned with salt and pepper, shaking to remove excess flour.

Heat the butter and oil in a large heavy skillet and brown the meats lightly. Lift out the meats with a slotted spoon and transfer to a casserole. Add the onions to the skillet and sauté over moderate heat until onions are soft. Add the apples and cucumber and sauté for 1 minute longer. Transfer vegetables to the casserole, season with salt and pepper, and add sage, bay leaf, tomato purée and stock. Add a little more stock if necessary barely to cover. Cover and simmer over low heat for about 1 hour, or until pork is tender.

SERVES 4.

LOIN OF PORK WITH APPLE AND ONION PURÉE

❖   ❖   ❖

Brian Prideaux-Brune of Plumber Manor, the family home of the Prideaux-Brunes at Sturminster Newton in Dorset since the early seventeenth century, and now a restaurant with rooms, is an unpretentious but highly original chef, not interested in cooking whims and fashions. Serve with a Beaujolais.

4 *tart green apples, such as* *Granny Smiths, peeled, cored,* *and chopped coarse*	12 *thin-cut boned pork loin chops*
2 *medium-size onions, chopped*	⅓ *cup dry vermouth, preferably* *Noilly Prat*
Salt, freshly ground pepper	1¼ *cups Veal Stock or Chicken*
4 *tablespoons butter*	*Stock (see Index)*
	⅔ *cup heavy cream*

Combine the apples and onions and ¼ cup water in a saucepan. Simmer, covered, until apples and onions are both soft. Drain; discard the excess liquid. Mash the mixture to a purée with a fork, or purée quickly in a food processor. Season with salt and pepper.

Heat the butter in a large skillet and sear the chops very quickly on both sides. Transfer chops to a baking pan large enough to hold them in a single layer, and spread them with the apple and onion purée. Cook in a preheated very hot oven (450°F.) until done, about 7 minutes. Transfer chops to a platter and keep them warm.

Pour the vermouth into the baking pan on top of the stove and simmer over moderate heat, scraping up the brown bits. Add the stock and simmer until the liquid is reduced to about ½ cup. Add the cream and simmer until sauce is lightly thickened. Taste for seasoning and add salt and pepper if necessary.

Spoon the sauce onto 4 heated plates and arrange the pork chops on top.

S E R V E S 4.

GARNISHED PORK SCALLOPS

❖   ❖   ❖

This recipe is another from Michael Collom, head chef at the Priory Hotel in Bath, Avon. The hotel, built in Gothic style, is set in spacious gardens near the center of the charming Georgian town. Michael's cooking is consistently excellent. His aim is to put together ingredients that will create the right harmony in a dish. He is open to new ideas but refuses to follow the whims of fashion, as this dish shows. Serve with a Côte du Rhône.

4 eggs
1 cup grated Gruyère cheese
½ cup grated Parmesan cheese
Salt, freshly ground pepper
⅛ teaspoon cayenne pepper
2 tablespoons butter
2 cups thin-sliced mushrooms
¼ pound lean ham, cut into
  julienne strips

¼ cup Veal or Chicken Stock
  (see Index)
6 pork scallops, each about 6
  ounces
Flour
Oil for deep-frying
Savory Rice (see Index)
Garnish: watercress sprigs

Break the eggs into a bowl, stir to mix, and add the Gruyère and Parmesan cheeses. Season with salt, pepper and cayenne. Set aside.

Heat the butter in a skillet and sauté the mushrooms over moderately high heat until they have given up all their liquid, about 6 minutes. Add the ham and cook for 1 minute longer. Transfer the mixture to a small saucepan, pour in the stock, and set aside.

Dredge the pork scallops with flour seasoned with salt and pepper; shake to remove excess flour. In a large skillet heat about 2 inches of oil. Dip each scallop into the egg and cheese mixture and deep-fry in the oil until crisp and golden, turning once or twice, about 15 minutes over moderate heat. Drain on paper towels. Warm the ham and mushroom mixture.

Have ready the Savory Rice. Serve the pork scallops on top of a serving of rice with the ham and mushroom mixture at the side. Garnish, if liked, with sprigs of watercress.

S E R V E S 6.

VENISON AND ORANGE STEW

❖ ❖ ❖

Martin Bredda is chef to the Earl and Countess of Normanton who make the family seat, Somerley in Hampshire, available for special lunch and dinner parties and weekend stays, as well as for banquets and business seminars. His aims are simple: a high standard of cooking and good presentation. This stew transcends his aims. It could hardly be easier to cook or more delicious to eat. Serve with a Rioja.

4 tablespoons vegetable oil
¾ pound sliced bacon, chopped coarse
6 tablespoons minced shallots
6 tablespoons tomato purée
4 cups dry white wine
7 cups brown stock
4 garlic cloves, minced
2 pounds mushrooms, sliced
3 tablespoons juniper berries, crushed

Bouquet garni: 1 bay leaf, 1 thyme sprig, 2 parsley sprigs, tied with a piece of thread
Grated rind of 1 lemon
3 oranges, well washed and halved, seeds removed
6 pounds boneless shoulder of venison, cut into 1½-inch cubes
Salt, freshly ground pepper
Flour for dredging the venison

In a large heavy casserole or kettle heat 1 tablespoon of the oil and add the bacon and shallots. Sauté over moderate heat for about 8 minutes. Add the tomato purée and stir well to mix. Add the wine, stock, garlic, mushrooms, juniper berries, bouquet garni, lemon rind and halved oranges. Bring the mixture to a boil and simmer, stirring from time to time, for 20 minutes.

Season the venison with salt and pepper and dredge with flour, shaking off excess flour. Heat remaining 3 tablespoons of oil in a large skillet and sear the venison cubes in it, in batches. Transfer to the casserole or kettle, cover, and cook in a preheated hot oven (450°F.) for 1¾ hours, or until the meat is very tender. Serve with potatoes or noodles and a green vegetable or salad.

S E R V E S 14 to 16.

The recipe can be halved.

VENISON WITH PEPPERY APRICOTS

❖ ❖ ❖

This was one of Alan Casey's dishes that I most enjoyed when he was head chef at Culloden House, Inverness in Scotland. Serve with a Côte du Rhône.

8 medallions (slices) of venison, each about 3 ounces
4 tablespoons butter
4 tablespoons brandy
1 cup Game Stock (see Index) or brown stock

4 whole cloves
1 bay leaf
1 tablespoon red-currant jelly
½ cup heavy cream
Salt, freshly ground black pepper
16 dried apricots, soaked

Flatten the venison medallions to ¼-inch thickness. In a skillet heat the butter and sauté the venison over fairly high heat, turning once, for about 3 minutes a side for rare, 4 minutes for medium rare. Pour 3 tablespoons of the brandy over the meat, and ignite it. Remove venison from the skillet, cover, and keep warm while making the sauce.

Into the skillet pour the game stock; add the cloves, bay leaf and red-currant jelly. Reduce to half, then stir in the cream and simmer until slightly thickened. Strain the sauce. Season to taste with salt and pepper and warm through.

Put the apricots and the water in which they have been soaking into a small saucepan and simmer them gently if they are at all hard. If they are soft, simply warm them through. Drain. Coat apricots liberally with freshly ground black pepper. Sprinkle with remaining tablespoon of brandy.

To serve put 2 medallions of venison on each of 4 heated plates and pour the warm sauce over them. Garnish with the apricots.

SERVES 4.

MEDALLIONS OF VENISON WITH GREEN PEPPERCORNS

❖   ❖   ❖

Philip Burgess, head chef at the Arundell Arms in Lifton, Devon, has a great respect for all types of food. He enjoys cooking with sophisticated as well as simple ingredients. His aim is to produce dishes that are not disguised with heavy garnishes or sauces and where natural flavors emerge from the cooking at their peak. Serve with a Côte du Rhône.

Marinade

1 garlic clove, crushed
1 medium-size onion, chopped
1 medium-size carrot, scraped
  and chopped

2 cups dry white wine
1½ tablespoons olive oil
1 bay leaf
Salt, freshly ground pepper

Venison

1½ pounds boneless venison loin,
  cut into 8 slices
Flour for dredging
1 tablespoon vegetable oil
4 tablespoons butter
¼ cup dry white wine

1 tablespoon green peppercorns,
  crushed
1 cup heavy cream
½ cup lightly thickened rich
  brown stock

Combine all the ingredients for the marinade in an earthenware, stainless-steel or enamel bowl, add the venison, and refrigerate for 24 hours.

Lift the venison out of the marinade and pat dry with paper towels. Lightly flatten the slices to about ½-inch thickness. Dredge with flour; shake to remove excess flour. In a large heavy skillet, heat the oil and butter and sauté the venison for 5 to 7 minutes, turning occasionally. The meat should remain pink inside. Lift meat out of the skillet onto a plate, cover, and keep warm.

Pour excess fat from the pan. Add the wine, peppercorns and cream and reduce over moderate heat by half. Add the brown stock and any juices that may have collected on the plate with the venison, and simmer until the sauce is slightly thickened. Taste for seasoning and add salt and pepper if necessary.

Arrange 2 medallions of venison on each of 4 heated plates and pour the sauce over them. Serve with rice or potatoes and a green vegetable.

SERVES 4.

VENISON COLLOPS WITH JUNIPER BERRIES AND APPLE AND CRANBERRY SAUCE

❖   ❖   ❖

David Harding of Bodysgallen Hall in Llandudno, Wales, is able to get very fine venison. He has developed this recipe to take advantage of it. The medley of flavors combines deliciously. Serve with a Rioja or Cabernet Sauvignon.

4-pound saddle of venison,
 boned, bones reserved
1 cup dry red wine
12 juniper berries, crushed
2 sprigs of thyme
2 sprigs of marjoram
1 bay leaf
1 tablespoon vegetable oil
1 medium-size onion, chopped
1 medium-size carrot, scraped
 and chopped
½ cup Sauce Demi-glace (see
 Index)

½ cup light cream
Salt, freshly ground pepper
4 tablespoons Clarified Butter
 (see Index)
1 tablespoon raw butter
½ cup fresh cranberries
1 tart apple, peeled, cored and
 diced
2 teaspoons sugar
2 tablespoons minced parsley

Put the venison into a dish just large enough to hold it comfortably. Pour in the wine, add the juniper berries, thyme, marjoram and bay leaf. Cover and refrigerate for 24 hours, turning 2 or 3 times.

Chop the venison bones. In a casserole heat the oil; add the bones, onion and carrot and cook over moderate heat, stirring from time to time, until bones are browned. Lift venison out of the marinade, pat it dry with paper towels, and set aside. Add the marinade to the

(recipe continues)

casserole with the bones and cook uncovered until the marinade is reduced by half. Add the demi-glace and simmer, uncovered, over low heat for 20 minutes. Strain the liquid through a fine sieve. Return it to the casserole, stir in the cream, taste for seasoning, and add salt and pepper if necessary. Keep hot.

Cut the venison into 8 equal slices (collops) and season with salt and pepper. Heat the clarified butter in a heavy skillet and sauté the collops for 1 minute on each side. They will be pink inside.

Put 2 slices of venison on each of 4 heated plates. Keep warm. Meanwhile in a small pan heat the tablespoon of raw butter and quickly sauté the cranberries and apple sprinkled with the sugar. Pour the sauce over the venison slices and top with the cranberries and apples. Sprinkle with the parsley.

SERVES 4.

VARIATION: In his Mignon of Venison with Black Currants, Ken Stott, head chef of Kildrummy Castle Hotel, in Grampian, uses the same cut of venison as David Harding with different but equally delicious results.

2 pounds boned saddle of venison, cut into 8 slices	½ cup Sauce Demi-glace (see Index)
4 tablespoons butter	½ cup heavy cream
¼ cup Crème de Cassis liqueur	Salt, freshly ground pepper
	1 cup black currants

Flatten the venison slices. Heat the butter in a large heavy skillet and sauté the slices quickly on both sides. Keep them rare as they should be pink inside. This takes only about 1 minute a side. Remove venison from the pan, place on a warm platter, and keep hot, covered. Pour the Crème de Cassis into the pan, add the demi-glace and cream, and simmer until slightly thickened. Season to taste with salt and pepper. Add the black currants, cook for 1 or 2 minutes longer, and pour over the venison.

SERVES 4.

NOISETTE OF VENISON WITH LAVERBREAD AND ORANGE SAUCE

❖   ❖   ❖

Laverbread, a Welsh specialty, is made from purple laver (*Porphyra umbilicalis*), a seaweed which looks very like sea lettuce except that it is purple-red or brown instead of green. It is cooked down and sold canned in specialty shops and health-food stores and is eaten as a garnish, either hot or cold, with seafood, meat or poultry. It makes a delicious, fresh-tasting and delicate sauce for the richly flavored venison. Cooked, very thoroughly drained and chopped spinach can be used instead as laverbread is not always easy to find. Tim Cumming, chef-patron of the Hole in the Wall restaurant in Bath, developed this unusual dish. Serve with a Rioja.

2¼ pounds boned and tied saddle   6 slices of bacon
of venison, preferably roe deer

Sauce

½ pound laverbread, or 1 pound   Grated rind of 1 lemon
spinach   1 tablespoon lemon juice
Grated rind of 1 orange   2 tablespoons butter
½ cup orange juice   Salt, freshly ground pepper

Wrap the venison in the bacon and place in a baking pan. Roast in a preheated hot oven (425°F.) for 10 to 12 minutes. Meat should remain pink in the middle. Remove and discard the bacon and cut the venison into 6 slices. Cover and keep warm.

If using laverbread, which is already cooked, put it into a saucepan with all the other sauce ingredients and heat it through, stirring to mix. Season it generously with black pepper. Taste and if necessary add a little salt.

If using spinach, wash and trim away any coarse stems. Drop the spinach into a large saucepan filled with briskly boiling salted water, bring back to a boil, and cook for 4 minutes. Drain and refresh in cold water. Drain again very thoroughly and chop. Put into a saucepan with all the other sauce ingredients exactly as for laverbread.

Spoon a layer of sauce on each of 6 heated plates and put a noisette of venison on top. Serve immediately.

S E R V E S 6.

ROE DEER WITH SOUR CREAM AND CAPERS

❖   ❖   ❖

Stephen Ross, chef-patron of Homewood Park, at Freshford, near Bath in Avon, likes his dishes to be well flavored with plenty of character. He particularly likes to cook with fine, local produce. This dish, like many others that he and chef Antony Pitt create in the Homewood Park kitchen, is the result of fine ingredients stimulating creative talent. If the haunch of a young roe deer is not available, use tenderloin or round of venison. Serve with a Rioja.

1 small haunch of roe deer	½ cup lemon juice
¼ pound (1 stick) butter	Grated rind of 2 lemons
1 small onion, chopped fine	1¼ cups sour cream
1 slice of bacon, chopped fine	2 tablespoons capers
½ cup dry white wine	Salt, freshly ground pepper
½ cup Chicken Stock (see Index)	

Have the venison cut into twelve ½-inch slices. In a skillet heat the butter and sauté the venison slices over fairly high heat, turning once, for about 1 minute a side. Remove to a serving dish, cover, and keep warm.

Add the onion and bacon to the skillet with the white wine and chicken stock and simmer, uncovered, to reduce by half. Add the lemon juice and grated rind, sour cream and capers. Season to taste with salt and pepper.

Put 2 slices of venison on each of 6 heated plates. Spoon the sauce over them and serve with rice or new potatoes.

S E R V E S   6.

MEDALLIONS OF VENISON IN GREEN PEPPERCORN JELLY

❖ ❖ ❖

Julian Waterer, who was head chef at Greywalls hotel in Scotland, great venison country, is now at the Salisbury restaurant at Old Hatfield, Hertfordshire. He serves this as an appetizer, attractive in a meal where the main course is fish. I find it makes a perfect main course for two for a warm weather lunch or dinner. It is well flavored and original in concept like all Julian's recipes. Serve with a Rioja.

Jelly

2½ cups clarified Game Stock or Beef Stock (see Index)
¼ cup dry red wine
¼ cup Tawny Port wine

1 envelope unflavored gelatin, 7 grams
1 tablespoon red-wine vinegar
2 tablespoons sugar

Venison and Sauce

12 ounces boned and tied saddle of venison
1½ teaspoons green peppercorns

3 bunches of watercress
Salt, freshly ground pepper
6 Oatcakes (see Index)

Pour the stock, red wine and Port into a medium-size saucepan and reduce over moderate heat to 2 cups. Sprinkle the gelatin over ¼ cup cold water and stir into the hot stock; simmer for a minute or two to dissolve the gelatin. Combine the vinegar and sugar in a small saucepan and simmer until the mixture is syrupy. Stir into the stock and simmer over low heat, stirring, until sugar is dissolved. Cool.

Roast the venison in a baking pan in a preheated hot oven (425°F.) for 8 to 10 minutes. It should be pink inside. Remove from the oven and cool.

If serving as an appetizer, pour a thin layer of jellied stock into 6 small (about 1-cup) ramekins or soufflé molds and refrigerate until set. Sprinkle with the green peppercorns. Cut the venison into 6 slices and put a slice into each mold. Pour in the rest of the jellied stock to cover the venison and refrigerate for at least 2 hours.

While the jelly is setting, make the watercress sauce. Wash the watercress and remove and discard the tough stems. Put the watercress

(recipe continues)

into a blender or food processor and process to a purée. Transfer to a bowl and season to taste with salt and pepper.

To serve, place an oatcake on each of the 6 plates. Make a border of watercress purée round each oatcake. Unmold the jellied venison and place one on each oatcake.

If serving as a main course for two or three, either serve 2 or 3 venison molds on larger plates per person, or make them in larger molds, cutting the venison into thicker slices. If liked, pour the watercress sauce onto the plates and serve the oatcakes separately. The crunchy flavor complements the venison.

S E R V E S 6 as an appetizer, 2 or 3 as a main course.

RABBIT

❖   ❖   ❖

RABBIT is an ideal meat from today's dietary point of view. It is lean, high in protein, with less fat and cholesterol than chicken or beef, yet it has been singularly neglected for years. Its popularity is now increasing. Excellent top-grade American packaged rabbits, weighing 2½ to 3 pounds, can be found in supermarket freezers, usually cut into serving portions, though some whole or halved rabbits can be found. Fresh rabbits are sometimes available in butcher shops. Domestic English rabbits are of very high quality, and sometimes a member of the kitchen staff of a country house hotel will raise a few domestic bunnies as a sideline. They have tender white flesh, and some of the best dishes I have eaten have been the rabbit dishes of inspired young chefs. I have collected the ones I enjoyed most.

RABBIT STEW MALTAISE

❖   ❖   ❖

Rabbit becomes something special when cooked according to this recipe, the creation of David Nicholls. I first met David and enjoyed his cooking when he was head chef at the Old Lodge at Limpsfield, Surrey, and found his enthusiasm infectious. He is now head chef at Waltons in London. His first job was as a footman to H.M. The Queen at Buckingham Palace, but cooking soon claimed him and at 18 he became the youngest *chef de partie* the London Waldorf Hotel ever had. His culinary philosophy demands simplicity and the freshest and best produce, and he cares a great deal about presentation. Serve with a Côte de Beaune or Côte de Nuits.

Marinade

2 large Bermuda-type onions,
    chopped fine
2 cups dry red wine
3 garlic cloves, crushed

4 parsley sprigs
1 teaspoon peppercorns
1 sprig of thyme
2 bay leaves

Rabbit

1 rabbit, 2½ to 3 pounds, cut
    into 8 serving pieces
Salt, freshly ground pepper

3 tablespoons vegetable oil
2 cups Veal or Beef Stock (see
    Index)

Garnishes

4 medium-size tomatoes, peeled,
    seeded and quartered
4 small heads of purple broccoli
    (calabrese), freshly cooked
4 large whole unpeeled garlic
    cloves, sautéed in butter

2 tablespoons minced parsley
Grated rinds of 1 orange and
    1 lemon

Combine all the ingredients for the marinade in a large bowl and add the rabbit pieces. Cover and refrigerate for 48 hours, turning the pieces 2 or 3 times.

Lift out the rabbit pieces and pat them dry with paper towels. Season with salt and pepper. In a heavy skillet heat the oil and sauté the rabbit until lightly browned all over. Transfer rabbit to a heavy casserole and pour in the marinade and the veal or beef stock. Bring to a simmer, cover, and cook in a preheated moderate oven (350°F.) for 2 hours, or until rabbit is tender. Lift out the rabbit pieces to a heated dish, cover, and keep warm. Over moderately high heat reduce the liquid in the casserole until it is slightly thickened. Taste for seasoning and add salt and pepper if necessary. Strain the sauce and discard the solids. Return sauce to the casserole and heat it through.

Arrange the rabbit pieces on 4 warm plates and spoon the sauce over them. Arrange the warm broccoli and a garlic clove beside the rabbit and the quartered tomato on the other side. Sprinkle with the orange and lemon rind, then with the parsley.

SERVES 4.

ROAST SADDLE OF RABBIT
WITH MUSTARD SAUCE

❖   ❖   ❖

Nick Gill, head chef at Hambleton Hall, Oakham, is the originator of this well-flavored, uncomplicated dish, a delight for all lovers of rabbit dishes. Serve with a Burgundy, either a Côte de Beaune or Côte de Nuits.

1 pound saddle of rabbit,
  thoroughly thawed if frozen
Salt, freshly ground pepper
½ teaspoon dried thyme
2 slices of bacon, halved
  crosswise
1 carrot, chopped
1 onion, chopped
1 celery rib, chopped
3 garlic cloves, minced

4 parsley sprigs
1 bay leaf, crumbled
1 cup dry white wine
1 tablespoon vegetable oil
½ cup heavy cream, or Fresh
  White Cheese (see Index)
1 tablespoon moutarde de
  Meaux, or other French
  coarse-grain mustard
Garnish: watercress sprigs

Remove as much as possible of the thin, silvery skin covering the top of the saddle of rabbit. Season the rabbit with salt, pepper and half of the dried thyme. Cover the top with the bacon slices. In a shallow flameproof casserole just large enough to hold the rabbit, make a bed of the carrot, onion, celery, garlic, parsley, bay leaf and the rest of the thyme. Pour ½ cup of the white wine over the vegetables and put the rabbit, bacon side up, on the vegetables. Brush the rabbit with oil and roast it uncovered in the middle of a preheated very hot oven (475°F.) for 10 minutes. Add remaining ½ cup of wine and roast rabbit for 10 minutes longer, or until it is tender. Remove the rabbit, cover and keep warm.

Transfer the casserole to the top of the stove and bring to a boil over moderate heat. Reduce the liquid by half. Add the cream and continue to cook the sauce until it has thickened slightly. Strain the sauce through a fine sieve into a saucepan and season with salt and pepper.

Remove the bacon from the rabbit and discard. Remove the 2 fillets from the saddle, each in one piece, and cut them at a 45-degree angle into ½-inch slices. Re-form the slices into 2 fillets and return them to the saddle bones. Transfer the rabbit to a heated platter. Bring the sauce to a boil over moderate heat. Off the heat stir in the mustard.

Pour the sauce over the rabbit and serve garnished with watercress sprigs.

S E R V E S 2.

V A R I A T I O N : Pierre Chevillard, head chef at Chewton Glen Hotel in New Milton, Hampshire, has his own version of the dish.

2 *large rabbit legs, each about 12*	¼ *cup dry white wine*
ounces	¼ *cup Veal or Chicken Stock*
Salt, freshly ground pepper	*(see Index)*
4 *tablespoons butter*	¼ *cup heavy cream, or Fresh*
2 *tablespoons minced shallots*	*White Cheese (see Index)*
1 *tablespoon moutarde de Meaux*	*Cooked spinach leaves*

Season the rabbit with salt and pepper. In a heavy skillet just large enough to hold the rabbit legs, heat 2 tablespoons of the butter. Add the rabbit, reduce the heat to low and cook the rabbit, basting it constantly, for 12 to 15 minutes, or until it is tender. Remove rabbit legs, cover, and keep warm.

Rinse out and dry the skillet. Add the shallots, mustard and wine to the skillet and reduce until the wine has evaporated. Add the veal or chicken stock and the cream. Bring to a boil, lower the heat, and cook for 1 minute. Add remaining 2 tablespoons of butter, shaking the skillet until the butter has melted into the sauce.

If liked, remove the main bone from each leg, but leave the bone in if preferred. Put each leg on a heated plate, surround it by cooked spinach, and pour the sauce over the rabbit.

S E R V E S 2.

ROAST SADDLE OF HARE
WITH BLACKBERRY SAUCE

❖   ❖   ❖

Hares belong to the same family as rabbits, Leporidae. They are dark-fleshed and larger than the white-fleshed rabbits and usually have to be bespoken from a specialty butcher unless caught by a hunter. They tend to have a lot of blood but are very flavorful and worth coping with. Julian Waterer of the Salisbury restaurant at Old Hatfield, in Hertfordshire, has come up with a very simple recipe just using saddles. I used the rest of my two hares to make a fine stew. Serve with a Côte du Rhône.

2 saddles of young hare	¾ cup sugar
Salt, freshly ground pepper	2 tablespoons red-wine vinegar
4 slices of bacon	1 cup rich Game Stock or Beef
2 tablespoons vegetable oil	Stock (see Index)
1 pound blackberries	1 tablespoon butter

Season the saddles with salt and pepper and tie the bacon slices on them. Heat the oil in a heavy skillet and sauté the saddles for 1 minute on each side. Put into a baking pan and roast in a preheated hot oven (425°F.) for 15 to 20 minutes, or until saddles are tender. Remove from the pan, take off and discard the bacon, and put saddles onto a heated plate. Cover and keep warm.

Put three quarters of the blackberries in a heavy saucepan; add water barely to cover and ½ cup of the sugar. Bring to a simmer and cook uncovered for 10 minutes. Put through a sieve and set the syrup aside.

Rinse out and dry the saucepan. Add remaining ¼ cup sugar and caramelize over very low heat until it is golden brown. Add the vinegar and simmer for 3 minutes, then stir in the reserved blackberry syrup and reduce to half. Gradually add the stock, a tablespoon at a time. The sauce should not be too thin and should remain tangy. It may not be necessary to add all of the stock. Simmer for 4 minutes, then stir in the butter, off the heat.

Remove the hare fillets from the saddles and cut them into thin diagonal slices. Arrange in a fan shape on each of 4 heated plates. Trickle the sauce round them, or if preferred pour the sauce onto the plates and then arrange the hare on top. Garnish with the remainder of the blackberries. Serve vegetables such as new potatoes and a green vegetable on a separate plate.

S E R V E S 4.

RABBIT AND PRUNE TERRINE

❖　　　❖　　　❖

This unusual terrine makes a pleasant main course for lunch or a summer dinner served with salads. It can also be served as an appetizer course. It is another of the rabbit dishes invented by head chef Pierre Chevillard of Chewton Glen Hotel in Hampshire. Serve with a Burgundy, either a Côte de Beaune or Côte de Nuits.

2 rabbits, 2 pounds each
1½ pounds boneless lean pork,
　chopped coarse
1½ pounds pork fatback

Salt, freshly ground pepper
½ cup shelled pistachio nuts,
　peeled
½ pound pitted prunes

Bone the rabbits, cutting off as much meat as possible. Chop the rabbit meat coarse and combine it in a food processor with the pork and 1 pound of the pork fatback, chopped. Process just long enough to mince the meats; or put the meats through a meat grinder. Season to taste with salt and pepper and add the pistachio nuts, mixing them in thoroughly.

Line an 8-cup terrine or loaf pan with the ½ pound pork fatback cut into strips, allowing the strips to overlap the terrine. Make a layer of half of the rabbit and pork mixture. Make a layer of the prunes in 2 parallel rows and finish with the rest of the meat. Fold the fatback strips over the terrine and cover with a lid or with aluminum foil. Set terrine into a baking pan with hot water to come about halfway up the sides. Bake in a preheated moderate oven (350°F.) for 1 to 1½ hours, until the meats have shrunk slightly from the sides of the terrine. Remove the terrine from the oven and let it cool. Refrigerate until the juices have set. Unmold the terrine and slice.

S E R V E S 6 for a main course, 10 to 12 as an appetizer.

DESSERTS

❖   ❖   ❖

DESSERTS BASED on fresh fruit are increasingly popular with today's young chefs who like a meal to end on a light note. There are always fresh fruit sorbets on the menu since the sorbet as a dessert has become a universal favorite. Many chefs serve a Champagne or similar type of sorbet as a palate freshener during the meal in the old tradition, but the fruit sorbets are now an established tradition in their own right as desserts. Ice cream is also used imaginatively.

There are still some very rich desserts for self-indulgent moments. A few old favorites like Trifle and Hot Butterscotch Pudding are enduringly popular.

A glass of sweet white wine with desserts rounds out a meal pleasantly. Drink a Barsac, Sauternes, Vouvray, Tokay dessert wine, the sweet wines of the Rhine and Moselle, Muscat de Beaumes-de-Venise or the sweet California wines such as the Stony Hill Vineyard's Semillon de Soleil, and of course, Champagne.

FRUIT SHERBETS

❖   ❖   ❖

NICK GILL, head chef at Hambleton Hall, in Leicestershire, has a special way with sherbets, which he serves freshly made, either singly, or together in smaller quantities with the various fruit colors making an attractive pattern on the plate. They make a subtle and refreshing ending to a meal.

NICK GILL'S ORANGE SHERBET

❖   ❖   ❖

3 cups fresh orange juice, strained
⅓ cup confectioners' sugar, or to taste

1 to 2 tablespoons orange liqueur, according to taste
Garnish: tangerine or mandarin orange segments

Combine the orange juice, sugar and liqueur in a bowl and stir to dissolve the sugar. Taste and add more sugar if liked. Freeze the mixture in an ice-cream freezer according to the manufacturer's instructions. Or the sherbet can be made in ice-cube trays with the dividers removed. When partly frozen, remove and beat until smooth. Beat the mixture 2 or 3 times during the freezing process.

If the sherbet is not to be served immediately, put it into the freezer or freezer compartment, then transfer to the refrigerator half an hour before serving to restore the soft texture. Scoop into serving dishes and garnish with a tangerine or mandarin section.

MAKES 3 cups.

NICK GILL'S LIME SHERBET

❖   ❖   ❖

2 cups fresh lime juice, strained
2½ cups confectioners' sugar, or to taste

Garnish: thin slices of unpeeled lime

Combine the lime juice and sugar in a bowl and stir to dissolve the sugar. Taste and add more sugar if liked. Freeze the mixture in an ice-cream freezer according to the manufacturer's instructions. Or the sherbet can be made in ice-cube trays in the same way as the orange sherbet.

Serve immediately, or put into the freezer or freezer compartment and transfer to the refrigerator half an hour before serving to restore the soft texture. Scoop into serving dishes and garnish with a slice of lime.

M A K E S 3 cups.

NICK GILL'S STRAWBERRY SHERBET

❖   ❖   ❖

4 cups hulled and sliced strawberries
½ cup confectioners' sugar, or to taste

2 tablespoons lemon juice
Garnish: mint leaves and raspberries

Purée the strawberries with 1 cup water in a blender or food processor, then rub the purée through a fine sieve into a bowl to get rid of the seeds. Add the sugar and lemon juice and stir until sugar is dissolved. Taste and add more sugar or lemon juice if liked. Freeze the mixture in an ice-cream freezer according to the manufacturer's instructions. Or the sherbet can be made in ice-cube trays in the same way as the orange sherbet.

Serve immediately, or put into the freezer or freezing compartment and transfer to the refrigerator half an hour before serving to restore the soft texture. Scoop into serving dishes and garnish with a raspberry and a mint leaf.

M A K E S 4 cups.

ALMOND TUILES

❖   ❖   ❖

Nick Gill serves his sherbets with Almond Tuiles, the crisp thin almond cookies that are shaped like curved tiles. They are easy to make. This is Nick's own recipe.

3 tablespoons unsalted butter,
    softened at room temperature
⅓ cup superfine sugar
2 large egg whites, lightly beaten
½ teaspoon vanilla extract

¼ teaspoon almond extract
½ cup blanched almonds, lightly
    toasted and ground
¼ cup all-purpose flour, sifted
½ cup sliced blanched almonds

Cream the butter and sugar together in a bowl until the mixture is light and fluffy. Whisk in the egg whites in 2 batches. Add the vanilla and almond extracts and whisk again until the mixture is lightly combined. Fold in the ground almonds and the flour, then stir in the sliced almonds.

Using one quarter of the batter drop it, a teaspoon at a time, onto a buttered baking sheet, 3 inches apart. Flatten each spoonful into a circle about 2½ inches in diameter. Bake in a preheated moderate oven (375°F.) for 6 to 8 minutes, until the edges are lightly browned.

Remove immediately from the oven; using a metal spatula, take the cookies one by one from the baking sheet and curve them around a rolling pin. Slide off and cool on a rack. Any that cool too much to be easy to curve can be returned to the oven very briefly to soften. Continue in the same way with the rest of the batter.

M A K E S   about 40.

WHITE PEACH SORBET

❖   ❖   ❖

This is a most delicious sorbet which Simon Hopkinson, the head chef of Hilaire restaurant in London, created to use his favorite white peaches, which are in season only for a short time. He discovered, rather to his amusement, that canned white peaches also produce a beautifully textured and flavored sorbet.

3 large white peaches, peeled and
    pitted
1 cup peach juice, or water
4 tablespoons confectioners'
    sugar, or to taste

6 tablespoons lemon juice
¼ cup blue plum eau-de-vie
    (Quetsch), or yellow plum
    eau-de-vie (Mirabelle)
    (optional)

Chop the peaches coarse and put them into a food processor or blender
with the peach juice or water, sugar, lemon juice, and *eau-de-vie* if
using it, and process to a purée. Taste and add more sugar, if necessary.
If using canned peaches, the peach juice in the can will be sweetened;
more sugar may be necessary if using fresh peaches. Freeze in an ice
cream or sorbet freezer according to manufacturer's instructions, usually for 15 to 20 minutes.

S E R V E S 6.

ICED BOMBE

❖   ❖   ❖

Terry Boswell, chef-patronne of Combe House Hotel in Gittisham,
Devon, invented this dessert to use up some leftover meringues. It
happened one summer day when there were also lots of fine strawberries and raspberries to be had. It is a really lovely excuse for creating
a dish that is anything but plain and leftoverish-dull. It is truly luxurious.

Meringues

4 large egg whites
Pinch of salt

¼ teaspoon cream of tartar
1 cup superfine sugar

Bombe

2½ cups heavy cream
½ teaspoon vanilla extract
½ cup plus 2 tablespoons
    confectioners' sugar
2 cups chopped strawberries or
    raspberries

1 tablespoon eau-de-vie de
    Framboise (optional)
Oil for terrine

(recipe continues)

To make the meringues beat the egg whites in a large bowl with the salt until they are frothy. Add the cream of tartar and beat until they begin to hold their shape. Gradually add ¼ cup of the sugar, beating until the whites hold stiff peaks. Continue to beat while gradually adding the rest of the sugar until the whites are stiff and shiny. Line a baking sheet with buttered and lightly floured parchment paper and spoon the meringue mixture by tablespoon onto it. Bake in a preheated very slow oven (200°F.), or as low as possible, and bake for 2 hours or until the meringues are crisp and firm. Take meringues out of the oven and let them cool. Crumble into pieces the size of walnuts. Set aside.

In a large bowl beat the cream with the vanilla and 2 tablespoons of confectioners' sugar until cream stands in peaks. Toss the strawberries or raspberries in the ½ cup confectioners' sugar and fold into the whipped cream, with the *eau-de-vie* if using it. Taste and add more sugar if necessary. Fold in the crumbled meringues gently but thoroughly.

Line a terrine or loaf pan 9 by 5 inches with aluminum foil brushed with oil and pour in the cream mixture, banging the pan on the table so that the mixture drops into the corners. With a spatula, level the top. Cover with foil and freeze.

Two hours before serving, transfer the bombe to the refrigerator to let it soften slightly. Turn it out onto a serving platter and slice. If liked, serve with heavy cream or puréed raspberries, sieved to get rid of the seeds.

S E R V E S 8 to 10.

Terry Boswell says this bombe invites the cook's imagination to invent other fillings. Add half a pound of melted chocolate with toasted almonds for example; or experiment with other soft fruits. Cranberry sauce might be interesting.

ICED CRANBERRY SOUFFLÉ

❖   ❖   ❖

Lyn Hall, principal of La Petite Cuisine School of Cooking in London, says her soufflé is ideal for holiday entertaining and at any time of the year, as cranberries, which freeze well, are always available. It is also easy to make and can be prepared well ahead of time.

Topping

1¼ cups sweet cider
1 cinnamon stick
Pinch of freshly grated nutmeg
¾ cup dry red wine

2 tablespoons lemon juice
Grated rind of 1 orange
Sugar
1½ cups cranberries

Soufflé

1 cup cranberries
¼ cup Ruby Port wine
2 tablespoons water
1 cinnamon stick
1¾ cups heavy cream
3 large eggs, separated
½ cup vanilla sugar, or use ½
   cup sugar and ¼ teaspoon
   vanilla extract

2 tablespoons crème de cassis
   liqueur
Garnish: ¾ cup heavy cream,
   whipped

To make the topping, combine all the ingredients in a saucepan, using sugar to taste, and cook over low heat until the cranberries burst. Remove immediately from the heat and leave for 3 hours for the cranberries to absorb the flavor of the liquid.

To make the soufflé, put 1 cup cranberries into a saucepan with the port, water and cinnamon stick. Cook over low heat until berries burst. Drain thoroughly, reserving the liquid. Discard cinnamon stick. Chop berries and set aside in a bowl. Reduce the cooking liquid over moderate heat to 2 tablespoons. Transfer to a cup and set aside.

In a large bowl beat 1¾ cups cream until stiff. Refrigerate. In another bowl beat the egg yolks with ¼ cup of the sugar until lemon-colored and fluffy. In a large bowl beat the egg whites until they stand in peaks. Gradually beat in remaining ¼ cup sugar, and the vanilla extract if not using vanilla sugar, and beat until whites are very stiff and shiny. Fold the egg-yolk mixture into the whites, then gently but thoroughly fold eggs and the chopped cranberries into the whipped cream. Add the crème de cassis and the 2 tablespoons of reduced cranberry liquid to the mixture, then pile it into a 3-cup soufflé mold prepared with a collar. Freeze, uncovered.

Remove from the freezer and put into the refrigerator for about 2 hours before serving, to soften. Pipe or spoon a border of whipped cream on the top of the soufflé. Drain the poached cranberries that have been soaking and spoon on top of the soufflé inside the whipped cream border. Remove the collar and serve.

S E R V E S 6.

HONEY ICE CREAM WITH WILD STRAWBERRIES

❖   ❖   ❖

This is a lovely summer dessert created by Shaun Hill, when he was chef-patron of Hill's restaurant in Stratford-upon-Avon, before joining Gidleigh Park, Chagford, Devon, as head chef. It takes little time and, since it can be made ahead, is useful for entertaining. Any strawberries can be used, but Shaun prefers tiny *fraises des bois*, wild strawberries, which look very pretty on a plain white plate with the golden ice cream beside them.

1 cup milk	1 cup heavy cream
1 cup superfine sugar	2 tablespoons lemon juice
6 large egg yolks	1½ pounds strawberries,
2 tablespoons clear honey	preferably wild strawberries

Heat the milk. In a bowl cream the sugar and egg yolks until they form a ribbon. Whisk the warm milk into the egg-yolk mixture and set the bowl over hot water. Cook over low heat until the mixture thickens enough to coat a spoon. Remove from heat, stir in the honey, cream and lemon juice, and pour into an ice-cream freezer. Freeze for 20 minutes.

Arrange the strawberries in a mound on a dessert plate with the honey ice cream beside them. Any imperfect berries may be puréed in a blender or food processor and poured onto the plates as a decorative accent.

SERVES 6.

STRAWBERRIES AND VANILLA ICE CREAM GRATIN

❖   ❖   ❖

Michael Collom, head chef at the Priory Hotel at Bath in Avon, has created a novel and attractive way of serving strawberries with vanilla ice cream. It takes little time to do and makes a most elegant dessert.

4 large egg yolks
¼ cup superfine sugar
1 tablespoon Kirsch liqueur
6 macaroons

6 scoops of vanilla ice cream
1 pound strawberries, sliced
    lengthwise

In the top pan of a double boiler set over hot water on low heat whisk the egg yolks, sugar and Kirsch together until the mixture is thick and creamy. Remove from the heat and continue to whisk until it is cold. Set aside.

Crumble the macaroons into the bottoms of 6 shallow flameproof ramekins or small soufflé molds. Put a scoop of ice cream in each mold and surround it with the strawberries. Spoon the egg-yolk mixture on top and glaze quickly under a preheated hot broiler about 4 inches from the source of heat just until the top is lightly browned. Serve immediately.

S E R V E S 6.

PEACHES AND STRAWBERRIES WITH ICE CREAM

❖   ❖   ❖

John King, head chef of the Ritz Club, London, has devised a simple and attractive use for fresh peaches and strawberries, turning them into a quite glamorous and very pretty-to-look-at dessert.

3 large ripe peaches
½ pound fresh strawberries,
    about 2 cups
2 tablespoons lemon juice, or to
    taste

¼ cup superfine sugar
1 pint banana ice cream
1 large ripe banana, sliced
2 sprigs of fresh mint

Drop the peaches into briskly boiling water for a few seconds; lift out and slip off the skins. Halve the peaches and remove the pits. Have ready 6 chilled dessert plates. Place a peach half, cut side up, in the center of each dish.

Set aside six of the best strawberries. Put the rest of the strawberries in a blender or food processor with the lemon juice and sugar and reduce to a purée. Pour into a jug.

Place a scoop of ice cream in the hollow of each peach. Put the sliced bananas round the edge of the ice cream. Slice or halve the strawberries and put them round the edge with the banana slices. Place a mint leaf on top of the ice cream. Pour the strawberry purée around the peach onto the plate.

S E R V E S 6.

BROWN BREAD ICE CREAM

❖   ❖   ❖

Peter Jackson, chef-patron of The Colonial Restaurant on the High Street in Glasgow, Scotland, enjoys brown bread ice cream, so he worked out his own version. It is very rich and good. The bread crumbs add a pleasant crunch to the soft ice cream.

2 large eggs
2 large egg yolks
¼ cup plus 1 tablespoon
superfine sugar
1 vanilla bean
1¼ cups milk

1¼ cups heavy cream, partially
whipped
4 to 5 tablespoons fresh brown
bread crumbs
1 tablespoon rum

In a large bowl beat the whole eggs, egg yolks and ¼ cup sugar until well blended. Split the vanilla bean and add it to the milk in the top pan of a double boiler set over hot water on very low heat. Cover and let the vanilla infuse for 10 minutes. Do not let the milk boil. If it gets too hot, remove it from the heat. Strain the milk onto the egg mixture, stirring constantly. Return the mixture to the double boiler and cook, stirring, over low heat until the custard coats the back of a spoon, about 7 minutes. Pour it into the bowl and whisk occasionally as it cools. When it is cool, fold in the partially whipped cream. Put into an ice-cream freezer and churn according to manufacturer's instructions.

Mix the bread crumbs and 1 tablespoon sugar together and put on a baking sheet. Put under a preheated, not very hot broiler to brown slowly. Do not let crumbs burn. Cool the crumb mixture. Stir it into the ice cream with the rum, or use a little vanilla if preferred. Leave it in the freezer to harden.

This is delicious with Kenneth Bell's Butterscotch Pudding (see Index), served sliced and chilled but without the sauce.

S E R V E S 6.

STRAWBERRIES IN ORANGE SABAYON

❖   ❖   ❖

When strawberries are at their largest and finest, red-ripe and lus-cious, Murdo MacSween, head chef at Oakley Court near Windsor, likes to serve them in an orange sabayon which brings out the tart sweetness of their flavor. It is a pretty dessert, and simple to make.

6 large egg yolks
1 cup sugar
¼ cup dry white wine
¼ cup orange juice

1½ pounds strawberries, large if
    possible, washed and hulled
6 mint leaves

In the top pan of a double boiler set over hot water beat the egg yolks with the sugar, wine and orange juice and cook over low heat until thick enough to coat a spoon. Pour the sauce onto 6 dessert plates.

Cut the strawberries lengthwise into halves and arrange, cut sides down, on top of the sabayon around the inner rim of the plate. Glaze under a hot broiler. Decorate each plate with a fresh mint leaf.

S E R V E S 6.

V A R I A T I O N : Sam Chalmers, formerly of Le Talbooth restaurant at Dedham, in Essex, has an interestingly different version of this, a rather more elaborate one. Instead of wine and orange juice, add 2 tablespoons Grand Marnier to the sabayon. Soak an assortment of sliced fresh fruits in Grand Marnier for 3 to 4 hours, then arrange the fruits on the base of a dessert plate. Pour the sabayon over the fruits, sprinkle with slivered almonds, and glaze under a hot broiler.

S E R V E S 6.

PAPAYA WITH LIME MOUSSE

❖   ❖   ❖

Baba Hine, of Corse Lawn House at Corse Lawn in Gloucestershire has created a very refreshing summer dessert in which the honey sweetness of the papaya is pleasantly contrasted with the tart sweetness of the fresh lime mousse.

¾ cup fresh lime juice or lemon
   juice
¾ cup superfine sugar

1 cup heavy cream
3 small papayas, halved, with
   seeds removed

Strain the lime juice into a bowl. Stir in the sugar and continue to stir until it is dissolved. In another bowl beat the cream until it stands in firm peaks. Gently fold in the lime juice mixture and beat again until it holds a soft peak. Fill the papaya halves with the mixture and refrigerate until ready to serve.

SERVES 6.

BLACKBERRY MOUSSE

❖   ❖   ❖

Roy Richards is the chef patron of the Manor House restaurant in Pickworth, Lincolnshire. His wife, Veronica, who cooks and more often than not creates the desserts, merits the title of chef-patronne as her desserts, even the more traditional ones, always have a touch of originality because of her creative use of ingredients. I am especially fond of this simple blackberry mousse.

1 envelope unflavored gelatin, 7 grams	½ cup heavy cream, chilled
1 pound blackberries	4 large egg whites
¼ cup lemon juice	Pinch of salt
½ cup sugar	Pinch of cream of tartar

Sprinkle the gelatin over ¼ cup cold water in a small bowl and leave it to soften. Combine the blackberries, lemon juice and sugar in a saucepan, bring to a simmer over moderate heat, and cook uncovered for 5 minutes. Cool slightly, then pour into a blender or food processor and reduce to a purée. Strain through a fine sieve set over a bowl, pushing down hard on the solids. Only the seeds should remain in the sieve; discard them. Return the purée to the saucepan. Stir in the gelatin and warm the mixture just until the gelatin is dissolved. Set aside.

In a bowl beat the cream until it stands in stiff peaks. In a large bowl beat the egg whites with the salt and cream of tartar until they stand in stiff peaks. Fold the cream and egg whites gently but thoroughly into the blackberry purée. Spoon the mousse into a glass serving bowl and chill in the refrigerator for 4 hours, or until it is set.

To serve, divide the mousse among 6 individual glass dishes.

S E R V E S 6.

RUM AND BRANDY MOUSSE

❖   ❖   ❖

This is a simple-to-make, quick and good dessert, the creation of John Evans, chef-patron of Meadowsweet Hotel and Restaurant at Llanrwst, Gwynedd, North Wales. It is useful for a dinner party as it is made ahead of time.

5 large eggs, separated
½ cup superfine sugar
1 tablespoon rum
1½ tablespoons brandy

1¾ cups heavy cream
1 envelope unflavored gelatin,
  7 grams

In a bowl whisk together the egg yolks and sugar until they are thick and creamy. Whisk in the rum and brandy. In another bowl beat the cream until it stands in soft peaks. Fold into the egg-yolk mixture. Pour ¼ cup cold water into a small saucepan and sprinkle the gelatin over it to soften, then heat gently, stirring, until the gelatin has dissolved. Cool slightly and stir into the mixture. In a large bowl beat the egg whites until they stand in firm peaks. Fold the egg whites into the egg-yolk and cream mixture gently but thoroughly. Pour into a large decorative glass dessert bowl and chill in the refrigerator until set.

Serve with brandy snaps. If liked, the mousse may be spooned into individual dessert glasses and chilled.

S E R V E S 6 to 8.

MOUSSE OF TWO CHOCOLATES

❖   ❖   ❖

This simple-to-make dessert lends itself to all manner of attractive presentations. Its creator, Paul Vidic, head chef at Michael's Nook, a country house hotel in Grasmere in the English Lake District, spoons layers of each mousse alternately into glass dessert dishes. It also looks attractive served in two small molds, one of white chocolate mousse, the other of dark. It is very good served with halved strawberries set upright around the edge of the dish with a whole strawberry in the middle. The flavors marry well.

Dark Chocolate Mousse

4 ounces (squares) semisweet   ½ cup heavy cream, whipped
    dark baking chocolate   Pinch of salt
2 eggs, separated

White Chocolate Mousse

4 ounces (squares) white   ½ cup heavy cream, whipped
    chocolate   Pinch of salt
2 eggs, separated

Melt the two chocolates separately. Place each in the top pan of a double boiler with 2 to 3 tablespoons water, set over hot water on low heat. Stir constantly with a wooden spoon until the chocolate has melted and is smooth, about 5 minutes or less. Cool. Stir the egg yolks into each chocolate. Fold the cream into the mixture.

It may be more convenient to whip all the egg whites together with a pinch of salt and fold half into each chocolate mixture instead of beating them separately. When the whites stand in firm peaks, fold half into each mixture and spoon the batters in alternate layers into 6 chilled dessert glasses. Refrigerate for at least 6 hours.

Decorate according to personal taste with strawberries, crystallized violets, chopped crystallized gingerroot, or rosettes of whipped cream; or if preferred, leave plain.

SERVES 6.

PEACHES WITH LEMON AND BRANDY

❖   ❖   ❖

George Perry-Smith of the Riverside Restaurant at Helford, Corn-wall, has created a deceptively simple dessert which turns out to be exquisitely flavored. It makes the peach season worth waiting for.

6 *large peaches*   3 *large lemons*
2¼ *cups water*   3 *tablespoons brandy*
¾ *cup sugar*

Drop the peaches into boiling water for 1 minute, plunge them into cold water, and remove the skins. In a saucepan combine 2¼ cups water and sugar. Trim the ends of the lemons and cut them into very thin slices. Remove any seeds. Add lemons to the saucepan with the sugar and water and simmer, uncovered, for 10 minutes. Add the peaches and simmer until they are tender, about 10 minutes. The time will vary so test with a toothpick after 5 minutes. Lift peaches out as soon as they are done. Continue to cook the lemon slices until they are translucent, about 30 minutes. Cool. Stir in the brandy, then pour the syrup over the peaches and chill in the refrigerator.

S E R V E S 6.

MIXED FRUITS IN SAUTERNES JELLY

❖　　　❖　　　❖

Joyce Molyneux, chef-patronne of the Carved Angel restaurant in Dartmouth, Devon, often finds herself with an excess of fresh fruit. This simplest of recipes is an excellent way of turning it into a light, refreshing dessert.

1 pound fruits—apples, pears and
  peaches
1 cup sugar
1 cup water
1 cup sweet white wine such as
  Sauternes

1 envelope unflavored gelatin,
  7 grams
1 tablespoon lemon juice, or to
  taste
Garnish: mint sprigs

Peel and core the apples and pears and cut into 8 lengthwise slices. Drop the peaches into briskly boiling water for a few seconds, lift out, and slip off the skins. Cut into halves, remove the pits, and cut each peach half into 4 lengthwise slices.

In a medium-size saucepan combine the sugar, water and wine and simmer just until the sugar has dissolved. Add the fruits and poach, uncovered, until fruits are tender, 10 to 15 minutes. Lift out the fruits with a slotted spoon into a bowl.

Measure the liquid and reduce it, if necessary, to 2 cups over moderately high heat. Pour ¼ cup water into a small bowl and sprinkle the gelatin over it. When the gelatin has softened, stir it into the syrup and cook, stirring, until the gelatin has dissolved. Taste and add the lemon juice, adding more if necessary. Pour half of the jelly mixture into 3 or 4 dessert dishes and chill in the refrigerator until it is set. Arrange the fruits on top of the jelly and pour in the rest of the jelly. Refrigerate until set. Garnish with mint sprigs.

S E R V E S 3 or 4.

V A R I A T I O N S : The jelly can be flavored with other wines or liqueurs. If preferred, a single fruit may be used, for example, pears in red wine and Port wine jelly. The jelly may be unmolded and served with yogurt, cream, or ice cream and sweet biscuits, or served plain garnished with a sprig of mint.

STRAWBERRY OMELET

❖ ❖ ❖

Willie MacPherson, when he was head chef at the Feathers Hotel, Woodstock, Oxfordshire, delighted me by having Strawberry Omelet on the menu. Dessert omelets are not often served on menus with food as innovative and modern as Willie's. It is an essential part of his cooking philosophy to unite the good things of the past with the best of the new. I had forgotten how luscious a strawberry omelet can be.

1 cup strawberries	1 large egg
¼ cup Grand Marnier or Curaçao or other orange liqueur	1 large egg yolk
	1 tablespoon whipped cream
	Pinch of salt
1½ teaspoons superfine sugar	1 tablespoon butter
	Confectioners' sugar

Put half of the strawberries, half of the orange liqueur and ½ teaspoon sugar in a small saucepan and cook over low heat for a few minutes, just until the strawberries have softened. Transfer to a blender or food processor and purée. Scrape out the purée into the saucepan and set aside.

Cut the other half of the strawberries into quarters and put into another small saucepan with the rest of the liqueur, and cook over low heat until the strawberries have softened. Set aside.

In a bowl combine the whole egg, egg yolk, cream, remaining sugar and the salt and mix well. Heat the butter in an omelet pan and pour in the egg mixture, tilting the pan rapidly back and forth and stirring the egg with the back of a fork to spread the mixture evenly. As soon as it begins to set, in about 4 seconds, spoon in the quartered strawberry mixture and fold the omelet in half. Slide it off onto a buttered ovenproof dish, sprinkle with confectioners' sugar, and brown it quickly under a preheated broiler.

While the omelet is cooking, warm the strawberry purée and pour it onto a plate. Lift the omelet onto the plate, using a fish slice. Serve immediately.

S E R V E S   1.

PANCAKES WITH MERINGUE AND EXOTIC FRUITS

❖   ❖   ❖

Jean Norton is a distinguished prizewinning woman chef whom I met when she was chef-patronne of Rookery Hall near Nantwich in Cheshire. She is one of the few women appointed a Master Chef member of the British Chapter of the Institute of Master Chefs. This is one of her own recipes.

4 pancakes, 6 inches across
   (follow Crêpe recipe, see
   Index, but add 1 teaspoon
   superfine sugar; or use any
   crêpe or pancake recipe)
2 large ripe mangoes
1 tablespoon brandy

3 large egg whites
1 tablespoon confectioners' sugar
Oil
1 cup thin-sliced fresh fruits such
   as strawberries, kiwi fruit,
   fresh figs, etc.
Confectioners' sugar

Make the pancakes and set them aside. Peel the mangoes. Using the point of a small sharp knife, locate the mango seed. Set the mango on its side and cut down each side to remove the flesh. Do the same with the second mango. Cut off any flesh around the pit. In a blender or food processor purée mangoes, chopped, with the brandy. Pour into a sauceboat and chill.

In a large bowl beat the egg whites until they stand in firm peaks. Fold in the tablespoon of confectioners' sugar. Lightly brush a baking sheet with oil and lay the 4 pancakes on it. Make a layer of the sliced fresh fruit to cover one side of each pancake. Top with the meringue and fold over lightly. Bake in a preheated hot oven (425°F) for 10 minutes, or until the meringue is firm and golden.

Carefully lift out pancakes onto 4 dessert plates. Sprinkle with confectioners' sugar and serve with the mango purée.

S E R V E S 4.

JOAN SUTHERLAND BAVAROIS

❖   ❖   ❖

I never did find out why this dessert is named for Joan Sutherland, the singer, as I was too busy enjoying it, as I always enjoy the cooking of Francis Coulson, chef-patron of Sharrow Bay hotel, Lake Ullswater, in Cumbria's Lake District.

4 *large egg yolks*	*1 tablespoon Curaçao liqueur*
½ cup superfine sugar	*1¼ cups heavy cream, whipped*
1¼ cups milk heated with a	*4 tablespoons apricot jam*
vanilla bean, or add 1	*2 tablespoons apricot brandy*
teaspoon vanilla extract	*Garnish: whipped cream and*
1 envelope unflavored gelatin,	*halved apricots (optional)*
7 grams	

In the top pan of a double boiler beat the egg yolks and sugar together until they form a ribbon. Remove the vanilla bean from the hot but not boiling milk and pour the milk slowly into the egg and sugar mixture, stirring constantly. If using vanilla extract instead of the vanilla bean, stir it in. Set the double boiler over hot water on low heat and cook, stirring with a wooden spoon, until the custard has thickened and coats the back of the spoon, about 7 minutes. Remove from the heat. Sprinkle the gelatin over ¼ cup cold water to soften, then stir it into the hot custard and continue to stir until gelatin is dissolved. Let the custard cool, then stir in the Curaçao. Taste and add a little more liqueur if necessary. When the custard is cold, fold in the whipped cream.

In a small bowl mix together the apricot jam and apricot brandy until smooth. Pour into the bottom of a 1-quart soufflé mold or glass dessert bowl. Spoon the custard on top and chill thoroughly in the refrigerator until set, 3 to 4 hours.

When ready to serve, decorate with rosettes of whipped cream and halved apricots, if liked. Glaze, if liked, with a little warmed and strained apricot jam.

S E R V E S   4 to 6.

CRÈME BRÛLÉE WITH TANGERINES

❖   ❖   ❖

Allan Holland, chef-patron of Mallory Court at Bishop Tachbrook near Leamington Spa in Warwickshire, has transformed an ancient English dessert, burnt cream, into something excitingly special. The unctuous custard contrasts with the deliciously tart fruit.

6 tangerines, peeled and sectioned
2½ cups heavy cream
8 large egg yolks
¼ cup superfine sugar

2½ tablespoons Mandarin
    Napoleon liqueur, or any
    tangerine liqueur
Light brown sugar

Peel the tangerine segments and remove seeds, if any. Divide the segments among 6 small soufflé molds, about 1-cup size.

Rinse a heavy saucepan with cold water and leave wet. Pour in the cream and heat to just below simmering point. Beat the egg yolks and sugar together in a bowl until they form a ribbon. Pour the hot cream slowly onto the egg-yolk and sugar mixture, stirring constantly with a wooden spoon. Gradually stir in the liqueur. Pour the mixture into the top pan of a double boiler and set over simmering water on very low heat. Cook the custard, stirring constantly, until it is thick enough to coat a spoon. Pour the custard into the molds and refrigerate for at least 6 hours, or overnight.

An hour before serving sprinkle a layer of soft brown sugar, about ¼ inch thick, over the custards. Put the molds under a preheated broiler just long enough to caramelize the sugar, only a few minutes. Set in a cool place but do not refrigerate.

SERVES 6.

RHUBARB BRÛLÉE

❖   ❖   ❖

This is a deliciously fresh-tasting dessert created by Sheena Buchanan-Smith, chef-patronne of the Isle of Eriskay Hotel at Ledaig, Strathclyde, in Scotland, to take advantage of an abundance of fresh rhubarb. I have found that it also works well with frozen rhubarb when fresh is not available.

1 pound fresh rhubarb, cut into ½-inch pieces, or 1 pound frozen chopped rhubarb, thawed

⅓ cup sugar
1 cup chilled heavy cream
½ cup firmly packed light brown sugar

Put the rhubarb, fresh or frozen, into a saucepan with just enough water to prevent it burning. Add the sugar, cover, and simmer over low heat for about 8 minutes, or until rhubarb is soft. Cool and spoon into a 1-quart gratin dish. In a chilled bowl beat the cream until it holds firm peaks. Spread the cream over the rhubarb and chill in the refrigerator for at least 1 hour, preferably longer.

Sift the brown sugar over the cream and set under a preheated broiler, about 4 inches from the source of heat, for about 2 minutes, until the sugar is just melted. Serve the dessert immediately, or chilled.

S E R V E S 6.

TRIFLE

❖   ❖   ❖

Christopher Pitman, head chef of the George of Stamford in Lincolnshire, has an interestingly different version of the traditional English trifle. The addition of black coffee sounds very odd, but it works well.

1 day-old sponge cake, cut into
   1-inch cubes, about ¾ pound
2 pounds blackberries,
   strawberries or raspberries,
   according to taste and the
   season

4 tablespoons apricot or other jam
½ cup strong black coffee
½ cup medium-dry sherry wine

Custard

4 large eggs
⅓ cup superfine sugar
¼ teaspoon salt
1½ cups milk

1 cup heavy cream
½ teaspoon vanilla extract
Garnish: 2 cups whipped cream,
   seasonal fruits

Put the cake cubes into a large glass bowl. Cover with the fruit. In a small saucepan mix the jam with the black coffee and sherry and heat, stirring, just long enough to make a smooth mixture. Cool and pour over the cake and fruit. Refrigerate for 24 hours.

Make the custard. In the top pan of a double boiler beat the eggs lightly. Beat in the sugar and salt. In a small saucepan heat the milk with the cream to just under a boil. Cool slightly and gradually pour into the egg mixture in the double boiler set over hot, not boiling, water on very low heat. Stir in the vanilla. Cook, stirring constantly, until the mixture coats the spoon, about 7 minutes. Remove from the heat and cool. Pour it over the trifle and refrigerate until the custard has set. Garnish with whipped cream and seasonal fruits.

S E R V E S 6 to 8.

BUTTERSCOTCH MERINGUE PIE

❖   ❖   ❖

This simple, old-fashioned dessert was developed by Ken Stott, head chef at Kildrummy Castle Hotel in Grampian, Scotland, from a traditional recipe. Scots chefs never lose their old favorites, but constantly and subtly update them so they fit happily into modern menus. This one is a delight.

1 recipe Short-Crust Pastry (see Index)
Raw rice for weighting the shell
1 cup firmly packed light brown sugar
½ cup all-purpose flour
1 cup milk
4 large eggs, separated

4 tablespoons (½ stick) butter, cut into bits
1 teaspoon vanilla extract
Pinch of salt
Pinch of cream of tartar
¼ cup superfine sugar

On a lightly floured surface roll out the dough to about 1/8-inch thickness and fit it into a 9-inch pie plate. Crimp the edge with the fingers, prick the bottom of the shell with a fork, and chill in the refrigerator for 30 minutes. Line the shell with wax paper, fill with the rice, and bake in a preheated hot oven (425°F.) for 15 minutes. Remove the paper and rice and bake the shell for 10 minutes longer, or until the pastry is golden. Let it cool on a rack.

In a saucepan mix together the sugar and flour. Whisk in 1/4 cup water and the milk. Simmer over low heat, stirring, for 5 minutes, or until the mixture is smooth and thick. Off the heat whisk in the egg yolks, one at a time, then the butter and the vanilla. Cool the mixture, stirring from time to time, and pour it into the pie shell.

In a bowl beat the egg whites with the salt and cream of tartar until they stand in firm peaks. Pipe or spoon the meringue onto the filling, covering it completely. Bake in a preheated slow oven (300°F.) for 20 minutes, or until the meringue is golden brown. Serve with cream or ice cream or by itself.

S E R V E S 6.

HOT BUTTERSCOTCH PUDDING

❖ ❖ ❖

This is a fine, old-fashioned English dessert to which Kenneth Bell, chef-patron of Thornbury Castle, Thornbury, near Bristol, has given his own inimitable touch. It is a wonderful hot pudding. If fresh dates are available, they add to both texture and flavor.

Pudding

¾ cup sugar
4 tablespoons butter
2 large eggs
1 teaspoon vanilla extract
½ teaspoon baking powder

2 cups all-purpose flour
1 cup milk, warm
1 teaspoon baking soda
1 cup chopped dates or raisins
   tossed in flour

Sauce

¼ pound (1 stick) butter
½ cup dark brown sugar

1 cup heavy cream
¼ cup dark rum (optional)

In a bowl beat the sugar and butter together until the mixture is light and fluffy. Beat in the eggs, vanilla, baking powder and flour, stirring to mix. Pour in the warm milk and add the baking soda. Fold in the dates or raisins, or fresh dates, pitted and chopped, if available. Butter a nonstick cake pan, 9 by 5 inches, and pour in the pudding mixture. Let it stand for 1 hour. Bake in a preheated moderate oven (350°F.) for 1 hour, or until a cake tester inserted in the middle comes out clean.

While the pudding is baking, make the sauce. In a small saucepan melt the butter and stir in the dark brown sugar. When the sugar has dissolved, add the cream and continue to cook, stirring, until well blended. Stir in the rum, if using, as it greatly improves the sauce.

Turn the pudding out onto a serving dish and cut into 8 to 10 slices. Arrange the slices on dessert plates and pour some of the sauce over them. Serve the rest of the sauce separately. If liked, the pudding may be cut into more generous slices to serve 6.

S E R V E S 6 to 10.

CHOCOLATE TRUFFLE CAKE

❖ ❖ ❖

John Martin Grimsey, the young head chef of the White Hart Hotel at Coggeshall in Essex, describes this as a rather rich dessert made with the minimum of effort, and ideal for a dinner party as one can prepare it at least 24 hours beforehand. I endorse all of that except that I'd change rather rich to very rich and add that the cake should delight all chocolate lovers, that it keeps well, and that it goes a long way. Serve it in thin slices, as it is most satisfying.

8 ounces (squares) semisweet baking chocolate
2 large eggs
¼ cup sugar
¼ pound (1 stick) butter, melted and cooled
½ pound graham crackers, crushed (3 cups)

½ pound shelled mixed nuts (walnuts, pecans, cashews, almonds, filberts), chopped
½ cup chopped candied cherries
¾ cup dark rum
Garnish: Whipped cream, candied cherries and nuts

Break the chocolate into bits and put it with 4 tablespoons water into the top pan of a double boiler set over hot water on low heat. Stir constantly with a wooden spoon until the chocolate has melted and is smooth, about 4 minutes.

In a bowl cream the eggs and sugar until they are light and fluffy. Stir in the butter, then the melted chocolate, the cracker crumbs, nuts, cherries and rum. Leave the mixture to set in a cool place or in the refrigerator for 12 hours to let the flavor develop.

Unmold the cake on a serving dish. The easiest way to do this is to put the bowl in a shallow dish of warm water for a few minutes. Garnish the cake with rosettes of whipped cream, candied cherries and nuts.

S E R V E S 8 to 10.

CHOCOLATE LAYER CAKE WITH COFFEE CUSTARD SAUCE

❖   ❖   ❖

This is not a difficult dessert to make but it does take time. It is richly flavored with a delicious sauce. It is worth the effort for a special occasion. Mark Napper, a young Englishman, created the cake when he was head chef at Cromlix House, in Dunblane, Central Region, Scotland.

Cake

2 large eggs
¼ cup superfine sugar
⅓ cup all-purpose flour
2 tablespoons unsweetened cocoa
   powder

2 tablespoons Clarified Butter
   (see Index)

Pastry Cream Fillings

2½ cups milk
6 large egg yolks
½ cup superfine sugar
½ cup plus 2 tablespoons all-
   purpose flour
¼ pound (1 stick) butter, cut
   into bits and softened at room
   temperature

2 teaspoons vanilla extract
2 teaspoons instant espresso
   coffee powder dissolved in
   1 tablespoon hot water

Chocolate Cream Filling

½ cup heavy cream
4 tablespoons dark rum
12 ounces semisweet chocolate,
   chopped fine

2 tablespoons butter, cut into bits
   and softened at room
   temperature

2 tablespoons dark rum to brush
   on cake layers

Coffee Custard Sauce

2½ cups milk
3 tablespoons ground espresso
  beans

6 large egg yolks
½ cup superfine sugar

Make the cake: Line the bottom of a buttered loaf pan, 9 by 5 by 3 inches, with buttered wax paper. Dust the pan with flour, shaking out excess flour. In a bowl beat the eggs and sugar together until the mixture is light and fluffy. Set the bowl over a saucepan of hot water and let it warm, stirring from time to time. In a blender or food processor beat the mixture until it is very light and increased in volume. Scrape the mixture into a bowl and sift the flour and cocoa over it. Fold in the butter, a tablespoon at a time, until the mixture forms a smooth batter. Spoon the batter into the pan and smooth the top with a spatula. Bake in a preheated moderate oven (350°F.) for 25 to 30 minutes, or until a cake tester comes out clean. Cool the cake in the pan on a rack for 5 minutes, then invert the cake onto the rack. Remove the wax paper and let the cake cool, then chill in the refrigerator, covered, for 2 hours, or overnight if convenient.

Make the pastry creams: In a saucepan scald the milk. In a bowl whisk the egg yolks until they are combined, then whisk in the sugar and the flour, then pour in the scalded milk, whisking constantly. Transfer the mixture to a saucepan and cook over moderate heat, stirring constantly, until it has thickened. Simmer over low heat for 5 minutes. Strain into a bowl and stir in the butter and vanilla. Divide the custard evenly between 2 bowls. Stir the dissolved espresso coffee powder into one bowl, mixing thoroughly. Cover both bowls and chill in the refrigerator for about 1 hour.

Make the chocolate cream: In a saucepan combine the cream and the rum, bring to a boil, then remove from the heat. Add the chocolate and stir until the mixture is smooth. Cool slightly and stir in the butter, mixing well. Chill until the mixture has thickened and holds its shape in a spoon.

Make the coffee custard sauce: Combine the milk and the ground espresso in a saucepan and bring to a simmer over moderate heat, whisking the mixture. Remove from the heat and let the mixture stand for 5 minutes. In a large bowl beat the egg yolks, adding the sugar a little at a time, until the mixture is thick. Gradually whisk in the milk. Transfer the mixture to a saucepan and cook it over low heat, stirring constantly, until it is lightly thickened. Do not let it boil.

(recipe continues)

Strain the custard into a bowl and chill it, covered, for at least 1 hour.

Using a serrated knife, slice the cake carefully into 4 layers, brushing each layer on both sides with some of the rum. Clean the loaf pan and butter the bottom and sides of it lightly. Put the bottom layer of the cake, cut side up, in the pan and spread it with the plain pastry cream. Cover with another layer of cake and spread with the coffee-flavored pastry cream. Top with a third layer and spread with the chocolate cream. Top with the last layer, cut side down. Cover the pan and chill the cake in the refrigerator for 4 hours or overnight.

Invert the cake on a serving plate and use a hot knife to slice it. Pour the coffee custard sauce on 6 plates and top with a slice of cake. Decorate with chocolate leaves, if liked.

S E R V E S 6, or 8 if cut into thinner slices.

GLAZED PRUNE TART

❖   ❖   ❖

I have always admired the versatility of prunes in cooking, since they are equally at home with braised pork, in a pâté or, as here, in a tart. Pierre Chevillard, head chef at Chewton Glen Hotel in Hampshire, created this delicious tart.

1 recipe sweet Short-Crust Pastry (see Index)	3 large eggs, lightly beaten
	½ cup superfine sugar
1 pound pitted prunes	½ cup apricot jam
2 cups heavy cream	

Make the pastry and roll it out on a lightly floured surface into a round about 1/8 inch thick. Fit it into a 10-inch flan pan with a removable rim and trim the edge. Prick the shell with a fork and chill it for 30 minutes.

Put the prunes into a saucepan with water barely to cover. Cover, and simmer over low heat for 10 minutes. Cool the prunes, drain thoroughly, and arrange them in the flan shell. In a bowl combine the cream, eggs and sugar, whisking to mix well. Put the flan ring on a baking sheet and pour the custard over the prunes. Bake in a pre-heated moderate oven (350°F.) for 30 to 35 minutes, or until the custard is set. Cool the tart at room temperature, then carefully remove the rim.

Slide the tart from the baking sheet onto a serving plate. Melt the apricot jam in a small saucepan over low heat just until it begins to bubble. Rub the jam through a sieve to get rid of any bits of skin and brush it over the tart.

S E R V E S 6.

V A R I A T I O N : John Armstrong, head chef of Martin's Restaurant in London, has an interesting version of Prune Tart—Prune and Almond Tart, Flavored with Armagnac. The pastry is made in the same way as for Glazed Prune Tart, using an 8-inch flan pan. Soak ½ pound pitted prunes in warm water for 15 minutes; lift out and pat dry with paper towels. Arrange the prunes on the pastry. In a bowl whisk together 2 eggs, 5 tablespoons heavy cream, 4 tablespoons superfine sugar, 3 tablespoons fine-ground almonds and 2 tablespoons Armagnac, or other brandy if Armagnac is not available. Melt 2 tablespoons butter in a small saucepan; when it is cool whisk it into the egg and cream mixture. Pour the mixture over the prunes and bake in a preheated moderately hot oven (400°F.) for 20 to 25 minutes, or until the custard is set. Sprinkle the tart with 2 tablespoons Armagnac and serve warm.

S E R V E S 6.

PASSION FRUIT SOUFFLÉ

❖   ❖   ❖

Passion fruit has an exquisite flavor. Nick Gill, head chef at Hambleton Hall hotel at Oakham, has worked out a simple and delicious soufflé recipe using the fruit. The presentation of the dish is charming.

Butter, flour and sugar for the
  soufflé molds
12 ripe passion fruit
¾ cup fresh orange juice
8 large eggs, separated
1½ cups vanilla sugar, or use
  plain sugar and add 1 teaspoon
  vanilla extract to the egg whites

Grated rind of 1 lemon
Pinch of salt
Confectioners' sugar

Butter, flour and dust with sugar six 1-cup or slightly larger individual soufflé molds. Set aside.

Halve six of the passion fruit and scoop the contents into a bowl. Add the orange juice, stir to mix, and strain the mixture to remove the passion fruit seeds. Beat the egg yolks with ¼ cup of the sugar, the grated lemon rind and the passion-fruit and orange-juice mixture in the top pan of a double boiler set over hot water on very low heat, until the mixture is light and frothy. In a large bowl beat the egg whites with the salt until they stand in firm peaks. Whisk in remaining ¾ cup sugar. Mix half of the egg whites into the egg-yolk mixture, off the heat, then gently but thoroughly fold in remaining egg whites. Spoon the mixture into the prepared soufflé molds and smooth the tops with a spatula. Cook in a preheated hot oven (425°F.) for about 8 minutes, or until the soufflés are well risen and lightly set. Remove from the oven and dust with confectioners' sugar.

Serve immediately with the remaining 6 passion fruit, tops sliced off, and put into 6 small egg cups. The passion fruit should be spooned into the soufflé after the first spoonful has been eaten. If liked, serve with Almond Tuiles (see Index).

S E R V E S 6.

V A R I A T I O N : Hot Passion Fruit Soufflé. Michael Croft, head chef of the Royal Crescent Hotel in Bath, Avon, has a slightly simpler passion fruit soufflé recipe, conveniently scaled down for one, though it can easily be doubled.

2 egg yolks
½ cup superfine sugar
4 egg whites

1 cup passion fruit pulp, sieved to
   remove seeds
Confectioners' sugar

In a bowl beat the egg yolks with half of the sugar until light and fluffy. In another bowl beat the whites, adding the rest of the sugar bit by bit until they stand in firm, shiny peaks. Add 3 tablespoons of the passion fruit pulp to the yolks, mix well, then stir in one quarter of the egg whites. Fold in the rest of the egg whites gently but thoroughly. Have ready a 1-cup soufflé mold, buttered and sprinkled with sugar. Pour in the soufflé mixture and bake in a preheated hot oven (425°F.) for about 10 minutes, or until the soufflé is puffed and lightly browned.

Dust with confectioners' sugar and serve immediately with a sauce of the rest of the passion fruit pulp, warmed, and sweetened if necessary.

S E R V E S 1.

N O T E : Passion fruit are frequently available fresh. They are also available canned as passion fruit pulp in specialty food shops. The canned pulp is sweetened so this should be taken in consideration and the amount of sugar reduced.

BURNT GLAYVA CREAM

❖　　　❖　　　❖

John McGeever, head chef of Congham Hall, a country house hotel at Grimston, near King's Lynn in Norfolk, loves to create new and attractive dishes. This one is developed from the traditional Crème Brûlée, or Burnt Cream, which originated a very long time ago at Trinity College, Cambridge, in England where it is a specialty. Glayva is a Scottish liqueur, based on whisky. If it is not available, use any liqueur based on Scotch.

4 large egg yolks
2 tablespoons sugar
1 teaspoon cornstarch
1¼ cups heavy cream
¼ cup Glayva (liqueur based on
　Scotch whisky) or other
　Scotch-based liqueur

2 tablespoons brown sugar,
　approximately

In a bowl whisk together the egg yolks, sugar and cornstarch. In a small saucepan heat the cream to just under boiling and whisk it into the egg mixture. Stir in the liqueur, return the mixture to the saucepan and simmer, stirring, over low heat until it is thick. Pour it into four ½-cup ramekins or small soufflé molds. Cool and refrigerate for 15 to 30 minutes.

Sprinkle with the brown sugar and glaze under a preheated very hot broiler.

S E R V E S 4.

HOT STRAWBERRIES WITH GREEN PEPPERCORNS

❖　　　❖　　　❖

Melvin Jordan, head chef at Pool Court in Pool-in-Wharfedale, West Yorkshire, devised this delicious way of serving strawberries. The medley of flavors is unusual and delicious.

½ cup sugar
¼ cup brandy
4 tablespoons lemon juice
1 cup fresh orange juice
10 green peppercorns

1 pound strawberries, hulled and
   washed
Vanilla ice cream, preferably
   homemade

In a small heavy saucepan caramelize the sugar to a light golden color. Off the heat add the brandy, taking care to step back as it will flare up. When the flames die down, stir in the lemon and orange juices and the green peppercorns. Stir over low heat to dissolve the caramel, 5 to 10 minutes. When ready to serve, add the strawberries and cook for 1 minute.

Serve the strawberries and their sauce poured over ice cream in glass dessert dishes.

S E R V E S 4.

PANCAKES STUFFED WITH PEARS

❖ ❖ ❖

This was a favorite dessert of Raymond Baudon during the time he was head chef at Johnstounburn House Hotel, at Humbie near Edinburgh in Scotland. The pancakes can be made ahead of time, which makes this a quick dessert to put together for family or friends.

1 cup heavy cream
¾ cup sugar
¼ cup Cognac or other brandy
4 large ripe pears, peeled, cored
   and diced

¼ pound (1 stick) butter
8 Crêpes (pancakes) (see Index)
Garnish: fresh fruit, sliced thin

In a large bowl whip the cream with ¼ cup of the sugar and the brandy. Sauté the pears in the butter in a heavy skillet until the fruit is golden but not soft. Sprinkle with the rest of the sugar and cook for a few minutes longer. Divide the pear mixture among the pancakes and top with the whipped cream. Fold or roll the pancakes, transfer to a heated serving dish, and serve garnished with thin-sliced fruits. Serve immediately.

S E R V E S 4.

ALMOND MERINGUE
WITH GRAPES

❖   ❖   ❖

This is one of the uncomplicated, pleasing desserts created by Brian Prideaux-Brune at the family home, now a restaurant with rooms, Plumber Manor at Sturminster Newton, Dorset.

6 large egg whites	*1 cup slivered almonds*
Pinch of salt	*2½ cups heavy cream*
1½ cups superfine sugar	*2 cups halved and pitted grapes*

In a large bowl beat the egg whites with the salt until they stand in firm peaks. Fold in the sugar and the almonds. Line 2 baking sheets with oiled wax paper and spread the egg-white mixture evenly over them. Bake in a preheated slow oven (275°F.) for 1¼ hours. Cool.

Beat the cream in a large bowl with a little sugar until it stands in peaks. Fold in the grapes. Lift one of the meringues onto a large flat dish. Spread the cream and grape filling over it and top with the second meringue. Chill in the refrigerator until ready to serve, then slice and serve.

S E R V E S 6 to 8.

V A R I A T I O N : Nigel Lambert, head chef at the Elms in Abberley near Worcester, describes his cooking as English country with modern influences. He likes good, fresh, honest cooking and tries to make it original and interesting at the same time, as he has done with this traditional English dessert—English Sticky Meringue with Soft Summer Fruits. Make the meringue in the same way as in Almond Meringue with Grapes, only make it into one large circle like a cake. It may need a little longer cooking. When done it should be crispy, lightly brown on the outside, and a little soft and sticky inside. For the filling whip 2 cups heavy cream until the cream stands in peaks and spread it onto the cooled meringue base. Top with 2 pounds mixed summer fruits such as raspberries, strawberries or loganberries.

S E R V E S 6 to 8.

RASPBERRY SOUFFLÉS

❖   ❖   ❖

Robert Gardiner, head chef of Ardsheal House, at Kentallen of Appin, Argyll in Scotland's Highlands loves the fine quality of the summer fruits of his country, especially the big, luscious raspberries. He developed this soufflé to take advantage of their goodness in summer. He freezes a supply so that he can make his favorite soufflé long after the season is over.

Butter and superfine sugar
  for the soufflé molds
2 cups raspberries
1 tablespoon lemon juice
½ cup plus 3 tablespoons
  confectioners' sugar

2 large egg yolks
8 egg whites
Pinch of salt
Heavy cream (optional)

Butter eight ½-cup soufflé molds generously, making sure the rims of the molds are well coated. Refrigerate for 15 minutes. Repeat this process, then coat the insides of the molds with sugar. Refrigerate until ready to use.

In a blender or food processor combine the raspberries, lemon juice and ½ cup confectioners' sugar and process until smooth. Add the egg yolks and blend for 30 seconds longer. Scrape the purée into a large bowl. Set aside.

In another bowl beat the egg whites with the salt until they stand in soft peaks. Add 3 tablespoons confectioners' sugar, 1 tablespoon at a time, beating constantly. Beat for about 30 seconds longer after the sugar has been added, or until the whites are stiff and shiny. Mix one quarter of the egg whites into the raspberry purée, then fold the raspberry mixture gently but thoroughly into the egg whites. Spoon the soufflé mixture into the prepared molds and arrange on a baking tray. Bake in a preheated hot oven (425°F.) for 8 to 9 minutes, or until they are puffed and lightly set. Serve immediately with the heavy cream, if liked.

SERVES 8.

WHISKY AND MARMALADE SOUFFLÉ

❖   ❖   ❖

Another Scot, Campbell Cameron, head chef of Culloden House at Inverness, Scotland, created this dish using the native drink, Scotch, and marmalade, also credited to Scotland. It makes a very luscious hot dessert.

1 cup milk	2 large eggs, separated
¼ cup sugar	4 tablespoons Scotch whisky
1 small egg yolk	½ cup heavy cream
1½ tablespoons flour	Confectioners' sugar
2 tablespoons marmalade	

Pour the milk into a small saucepan and bring it to just under a boil. In a bowl cream together the sugar and the egg yolk until it makes a ribbon. Stir in the flour and mix well. Pour in the milk, stirring constantly. Transfer the contents to the saucepan and simmer, stirring, for 2 to 3 minutes. Remove from the heat.

Stir in the marmalade, egg yolks and 2 tablespoons whisky. Beat the egg whites until they stand in firm peaks. Fold gently but thoroughly into the egg-yolk and milk mixture and spoon into four 1-cup soufflé molds. If liked, the molds may be buttered and sprinkled lightly with sugar before being filled. Bake the soufflés in a preheated moderately hot oven (400°F.) for 13 minutes, or until lightly set and well risen.

Serve with a sauce made from ½ cup lightly whipped heavy cream flavored with 2 tablespoons Scotch whisky and confectioners' sugar to taste, if liked. Serve the soufflés hot as soon as they are cooked.

SERVES 4.

NOTE: I prefer the hot soufflé without the sauce, but I have found that when chilled the soufflé makes a most pleasant dessert with the cream and whisky sauce, even though it falls and loses its looks.

WHISKY AND OATMEAL SYLLABUB

❖   ❖   ❖

This is a very Scottish recipe, reflecting Murdo MacSween's feeling for his native Scotland, but it is not just traditional; it has the special MacSween touch and is very much his creation. He is now head chef at Oakley Court near Windsor, in Berkshire.

1⅓ cups oatmeal
2 cups heavy cream, whipped
4 tablespoons lemon juice
3 tablespoons golden syrup, or
   corn syrup if golden syrup is
   not available

4 tablespoons Scotch whisky

Sprinkle the oatmeal onto a baking sheet and toast in a preheated moderate oven (350°F.) for 5 to 10 minutes, or until lightly colored. In a bowl combine the oatmeal and all the rest of the ingredients, mixing gently but thoroughly. Spoon the mixture into 6 dessert dishes and refrigerate for 1 hour before serving. The oatmeal will expand and the mixture be very thick.

S E R V E S 6.

INDEX